Head Hunters in the
Malayan Emergency

Head Hunters in the Malayan Emergency

The Atrocity and Cover-Up

Dan Poole

Pen & Sword
MILITARY

First published in Great Britain in 2023 by
Pen & Sword Military
An imprint of Pen & Sword Books Limited
Yorkshire – Philadelphia

Copyright © Dan Poole 2023

ISBN 978 1 39905 741 7

The right of Dan Poole to be identified as
Author of this Work has been asserted by him in accordance
with the Copyright, Designs and Patents Act 1988.

A CIP catalogue record for this book is
available from the British Library

All rights reserved. No part of this book may be reproduced or
transmitted in any form or by any means, electronic or mechanical
including photocopying, recording or by any information storage and
retrieval system, without permission from the Publisher in writing.

Typeset by Mac Style
Printed in the UK by CPI Group (UK) Ltd, Croydon, CR0 4YY.

Pen & Sword Books Limited incorporates the imprints of After
the Battle, Atlas, Archaeology, Aviation, Discovery, Family History,
Fiction, History, Maritime, Military, Military Classics, Politics,
Select, Transport, True Crime, Air World, Frontline Publishing, Leo
Cooper, Remember When, Seaforth Publishing, The Praetorian Press,
Wharncliffe Local History, Wharncliffe Transport, Wharncliffe True
Crime and White Owl.

For a complete list of Pen & Sword titles please contact

PEN & SWORD BOOKS LIMITED
47 Church Street, Barnsley, South Yorkshire, S70 2AS, England
E-mail: enquiries@pen-and-sword.co.uk
Website: www.pen-and-sword.co.uk
or
PEN AND SWORD BOOKS
1950 Lawrence Rd, Havertown, PA 19083, USA
E-mail: Uspen-and-sword@casematepublishers.com
Website: www.penandswordbooks.com

Contents

Scandal Timeline 1952 April–May viii
Additional Information x

Introduction xi
What was the British Malayan Headhunting Scandal? xi
From allies to "terrorists": Who were the victims of headhunting? xiii
The Malayan Emergency (1948–1960): Britain's Vietnam xv
Introducing the Ibans: Britain's headhunters from Borneo xviii

Chapter 1   The Headhunting Scandal Begins 1
The first decapitation photograph is published (28 April) 1
British Government Denial 2
The Admiralty's investigation 3

Chapter 2   Journalism on the Offensive 5
The second decapitation photograph is released (30 April) ... 5
The MacDonald Family 5
Legality of the headhunting 6
Soldiers and eyewitnesses 7
Gordon Knapp, one soldier's protest against headhunting 10
Winston Churchill and government awareness 12
Churchill forbids headhunting 14
Government confirms the photographs are authentic 15
J.R Campbell intensifies his anti-war campaign 16

**Chapter 3   "This Horror Must End": The Scandal Reaches its
                        Boiling Point** 19
The war's most graphically violent images are revealed (10 May) ... 19
Headhunting's final mention in Parliament 20

The deployment of Iban soldiers continues   21
Headhunting in Malaya continues   23

Chapter 4   The Aftermath of the Headhunting Scandal   27
Trade union reaction to the headhunting scandal   28
The Dunlop Rubber Company protest   30
British media reaction to the photographs   31
Foreign Media reaction to the photographs   35

Chapter 5   Debate: Military Necessity and the Intelligence Gathering Theory   38
Hen Yan – the only known communist victim of British headhunting   38
Lim Tian Shui, the first decapitation victim?   41
Sources, content, and treatment of both heads and photographs   44
Skulls and scalp trophies   48
Soldier eye-witness testimonies cast doubt on the official story   50
The availability and reliability of cameras   55
The availability of alternative tactics   57
Intelligence Gathering Theory Conclusion   59

Chapter 6   The Historiography: Questions and Comments by Researchers   62
Soldiers' relatives and their reactions to headhunting   63
Arguments and theories presented by modern researchers   65
Headhunting from the victim's perspective   68

Chapter 7   The Public Display of Corpses   72
Corpse displays as tools of terror   73
Corpse displays as tools of reassurance and intelligence   78
Known victims of the public corpse displays   84
The Telok Anson Tragedy, August 1952   86
The Kulim Tragedy, September 1953   88
Conclusion on the public corpse displays   92

Conclusion	94
Additional Information	97
Acknowledgements	108
Tips for researchers	109
Notes	111
Sources for Images/Figures	139
Index	141

Scandal Timeline 1952 April–May

28 April: The *Daily Worker* publishes the first known decapitation photograph from Malaya within an article entitled *"This is the war in Malaya"*.

29 April: Royal Navy spokesperson claims the photograph is fake. However confidentially, British officials successfully identified the photographer and a man in the photograph who both confirmed that the photograph is genuine.

30 April: The *Daily Worker* publishes a second decapitation photograph within an article titled *"These are No Fakes"*, in response to claims that their first photograph was a forgery.

5 May: The Colonial Office refuses to answer the *Daily Worker's* questions concerning the authenticity of the decapitation photographs.

6 May: The Secretary of State for the Colonies, Oliver Lyttelton receives a telegram from British General Gerald Templer defending the decapitations and arguing for its continuation, saying photographing of severed heads as depicted in the *Daily Worker* was "the only one of its kind which can be traced".

7 May: Lyttelton tells Parliament that the *Daily Worker's* decapitation photographs are authentic.

8 May: The *Daily Worker's* editor, J. R. Campbell, sends telegrams and atrocity photographs to Winston Churchill, MPs, newspaper editors, politicians, religious leaders, and other relevant people.

10 May: The *Daily Worker* publishes four never-before-seen headhunting photographs in an article *"This Horror must End"*, challenging the claims that their previously published photographs depicted an isolated incident.

These photographs are the most graphically violent images of the Malayan Emergency ever published.

21 May: After weeks of silence the British government declares it will not punish soldiers who took part in headhunting in Malaya.

Additional Information

The ethics of publishing headhunting photographs in research
Methodology: How was this research created?
Tips for researchers
Sources rejected from this research
Acknowledgements
Sources for images/figures

Introduction

What was the British Malayan Headhunting Scandal?

In 1952 Britain's largest socialist newspaper, the *Daily Worker*, published a horrific never-before-seen photograph showing a British soldier posing with the decapitated head of an anti-colonial rebel. The image was taken in British Malaya (known today as Malaysia) during a pro-independence uprising known as the **Malayan Emergency (1948–1960)**. The headhunting photograph deeply shocked politicians, military leaders, and many members of the British public, highlighting the brutal realities of British colonialism that often went unseen in the mainstream British press.[1] The *Daily Worker's* headhunting photograph subsequently sparked a political scandal known as the **British Malayan Headhunting Scandal of 1952**.

During the scandal it was revealed that the decapitation of corpses of anti-colonial rebels in Malaya was not only a common practice but had also been authorised by the highest levels within the British colonial occupation. The British military claimed that the heads of corpses needed to be removed for intelligence purposes, arguing that cameras were unreliable in jungle environments. It was also revealed that Britain had recruited over 1,000 mercenaries from the Iban people of Borneo to serve as trackers in Malaya, many of whom joined the war to collect human scalp trophies in the hopes of achieving a higher social status within their villages, a practice which the Royal Marines actively encouraged. Many of these scalps were smuggled out of the country, and at least one skull had been displayed in a British museum. The British military further encouraged Ibans to behead the corpses of anti-colonial guerrillas in Malaya by promising cash bounties in return for the severed heads.

Graphic photographs of the decapitated heads were collected, duplicated, and traded between British soldiers as trophies of war, alongside countless images of British soldiers posing with the corpses of Malayans they had killed. Recognising the potential of these gruesome images in turning public opinion against colonialism, the *Daily Worker* newspaper began collecting and publishing many more atrocity photographs from Malaya, alongside eyewitness testimonies and commentaries from journalists, cartoonists, and military veterans.

Government and military officials began to panic at the thought that public opinion could turn against colonialism. Some even attempted to cover up and deny the existence of the headhunting practice by claiming that the *Daily Worker's* decapitation photograph was fake. The *Daily Worker* responded to this accusation that their first photograph was fake by releasing a second photograph of British soldiers in Malaya posing with a severed head. Eventually this forced the Colonial Secretary to openly confess in Parliament that the *Daily Worker's* headhunting photographs were real. Despite the authenticity of the photographs being confirmed in Parliament, the Daily Worker believed that the government was attempting to downplay the photographs and treat them as though they depicted an isolated incident. A few days later the Daily Worker published an avalanche of newly uncovered atrocity photographs far grizzlier and more horrifying than any images of the war ever published.

In response to the *Daily Worker* headhunting photographs, Winston Churchill and his Cabinet ordered the military to end their practice of headhunting in Malaya. The reason he did this was not that he morally disagreed with severing the heads of guerrillas, but rather because he feared that photographs of such atrocities would become ammunition for pro-communist and anti-colonial causes. Despite Churchill's order to end headhunting in Malaya, British soldiers widely ignored the order and continued to decapitate the corpses of suspected anti-colonial guerrillas and collect their severed heads. Not a single soldier during the Malayan Emergency was ever punished for decapitating a corpse and collecting the head.

Despite the horrific nature of the *Daily Worker's* decapitation photographs they were virtually ignored by all mainstream British newspapers and failed to cause any noticeable public outrage, with the notable exception of British trade union and socialist activists. Soon afterwards it became common knowledge in the press that British soldiers and police officers had been publicly displaying the corpses of suspected pro-independence revolutionaries in town centres and police stations across Malaya.

Although the British military claimed that corpses were beheaded solely for intelligence purposes, there is little evidence that the British occupation ever benefitted from the practice of headhunting. The British went from claiming that the photographs were fake, to admitting they were genuine and that the taking of heads was conducted for "identification purposes".[2] This research was unable to find a single British newspaper in the 20th century which republished the *Daily Worker*'s headhunting photographs. The scandal quickly sank into obscurity and became a vague memory, largely forgotten by both journalists and historians. No British soldiers or officers have ever been punished for taking part in headhunting during the Malayan Emergency. The British government and military have never apologised for the atrocities they committed in Malaya, nor have they taken any steps to rectify them.

From allies to "terrorists": Who were the victims of headhunting?

Before this book begins the readers must understand the Malayan Emergency, the war from which these decapitation photographs originate and the events that led to this conflict. It is very interesting to note that the people whose heads were being chopped off by British soldiers were once funded and supported by Britain to fight against Japan during WWII.

In 1941 the Japanese invaded British Malaya in a campaign which became known as one of the worst military defeats in British history. Desperate to hamper Japan's swift advance, the British armed and trained communist guerrillas to form a resistance army against the Japanese occupation. Known as the Malayan People's Anti-Japanese Army (MPAJA) and commanded by the Malayan Communist Party (MCP), this guerrilla force soon became the largest and most effective resistance organisation to fight against the Japanese occupation of Malaya.[3] The Japanese invasion of Malaya also had a profound psychological effect on the cause for Malayan independence. The sight of British soldiers running in defeat from the Japanese caused many Malayans to doubt the notion that white Europeans were inherently superior to Asians. This changing mentality fractured the foundations of British colonialism in Malaya and emboldened calls for independence from Britain.

After Japan's defeat in 1945 the British recolonised Malaya and the MPAJA was formally disbanded. Being hailed as heroes by the British, MPAJA veterans marched through London as part of the 1946 victory day parades and built a mock guerrilla camp in Hyde Park.[4] The most famous of the MPAJA commanders, the veteran anti-fascist and working-class hero Chin Peng, was presented the Order of the British Empire award (OBE) which was personally presented to him by Lord Mountbatten. Despite publicly disbanding and surrendering most of their guns to the British, the MPAJA secretly hid collections of weapons in the jungle and retained a skeletal force of fighters in the event that the British were ever to suppress the rights of Malayans.

Riding upon the wave of respect and fame which followed their role in resisting Japanese fascism, the communists became leaders of Malaya's trade unions and began fighting for the rights of Malayan workers, campaigning for higher wages for labourers, equal rights for women, and racial equality between all of Malaya's various ethnic groups. However despite their commitment to racial equality, the Malayan communist movement struggled to recruit members from outside the ethnic Chinese community which made up an approximate 40% of the country's population. For much of the early 20th century, the ethnic Chinese population suffered the worst conditions of any group of people in Malayan society. Many ethnic Chinese were barred from voting, lived under the constant threat of deportation, and were often the victims of intercommunal violence. During the Japanese occupation of Malaya, the Chinese suffered the worst of the violence and mass killings committed by the Japanese, who were seeking revenge on the Chinese for their military shortcomings in mainland China. To escape the Japanese, Malaya's Chinese populations were forced to flee to slums dotted along the edges of the jungles, where they remained even after the Japanese were defeated and the British returned. For these reasons and many more, the Chinese in Malaya had the most to gain from independence, and consequentially became attracted to revolutionary ideas which sought to address the hardships they faced.

The delicate peace between the communists and the British Empire failed to last, primarily due to the colonial occupation's continued looting of Malayan resources and their violent and often deadly suppression of Malayan trade unionists and leftist activists. Despite the incredible profits generated by Malaya's rubber plantations, most of this wealth was owned by a minority of white European bosses, while the majority of Asian workers lived in dire poverty. Furthermore the British had permitted the colour bar (racial segregation) across Malaya, suppressed voting rights, and was siphoning off much of Malaya's natural resources to pay off war debts to America. Malaya was one of the most profitable colonies in the British Empire due to its tin mines and rubber plantations, the money from which Britain would use to finance its post-war social services and the National Health Service.

To protect the profits of British capitalists from an increasingly organised working class, the colonial police and military used violence against labour activists, alongside other suppressive methods such as deportations, eviction from company housing, mass dismissals, and legal harassment.[5] There were several high profile cases of the colonial police beating workers to death in an attempt to break labour strikes and workplace occupations.[6] In one instance an estate was bought by a European company which proceeded to fire the entire workforce. When the workers refused to leave the estate and barricaded the property, the police attacked them, killing eight workers in an event known as the Segamat Massacre.[7] Communist rebels responded to this violence against labour activists by killing employers who were accused of mistreating their workers, shooting strikebreakers, and assassinating European plantation owners.[8]

The Malayan Emergency (1948–1960): Britain's Vietnam

In 1948 the assassinations of plantation bosses by Malayan communist revolutionaries were used by the British colonial occupation as a justification to arrest Malaya's leading left-wing and trade union activists, only for many of them to evade capture and escape deep into the jungles.[9] With all peaceful methods of enacting political change made impossible, the Malayan communists regrouped with fellow MPAJA veterans and founded the **Malayan National Liberation Army (MNLA)**, and waged a guerrilla war to liberate Malaya from British colonialism. The MNLA's long-term goal was to create an independent democratic socialist republic, with equal rights for women, racial equality, and for the nationalisation of Malaya's vastly profitable tin and rubber industries. The communist position on gender equality meant that a large portion of the MNLA's recruits were women who fought as equals beside their male counterparts, a fact which has often been overlooked by writers and documentary makers. The MNLA's guerrilla soldiers resisted the armed forces of Britain and their commonwealth allies for twelve years before being defeated, in a conflict now known to historians as the **Malayan Emergency (1948–1960)**.

Later dubbed "Britain's Vietnam" due to the war being a fight against communists in a jungle environment, the British made a conscious decision to describe the Malayan Emergency as an "Emergency" and never refer to the conflict as a "war". It is a commonly believed myth that the war was called an Emergency so that insurers would continue to protect British corporations in Malaya. However the term Emergency actually refers to the legal powers which the British Empire used to circumvent civilian law during instances of anti-colonial uprisings.[10] This wordplay was used by British forces as a justification to commit atrocities that broke international law, arguing that their actions could not be classified as 'war crimes' under the Geneva Convention because according to their commanders the conflict was an "Emergency" not a war. British propagandists often claimed that the MNLA was controlled and funded by communists from the Soviet Union and China, however both the British government and modern historians have been unable to find any evidence to support this now-discredited theory.[11, 12] Despite attempts by British propagandists to paint the Malayan communists as being controlled by the Soviet Union or China, the MNLA never received any orders, material support, funding, or training, from any government during their war against the British. On the other hand, Britain was joined by their colonial and Commonwealth allies Australia, New Zealand, Fiji, Rhodesia, and Kenya, all of which sent soldiers to help Britain fight the MNLA.

Although the British and their Commonwealth allies eventually won the Malayan Emergency, they did so by resorting to a number of extreme and controversial methods to crush both the MNLA and its civilian supporters. Such actions included:

- Forcefully evicting half a million (primarily Chinese) civilians and sending them to internment camps called New Villages.[13]
- Destroying rural aboriginal communities by evicting them from their homeland in the jungles, inadvertently leading to the deaths of thousands of tribespeople from disease.[14]
- Using Agent Orange for military purposes for the first time in history, a practice which was later used as a justification by America to use Agent Orange in Vietnam.[15]
- Using weapons such as flamethrowers and incendiary grenades which sometimes led to civilian casualties.[16,17]
- Printing millions of leaflets with the faces of dead pro-independence guerrillas and throwing them onto towns from aeroplanes between 1948–1952.[18]
- Distributing doctored ammunition designed to explode when fired and poisoning food supplies.
- Publicly displaying corpses to both terrify civilians and gather intelligence from onlookers. Such displays were often done in full view of children and relatives of the victim.[19,20]
- Racist mass deportation practices that led to people being deported to countries they had never lived in.[21]
- Collectively punishing civilian populations through food rationing and 22-hour curfews.[22]
- Torturing suspected socialists for information.[23]
- Hanging the former president of Malaya's largest trade union federation, despite pleas from India to grant him mercy.[24]
- Burning down villages whose inhabitants were suspected of having sympathy for socialists.[25]
- Committing the infamous Batang Kali Massacre of 24 unarmed villagers, which although not a part of official military policy, was covered up by the military for decades after the war ended.

Despite the many controversial and brutal actions undertaken to crush communists in Malaya, much of which relied heavily upon coercion and terror, the British military marketed their counterinsurgency as a flawless success, boasting to the world that they had been victorious because they had won the "hearts and minds" of the people they had colonised. This rare military victory over communist guerrillas was recognized by the United States which unsuccessfully attempted to replicate Britain's strategies in Vietnam, while also neglecting to take into consideration the vast social and geo-political differences between the two conflicts.[26] The result was an abysmal failure, inspiring the creation of America's disastrous "Strategic Hamlet" programme, and leading to countless civilian deaths and lifelong disabilities in Vietnam caused by exposure to Agent Orange.[27] Though the vast majority of the British public have forgotten about the Malayan Emergency, the war continues to be intensely studied by modern military leaders seeking lessons on how to defeat revolutionaries and insurgencies.

Despite the many controversial methods used to defeat the MNLA, the most unsavoury aspects of Britain's counterinsurgency in Malaya were often neglected by British mainstream publications. Most of the authors who wrote the first wave of literature on the Malayan Emergency were themselves former British soldiers and officials who had fought in Malaya and were thus typically unwilling to research topics that would potentially damage the reputation of their fellows. However come the early 21st century, British military shortcomings during the Iraq War sparked debates among historians and journalists, leading to heightened scepticism concerning the true effectiveness of Britain's past counterinsurgencies.

Introducing the Ibans: Britain's headhunters from Borneo

The decapitations in Malaya which were uncovered by the *Daily Worker* were rarely conducted by British troops themselves. The task of removing the heads from corpses was usually given to Iban trackers who the British had recruited from headhunting tribes in Borneo.

The Iban people, also known as 'Sea Dayaks', are one of over 200 ethnic subgroups belonging to the Dayak/Dyak people from the island of Borneo.[28] It was from these people that the British recruited their headhunters, whose actions sparked the British Malayan Headhunting Scandal once their headhunting activities in Malaya were revealed to the public by the *Daily Worker*.

Ibans were the subject of fascination by Europeans and were often fetishized as elite jungle warriors for their practice of headhunting, a cultural staple of Iban society perfected through centuries of inter-tribal warfare. Although headhunting had been a pillar of Iban culture for as long as recorded history remembers, the practice was often exacerbated by foreign interference in the region. Sarawak, the area of Borneo from which Ibans originate, was colonised by the incredibly wealthy British Brooke family whose male heirs ruled for over a century (1841–1946) as absolute monarchs known as "White Rajahs". The wife of the last White Rajah often jokingly referred to herself as the "Queen of the headhunters".[29] Despite instating the death penalty as punishment for headhunting to dissuade Ibans from taking heads, the White Rajah's involvement in Borneo's inter-tribal warfare during the 1800s had ironically led to an increase in headhunting.[30]

Foreign interference in Borneo yet again caused an increase in headhunting among Ibans when allied forces encouraged Iban warriors to attack and decapitate Japanese soldiers during WWII.[31,32] One Australian soldier in Borneo who fought in WWII describes being approached by a crowd of Ibans (Dayaks) hoping to claim cash rewards by presenting him with the severed heads of hundreds of Japanese soldiers:

> "Went out the end of the road from Sarawak one day and a great crowd of Dayaks, they were the local people. Must have been two or three hundred of them arrived with great big baskets. Baskets, well they would hold about fifty human heads each. And they came in with these things and they had been told by the British government, they claimed, that they would get five pounds sterling for every Japanese head and there must have been two or three hundred Japanese heads that were plonked down at my feet. And I didn't happen to have two or three hundred pounds in my pocket so we discreetly and very politely made our way back to Kuching and passed the matter over to the British attaché who had then arrived. What they did about it, I don't know."[33]

Within Iban society the practice of headhunting was exclusively performed by men and served to transform their reputation within their communities to that of brave and healthy warriors.[34] With bravery and fitness in Iban society being considered highly desirable traits for potential love interests, many Iban men were further encouraged to practice headhunting in the hopes of becoming more attractive to Iban women.[35] Headhunting was also believed by many Ibans to increase the fertility of women and encourage successful rice harvests.[36] During and shortly after WWII the attitudes of Iban women who were ecstatic at the sight of a potential lover returning with severed Japanese heads, was in stark contrast to the shock and disgust expressed by the lovers of American soldiers who had attempted to do the same.[37] Despite headhunting gradually becoming less common among Iban communities during the 20th century, it remained a central pillar of their culture, commemorated through dances, songs, funerals, romance, and festivals.[38]

The Ibans who fought alongside Britain during the Malayan Emergency were visually distinctive from their British counterparts. On average they were shorter than most British soldiers, they had long black hair often reaching to their waists, and many possessed large tattoos across their bodies.[39] It was common for Iban men to have all their natural teeth removed and replaced with gold teeth once they had saved enough money to afford them. Many Ibans carried charms around their necks and waists called pengarohs which were fabric containers filled with animal remains that they believed would protect them in battle.[40] Iban headhunters traditionally marked the successful taking of a human head with a tattoo on their thumb, a tradition that continued during the Malayan Emergency. Ibans often tattooed people they had befriended, which included many British soldiers in Malaya.[41] During the early years of the Malayan Emergency, most Ibans only wore loincloths, though as the war progressed it became customary to wear the same olive green uniforms as British soldiers. All of these features served to make Ibans visually distinctive and thus highly memorable in the eyes of British soldiers, who commonly noted the Ibans and their physical appearances in their diaries and memoirs.

The British military's deployment of Ibans during the Malayan Emergency began on August 8, 1948, when the first Ibans were sent to

Malaya to support a specialist jungle warfare unit known as Ferret Force.[42,43] Many of these Ibans signed up to fight alongside the British with the hopes of being allowed to collect the heads of their victims as trophies.[44] Most Iban recruits first arrived in Malaya at the coastal town of Port Dickson, often arriving armed with blowpipes and knives decorated with human hair.[45] Their deployment was supported by the Secretary of State for the Colonies, Arthur Creech Jones, who agreed to deploy them for 3 months. However amid rumours that they still practised headhunting, all the Ibans Britain had recruited were removed from the Malayan peninsula by December 1948.[46] Once the controversy had died down the Ibans were quietly redeployed in 1949 and fought until the end of the war.

Described by one British official as the most "faithful servants" of the British military,[47] Ibans were viewed by the colonial occupation as an extremely valuable asset due to their proficiency in jungle bushcraft.[48] During the early stages of the Malayan Emergency, Ibans were attached in small numbers to larger military units. Despite being armed and trained to fight as soldiers, the British chose to instead classify their Iban recruits as "civilians". In recognition of their civilian status some notable Ibans were awarded prestigious British decorations usually reserved for civilians such as the George Cross and the George Medal.[49,50] One famous Iban called Awang anak Raweng, was awarded the George Cross after he (allegedly) single handily repelled an attack by fifty communist guerrillas.[51]

Ibans were known to have worked with at least 42 different battalions belonging to Commonwealth armies during the Malayan Emergency.[52] During their service with these regiments, Ibans were expected to decapitate the bodies of suspected MNLA guerrillas and were often permitted to keep parts of the corpses (typically the scalp and hair) as trophies. Some notable examples of military organisations that used Ibans included:

- The Coldstream Guards
- The Scots Guards
- The Manchester Regiment
- The Lincolnshire Regiment
- The Worcestershire Regiment
- The Cameronians (Scottish Rifles)

- The Queen's Own Royal West Kent Regiment
- The Green Howards
- The Suffolk Regiment
- The Grenadier Guards
- The 40, 42, and 45 Royal Marine Commandos
- The Special Air Service Regiment (SAS)
- The Royal Air Force (RAF)

The Ibans imparted to the members of these military organisations much of their knowledge on jungle survival.[53,54] Later into the Malayan Emergency, Ibans also served alongside soldiers from Australia and New Zealand.[55]

In 1952, the British Army created two experimental Iban platoons, and by December over 1,168 Ibans had completed a tour of active service in Malaya.[56] In 1953 the British founded a regiment to host Iban soldiers called the Sarawak Rangers.[57] However, Britain and their Commonwealth allies rarely trusted Ibans to act independently and so their activities were constantly and closely monitored by a white European superior. The Sarawak Rangers were not exempt from this and were put under the command of a white British man called Christopher Baird.[58] Although most Ibans in Malaya joined the Sarawak Rangers, some continued to work while attached to large English speaking military units.

Some experts theorise that despite the strategic asset of the Iban's jungle bushcraft skills, the British military's faith in their abilities was largely influenced by the stereotype that as "primitive" people, the Ibans enjoyed a closer relationship with nature than Europeans.[59] Similarly, some historians argue that the British military's fetishization of traits they believed were inherent in certain ethnic groups, caused British soldiers to view Ibans as a martial race built for warfare.[60] Another misconception concerning Ibans that circulated among British troops was the mistaken belief that all Ibans were cannibals, a myth which was sometimes used to tease young and inexperienced British soldiers.[61] Despite their popularity, many British soldiers looked down condescendingly on Ibans, often referring to the Ibans they fought alongside as 'savages', sometimes comparing them to servants and pets.[62] Many British soldiers believed that Ibans possessed an almost supernatural ability to track communists via scents that no

European could smell. In numerous instances, Ibans were recorded to have successfully discovered MNLA guerrillas by following the scent of tobacco, the smell of which was allegedly undetectable to British troops.[63]

However despite their overwhelming popularity with British soldiers, the Ibans who fought in the Malayan Emergency suffered from numerous limitations and difficulties which brought into question their military effectiveness. Some were accused of lacking discipline and had difficulty holding fire when ordered.[64] Iban society had no social classes, making it especially hard for them to adhere to military discipline in Malaya.[65] There were cases of Ibans drawing their weapons and using them to threaten their superior officers.[66] Others were accused of aggressively pointing their rifles at unarmed people, stealing property from civilians, and looting corpses for valuables which they would later wear while posing for photographs.[67] Some Royal Marines also complained that Ibans were inaccurate when using firearms.[68] Despite being jungle trackers, Ibans were not native to the Malay peninsula and were as susceptible to jungle diseases in Malaya as their Commonwealth counterparts.[69] Some British commanders considered the Ibans very difficult to work with and believed that they harboured a strong racial hatred towards Malays. Due to this belief, Ibans were rarely trusted with automatic weapons, even after the Malayan Emergency.[70] Ibans were given far more lenience by their commanders in comparison to their British counterparts, and were routinely forgiven for behaviour which would have landed British troops in a military prison.

Many British officers found that recruits from Africa and other parts of the Commonwealth performed better as jungle trackers than Ibans.[71,72] In one instance, rumours arose among British troops that one Iban they had recruited was not actually an elite jungle tracker, but had actually spent most of his adult life living in a city working as a taxi driver.[73] Many Commonwealth officers found Ibans useless in combat scenarios due to the language barrier.[74,75] Difficulties in communicating with Ibans was further exacerbated by the fact that virtually every Iban recruited by the British was illiterate, and that the vast majority of the British soldiers they served alongside had no prior experience in Asian languages. Another common complaint of Iban soldiers was that their superstitious beliefs made them unreliable, and that it was common for Ibans to refuse to go on patrols after claiming to have received evil omens in the form of bad dreams.[76,77] In one instance a duo of Ibans in Malaya, one of whom was a practised headhunter, began to believe that they were surrounded by ghosts during a night patrol. This severely damaged the morale of an SAS patrol, who, due to the language barrier, mistakenly believed that the Iban duo were trying to warn them of an upcoming ambush.[78]

Ibans also appeared to have been involved in an abnormally high number of deadly friendly fire incidents during the Malayan Emergency, sometimes as the victims,[79,80] and at other times the perpetrators.[81] The first recorded Iban casualty during the Malayan Emergency occurred in 1951, when an Iban called Jaweng ak Jugah was shot dead by a special constable who ironically mistook him for a "communist terrorist".[82] Jugah's obituary in the official journal of the Royal Marines neglected to mention that he was killed by friendly fire. It is possible that the aforementioned communication difficulties were responsible for many of these friendly fire instances.

The news that Ibans were being deployed by the British military to fight in Malaya was already a widely publicised fact in British newspapers before the *Daily Worker* published their infamous decapitation photographs. When Ibans were first deployed in Malaya, British newspapers hailed their arrival and openly referred to them as headhunters.[83] Numerous frontpage articles appeared within British newspapers with titles such as "Head-hunters prepare for Jungle War in Malaya",[84] "Headhunters Train to Fight Terrorists",[85] "Head-Hunter Troops for Malaya?"[86] "Headhunters to Terrorise Terrorists,"[87] "Headhunters After Terrorist Scalps,"[88] and "Headhunters Called in to Track Rebels".[89]

British newspapers typically portrayed Ibans as though they were uncivilised and superstitious people who happened to have a soft spot for Europeans. In one such example, a British newspaper article supporting the deployment of Ibans in Malaya described them as "primitive and superstitious", claiming that Ibans "have a great faith in the white man and a great love for him" and that they often felt the urge to decapitate their Asian neighbours.[90] Even during the very earliest period of their deployment, Iban cultural practices were a cause for concern among the British as shown by multiple British newspapers reporting that Ibans deployed to Malaya were armed with poison darts.[91, 92] Within a private telegram to a fellow colonial official, the Secretary of State for the Colonies, Arthur Creech Jones, attempted to calm fears of headhunting among Britain's Iban recruits by claiming that none of the Ibans (Dyaks) fighting in Malaya still practised headhunting:

> "There is no truth whatsoever in the suggestion that they brought or used poison arrows. There is no truth in the suggestion that head hunting is prevalent (as it used to be years ago) among the Dyaks. There is no truth in the statement that the Dyaks were instructed or allowed to cut off bandits' heads or received or were promised any reward for doing so."[93]

This quote from Arthur Creech Jones was made a few months into the Malayan Emergency, and may have been true when he made it. However, eventually everything he argued in the above quote would eventually be proven false. Ibans recruited by Britain to fight in Malaya often possessed poison darts designed to be shot from blowpipes, headhunting was prevalent among them, and they were instructed to decapitate the corpses of their enemies, often under the impression that they would receive a financial reward and would be allowed to keep the scalp. These early concerns show how British officials were always conscious of the cultural importance and widespread practice of headhunting among the Ibans they were recruiting. In the month before the *Daily Worker*'s first article exposing the widespread practice of headhunting by Ibans against suspected MNLA guerrillas, there were 264 known Ibans attached to British forces in Malaya.[94]

As opposed to the majority of British newspapers which claimed Ibans had all abandoned headhunting, some newspapers attempted to make moral arguments in defence of allowing Iban mercenaries to decapitate anti-colonial guerrillas in Malaya. *News Chronicle* quoted American anthropologist Margaret Mead arguing that "using Dyaks who enjoyed head-hunting was no worse than sending white troops who had been brought up to regard killing as wrong."[95] Another British newspaper called *Truth* went even further and supported the practice of decapitating "terrorists" and turning their severed heads into trophies as an incentive to encourage Ibans (Dyaks) to kill MNLA guerrillas, which the article referred to as "Red Gangsters".

> "As was inevitable, the employment of Dyak head-hunters has provoked protests from sentimentalists, who are always ready to sympathise with the beast of prey which suffers the fate which it was about to wreck on its victim. It is held to be peculiarly wrong to employ Dyaks to kill, because they enjoy killing. This reminds one of the argument that it is more humane to condemn a fox to a lingering death in a trap than to hunt it down with a pack of hounds. Those in Malaya, especially the women and children, who live in ceaseless fear of the Red Gangsters will feel nothing but gratitude to the Dyaks who help to free them from the menace, and will not worry if a few terrorist heads are carried back as trophies."[96]

The *Daily Worker* was not the first publication to accuse the British military of allowing Iban headhunters to sever heads and take the scalps of Malayan guerrillas as trophies.

- In January 1951 *Commando News*, an official Royal Marine publication, published an article written by a Marine with the rank of Major, openly discussing how he allowed Ibans to scalp corpses in Malaya.[97] This article was later republished in *Globe and Laurel*, the official journal of the Royal Marines.
- In February 1951, two Australian newspapers published articles that put a positive spin on Iban headhunting and scalping in Malaya, quoting from the aforementioned article in *Commando News*, and telling their readers that Ibans were taking scalps from Malaya back home with them after their military service.[98, 99]
- In March 1951 a British newspaper called *The People* published an article accusing Ibans of taking the scalps from corpses in Malaya.[100, 101] However unlike the *Daily Worker* headhunting articles a year later, *The People* failed to publish any proof of these claims.

Declassified government documents show that British colonial officials viewed the article in *The People* as a potential propaganda threat and intended to cover up their headhunting allegations by releasing a War Office rebuttal to be published in a Malayan newspaper called the *Straits Times* designed to "kill the effects of the People's article".[102] Other British officials disagreed and believed it was best to avoid responding to such reports as to avoid drawing further attention to said accusations.[103] This method of ignoring media accusations of colonial wrongdoings as to not draw further attention to them would become a common tactic favoured by British officials against the *Daily Worker's* numerous accusations of British military atrocities in Malaya.

Several newspapers unintentionally raised concerns surrounding a common practice among Iban mercenaries which was the taking of macabre trophies from the corpses of suspected MNLA guerrillas. In one example, *The Yorkshire Post and Leeds Mercury* reported that Ibans in Malaya had been taking hair cuttings from corpses and were using it to decorate the scabbards of their knives.[104] In hindsight these hair cutting trophies taken from the bodies of suspected MNLA guerrillas should have been red flags for anyone who believed Britain's Iban recruits were not practiced headhunters.

The news that Britain was hiring Ibans, whose culture was known to have close links to headhunting, was picked up by the small yet active anti-war movement in Britain led by the Communist Party of Great Britain (CPGB) and used as an example of colonial atrocities committed by the British in Malaya. One example is the anti-colonial leaflet *Malaya: Stop the War*, written by the CPGB's leader Harry Pollitt, one of Britain's leading anti-colonial voices. Within his leaflet Pollitt describes various atrocities committed by British forces against Malayans, including being chased "by Alsatian wolf-hounds and by head-hunting Dyaks."[105] The CPGB whose activists founded and managed the *Daily Worker* newspaper, also supported the distribution of Malayan socialist and pro-independence literature throughout Britain and published numerous booklets and articles comparing British attempts to crush uprisings throughout Asia to Nazi atrocities committed in Europe.[106] In one notable example the communist poet Randall Swingler, a regular contributor to the *Daily Worker*, wrote a poem (which was likely influenced by the headhunting scandal) that compared British military atrocities in Malaya to the evils of Nazism.[107,108]

Interestingly the *Daily Worker's* printing of Malayan headhunting photographs in 1952 was not the first time that this newspaper published articles describing British allied forces decapitating anti-colonial fighters and socialists. In 1931 the *Daily Worker* published an article covering the use of decapitations by British colonial forces in Burma.[109] Then in 1947 the *Daily Worker* published articles describing the decapitated heads of Greek guerrillas by British allies. Just as the Malayan photographs would soon have, these articles from Greece left a strong impression on Winston Churchill.[110]

Chapter 1

The Headhunting Scandal Begins

The first decapitation photograph is published (28 April)

By 1952 the existence of Iban mercenaries in Malaya serving as jungle trackers and fighting alongside Commonwealth troops was public knowledge, having established themselves as capable jungle guides in the eyes of British soldiers and often being given features in British news media. Although rumours existed suggesting that these Iban were headhunters, there was no photographic proof that Ibans fighting alongside the British in Malaya were taking heads. The only published evidence showing that Ibans were decapitating people in Malaya existed in obscure military publications which were only read by a small number of British soldiers.[1]

This all changed on the 28 April 1952 when the *Daily Worker* published their frontpage article titled **"This is the War in Malaya"** which contained the first ever published photographic proof of Britain's headhunting practices in Malaya.[2] The article featured a photograph dated to 1951 showing a tall European man grinning with a decapitated head in his right hand and a rifle on his left, an Asian man pointing a rifle at the head, and a second armed Asian man wearing a large crucifix. The victim who had been decapitated by an Iban headhunter was said to have been a suspected communist and anti-colonial guerrilla fighter belonging to the Malayan National Liberation Army (MNLA). In the background four shirtless Royal Marines walk past a hut with the sign "40 commando hut R.M.".[3] The anonymous whistleblower who leaked the photograph said that the incident happened in the centre of a British military base near Kuala Kangsar in Perak, Malaya.[4] This ground-breaking article marking the beginning of the British Malayan Headhunting Scandal of 1952 contained only the first of many Malayan headhunting photographs which the paper would soon publish.

According to the official version of events as recorded in declassified Royal Navy archival documents and not released to the public until decades later, the *Daily Worker's* photograph had been taken in April 1951 after a Royal Marine patrol had been ambushed by MNLA guerrillas. The first volley of guerrilla gunfire killed two British Royal Marines, one of which was a Lieutenant and the other a Corporal.[5] The patrol returned fire and killed one of the guerrillas before the surviving guerrillas retreated back into the jungle. The British troops were accompanied by an Iban who ran away when the fight started. Once the fight had ended he returned and decapitated the corpse of an MNLA guerrilla which had taken part in the ambush. The severed head was then brought back to a British military base where the British soldiers, who according to their commanders had lost all sense of discipline after the attack, played with the decapitated head and photographed themselves posing while holding it.[6]

British Government Denial

Many officials believed that the decapitation of heads was necessary for military intelligence/identification purposes, believing that retrieving corpses from the deep jungles was impossible and that cameras could not operate in such environments. Despite the real difficulties of removing corpses from the jungle, the military failed to provide even a single instance in which decapitating a suspected MNLA fighter had helped to win an intelligence victory over the guerrillas or had in any way served a useful purpose to the Commonwealth forces during the war. Internally opinions were split on whether the decapitations were necessary for intelligence gathering and should continue, or if the risk of presenting ammunition to the communist's anti-colonial cause outweighed any potential intelligence victory over the MNLA.

Despite the shocking and violent nature of this photograph and the seriousness of its accusations, the initial reaction by the British government, journalists, and the wider public was underwhelming.[7] The main reason for this lack of reaction was because many of the people who saw this photograph initially believed it was fake.[8] The *Daily Worker's* support for Marxist-Leninist political ideology and the Soviet Union, coupled with its consistent opposition to British colonialism and support for racial equality, caused many British readers to suspect that the paper's decapitation photograph was a forgery created for the purpose of communist propaganda. One British newspaper even questioned whether the *Daily* Worker should be legally allowed to publish such a photograph, while also reporting that most people believed the photograph to be a fake.[9]

Government officials quickly responded to the *Daily Worker's* headhunting photograph by claiming that the image was a forgery. In one of the most bizarre cases of government denial, one official suggested that the decapitation shown in the *Daily Worker*'s photograph may have been done by the MNLA guerrillas themselves.[10] This spokesperson for the Colonial Office claimed that the decapitation "may have been done by the Communists because the victim was threatening to run away or surrender." He went onto say that: "It looks as if the soldier is holding up the head to show what the Communists sometimes do to their own people."[11] Another British government spokesperson, this time from the Admiralty (the commanders of the Royal Navy), also claimed that the photograph was fake.

The Admiralty's investigation

Publicly the authenticity of the *Daily Worker's* photograph was called into question by both the Royal Navy and the Colonial Office. However behind the scenes military officials had secretly run their own investigation which swiftly confirmed that the decapitation photograph published by the *Daily Worker* was real. The very next day following the first *Daily Worker* headhunting photograph, British officials had successfully identified the British soldier in the photograph and the photographer, both of whom confirmed that their version of events corroborated with what was published in the *Daily Worker*.[12] The British soldier holding the decapitated head in the first *Daily Worker* photograph was identified as "Marine Mills" and was described by one British military General as a "decent and reputable chap".[13]

Following the publication of the first headhunting photograph from Malaya, government officials began keeping a closer eye on the *Daily Worker* for clues that more potential British war crimes had been leaked.

This is shown by the number of scrapbooks containing *Daily Worker* articles on Malaya that appear within the historical archives of British government officials.[14]

When looking at declassified government archives covering the *Daily Worker's* exposure of headhunting in Malaya, a pattern emerges in the attitudes of government and military leaders. Many of them seem extremely confused by the *Daily Worker's* headhunting accusations and most appear entirely clueless concerning the exact details of the British military's headhunting practice in Malaya. Some British soldiers and their commanders would later accuse critics of headhunting of being out of touch with the realities of jungle warfare.[15] It would appear that in some ways many of them were correct, though this accusation can also apply to the headhunting practice's government supporters. Many of London's government workers, most of whom came from relatively wealthy families and lived very comfortable lives, were largely disconnected from the brutal realities of British colonialism and the violence inflicted upon its Asian and African subjects.

Despite the *Daily Worker's* headhunting photograph appearing to have been buried under the accusations that it was a forgery, military leaders behind the scenes took the *Daily Worker's* accusations far more seriously. The First Lord of the Admiralty (commander of the Royal Navy) held a meeting within his room in the House of Commons to discuss the *Daily Worker* photograph with fellow British military elites. Some of the more notable attendees at this meeting included the Commander General of the Royal Marines, the Civil Lord of the Admiralty and both the Secretary and the Principal Private Secretary of the Admiralty, among several others.[16] Some suggested that a press statement be created and released at the approval of Winston Churchill. Others lamented that their telegram to the British Empire's Far East Land Force (FARLAF) had been met with evasive answers surrounding the practice of headhunting in Malaya.[17] One official who appeared the most informed was a man known as Colonel Lumsden of the Royal Marines. He told those present at the meeting that Ibans working for the British were officially permitted to take parts of the scalp of dead MNLA guerrillas home with them for cultural reasons. He also said that patrols were equipped with No.0 Brownie cameras, though due to jungle conditions they could not always be used.[18]

Chapter 2

Journalism on the Offensive

The second decapitation photograph is released (30 April)

In response to the claims from newspapers and government spokespersons that the decapitation photograph was fake, the *Daily Worker* released yet another front-page article titled **"These are no Fakes"** containing a second never-before-seen photograph of British soldiers in Malaya posing with a decapitated head. The article also included a warning to the British government that the *Daily Worker* possessed many more such photographs of British atrocities in Malaya that they would publish in the future.[1] The *Daily Worker* also reported that Britain's Ibans in Malaya often decorated their headhunting knives with tufts of human hair, possibly taken from the corpses of people they had killed in Malaya.[2]

The MacDonald Family

To further link the British government to a policy of headhunting, the *Daily Worker* also printed a photograph showing Malcolm MacDonald, the son of Britain's first Labour Party Prime Minister (Ramsay MacDonald), welcoming Iban headhunters upon their arrival to Malaya.[3] Malcolm who was then serving as the British Commissioner-General for Southeast Asia, was far from ignorant of the practices of Iban headhunters.[4] He had previously spent time living amongst Ibans in Borneo, witnessing their headhunting trophies, partaking in "headhunter dances",[5] and going as far as to describe one veteran Iban headhunter whose house was decorated with human skulls as "one of the greatest men I had ever met".[6] Not only did Malcolm have an intimate knowledge of Iban headhunting but he had personally hand-picked a 17 year old Iban teenager to lead the first batch of Iban recruits sent to Malaya back in 1948.[7] Malcolm had even toured Malaya with American politicians during the Malayan Emergency, taking the opportunity to showcase Britain's Iban recruits to the fascination of his American guests.[8]

Interestingly the communist activist J.R. Campbell, then the editor of the *Daily Worker* and the man responsible for publishing the headhunting photographs, had a personal history with the MacDonald family. Decades earlier Campbell had inadvertently contributed to the destruction of Ramsay MacDonald's Labour Party government during an episode of British history known as the "Campbell Case". In 1924 Campbell was arrested on mutiny charges for publishing an article calling on British soldiers to mutiny in the event that their government starts another imperialist war. Ramsay suspended the prosecution which triggered a 'vote of no confidence', removing him as Prime Minister and causing the collapse of Britain's first ever Labour Party government. Now decades later, Campbell had yet again become involved in the politics of the MacDonald family, this time as the editor of a newspaper that was insinuating that Ramsay's son Malcolm was involved in war crimes. Interestingly, Campbell also shared a history with Winston Churchill against whom he ran during the 1951 General Election in his local constituency. Now less than a year later, Campbell was accusing his former election opponent of overseeing brutal atrocities against Malayan freedom fighters.

Legality of the headhunting

Despite publicly claiming that the decapitation photographs were fake, government officials privately discussed how to best deal with the *Daily Worker's* exposure of Britain's war crimes in Malaya. One legal advisor for the Admiralty admitted that "there is no doubt that under International Law a similar case in wartime would be a war crime."[9, 10] Although at first glance this may appear to be a confession by a legal professional that the decapitations were indeed war crimes, the wording and context shows otherwise. When the legal advisor said that "a similar case in wartime would be a war crime", he is following the British government's official line of denying the existence of a war in Malaya. The Malayan Emergency was officially described by the British as an "emergency" and not a "war". The advisor is using wordplay to argue that the decapitations were not war crimes because Britain had decided there was no war. Regardless of whatever strategies British propagandists had decided would be best, nothing could change the fact that they were fighting against an organised guerrilla army in a war in which thousands of people had already been killed.

There are zero known cases in which a British soldier was punished for decapitating a corpse during the Emergency or collecting photographs of said decapitations. However the testimony of at least one British soldier acknowledged that removing the body parts from corpses in Malaya was seen as a court-martial offence. The soldier called M. Engel recounts his experiences in 1949 when he and his men in fighting in Malaya's Gunong Bonsu Forest Reserve on the Kedah/Perak Border, removed the hands and head of a single CT, an abbreviation for "Communist Terrorist" used by British propagandists to dehumanise the MNLA. The soldier describes taking the severed body parts to Kulim Police Station:

> "We rejoined the main body of the patrol and made our way back to the start line, where a major in the Malay Regiment told me he had heard firing. When I had told him we had killed a CT, he wanted to know what we had done with the body, so I opened my pack, allowing a severed head and two hands to roll out onto the ground in front of him. He became very excited and got on the radio to his brigadier who stormed up, red-faced and furious. Apparently, our friends from Nepal had been upsetting everyone by doing this sort of thing and it had now become a court martial offense. In the end, I was ordered to go back and recover the rest of the CT and the various bits and pieces were taken to Kulim Police Station, where the usual photo-graphs were taken, 'pour encouragers les autres'."[11]

Soldiers and eyewitnesses

In early May 1952 following their second decapitation photograph, the *Daily Worker* began receiving countless telephone calls and letters from British soldiers who had been deployed to Malaya. These soldiers shared their eyewitness accounts of the war and their reactions to the paper's atrocity photographs, much of which the paper began publishing. William

Hutton, a Royal Artillery veteran of four years with a certificate of good service, told of how he showed a *Daily Worker* decapitation photograph at an appeal tribunal in London and used the photograph as a justification to oppose being recalled into military service:

> "What things we have done in Malaya! Concentration camps, destruction of villages-and now this."
>
> "These atrocities show a terrible attitude to human life. If I needed any further confirmation of my point of view in objecting to being recalled, there it is."[12]

In a similar instance of protest, one British soldier who had fought for three years in Malaya marched into the *Daily Worker*'s offices and gave reporters his eyewitness account of the decapitations, among other horrors that he experienced:

> "I have seen worse myself."
>
> "There are plenty of such photographs. But many were confiscated by Public Relations Officers and destroyed."
>
> "The Liberation Army has the support of all the peasants and workers."[13]

The same soldier then told reporters that he had witnessed Gurkhas in Bentong emptying sacks filled with severed heads, stressing to reporters that this was a very common occurrence.[14] Although most cases of headhunting during the Malayan Emergency appear to have been conducted by Ibans, Gurkhas also gained a reputation for headhunting.[15,16] The names and exact ethnic identity of the Asian men in the first two *Daily Worker* headhunting photographs is currently unknown, though it is likely the most prominent one wearing a crucifix is an Iban. However, due to the dark skin and Asian facial features of the men, some viewers of the photographs assumed them to be Gurkhas. This was such a prominent issue that the British embassy in Nepal warned the Foreign Office that grizzly images from Malaya were harming their attempts to recruit Gurkhas.[17] One British man who served the British military alongside Gurkhas and believed them to have

Journalism on the Offensive   9

been shown in the *Daily Worker* photograph, describes their reputation for headhunting:

> "Now in the early days of the Emergency, when the Gurkhas made a kill, they would decapitate the bandit, and carry the head, or heads, back to the camp, to prove to their officers that they had killed! Unfortunately, a communist paper in the UK called the Daily Worker, had a front page picture of a Gurkha holding the heads, with a caption stating that ... "This is what British troops are doing to the enemy," or some such similar statement. It was therefore decided at that moment, that every patrol should be issued with a camera, to record a kill."[18]

The fact that headhunting was a very common practice among British soldiers, Ibans, the police, Gurkhas, and possibly other Commonwealth soldiers in Malaya, is corroborated by many similar eyewitness accounts outside those published in the *Daily Worker*. One of the most famous of these soldiers was the former Royal Marine commando and journalist Neil Ascherson. During the Malayan Emergency, Ascherson witnessed an MNLA guerrilla die in a vain attempt to pull another guerrilla to safety, and also witnessed the racist oppression of ethnic Chinese people under British colonialism. These experiences among many others changed his view of the war, later turning him into a life-long anti-imperialist and campaigner for Scottish independence. When recollecting his experiences of the Malayan Emergency, Ascherson recalled that the decapitation of suspected MNLA members by Commonwealth forces was a common practice during the war.[19] The decapitation of heads was so common that it even seeped into the culture of certain regiments, with some soldiers creating wooden versions of decapitated heads which were attached to the poles of large tents.[20]

The soldiers whose eyewitness accounts were published in the *Daily Worker* were certainly not alone in their disgust at the decapitations. One British man stationed in Malaya immediately demanded to be sent home after an officer told him that he could be ordered to decapitate corpses and cut off their fingers.[21] Another British soldier witnessed his fellow soldiers having mental breakdowns and crying in their sleep after they were ordered by their lieutenant to decapitate the corpse of a suspected MNLA member.[22] Other British soldiers were so sickened by the practice of headhunting and the resulting photographs that they lost all faith in the British military. Many of the British soldiers who felt disgusted at the practice of headhunting and other British colonial atrocities in Malaya had a tendency to become life-long socialist and anti-imperialist activists.[23]

The attitudes of British soldiers who had witnessed and taken part in headhunting were extremely varied. Some soldiers were enthusiastic supporters of headhunting, arguing that the decapitations were a matter of practicality and that such actions were to be expected in the brutal realities of jungle warfare. Some soldiers would proudly brag about their involvement in headhunting, justifying their actions by claiming that their victims were "terrorists".[24]

Gordon Knapp, one soldier's protest against headhunting

Of the many letters and interviews from British soldiers received and published by the *Daily Worker*, one British soldier stands out from all the others for the length and detail of his reaction to the *Daily Worker's* articles exposing the practice of headhunting in Malaya. Gordon Knapp was a WWII veteran and former Royal Marine Commando who had been involved in raids against the Nazis in Holland. Knapp also happened to work as a photographic processor and used his professional knowledge to authenticate the *Daily Worker* headhunting photographs. Knapp wrote to the *Daily Worker* with news of his protests against the British military's headhunting atrocities and his disgust at the actions depicted by the *Daily Worker's* decapitation photographs.

> "It depicts a scene which I am ashamed to admit smears in the lowest form the good and glorified name of the Commandos. I am in no way a Communist and am not influenced by them, but I have discussed the print with my fellow-photographers at work, and we have decided it is not faked but original."

"As an ex-wartime member of the No.4 Army Commando, I feel ashamed that any member of units bearing our name should lower himself to parade before a camera in such a bestial manner."[25]

Knapp had also angrily informed the General Secretary of the Army Commando Association of his disgust over the atrocities his fellow Royal Marines were committing in Malaya, and returned his Old Comrades badge and membership book in protest against Britain's treatment of Malayans. In further protest, he rejected an invitation to a British war memorial unveiling because the *Daily Worker* decapitation photographs had made him too ashamed to appear at such events.

Although the *Daily Worker* received and published many responses by both British soldiers and members of the public responding to their headhunting photographs, Knapp was by far the most qualified of any person to comment on them. Not only was he a professional photographic processor, cameraman and Royal Marine Commando Veteran, but he had allowed his response to be printed alongside a detailed photograph of his face, his full legal name, and even an address.[26]

This wave of new evidence provided by eyewitnesses sharply increased the *Daily Worker's* credibility and emboldened them to put greater effort into publicising their ground-breaking journalistic work on the Malayan Emergency. Recognising the potential of their atrocity photographs in shifting public opinion against colonialism, the *Daily Worker* reported that over the course of a week since their first headhunting article they had sold and dispatched over 200,000 leaflets containing proof of the decapitations happening in Malaya.[27,28]

However despite multiple soldier eye-witness testimonies, the opinions of photographic experts, the publication of genuine photographic evidence, and the private admittance of Britain's military leaders that the decapitation photographs were indeed genuine, the Colonial Office was still refusing to answer public inquiries about the authenticity of the *Daily Worker's* decapitation photographs.[29] The rush to find a suitable justification for such seemingly indefensible acts, coupled with the hope that people will simply move on and the scandal will be forgotten, had effectively caused the government to become silent and refuse to answer any questions related to headhunting.

Winston Churchill and government awareness

Despite shunning public questions on the issue, behind closed doors British military and government officials were panicking over how to best proceed in the face of the *Daily Worker's* photographs and accusations. Winston Churchill, then serving his second term as Prime Minister (1952–1955) was quickly made aware of the *Daily Worker's* accusations that his government had been involved in war crimes shortly after the *Daily Worker* published the first decapitation photograph. The First Lord of the Admiralty J. P. L. Thomas sent Churchill a letter expressing his belief that decapitations should be entirely forbidden even though intel may be lost as a result. He also asked Churchill for permission to publish a public statement on the decapitations and claimed that although his Marines had taken part in these atrocities, he himself was not responsible since they were acting under Army operational control while in Malaya.[30] Attached to his letter to Churchill was a press statement which Thomas had taken the liberty of writing.[31]

Amid growing pressure on the government to respond to the headhunting accusations, the subject of the *Daily Worker* decapitation photographs was tabled for discussion within the House of Commons. Even though both the recruitment of Iban mercenaries and the severing of heads in Malaya began under Clement Attlee's Labour Party government, it was left-wing Labour Party MPs who were the most vocally critical politicians of the Malayan Emergency.[32] British communists recognised this difference and attempted to swing the opinions of left-wing Labour MPs and their supporters against colonialism, while also attacking the Labour Party leadership for its racist and imperialist policies.

The politician charged with formulating the official government response to upcoming MP questions concerning headhunting in Malaya was Oliver Lyttelton, the Secretary of State for the Colonies (1951–1954). Lyttelton was no stranger to the Malayan Emergency and the Ibans, having visited Malaya where he was photographed with an Iban mercenary shortly before the *Daily Worker's* first headhunting photograph.[33] Searching for more information to prepare himself for the government's official statement on the *Daily Worker* headhunting photographs, Lyttelton sent a telegram to General Gerald Templer, the man in charge of implementing Britain's military strategies in Malaya. Within the telegram, Lyttelton asked for Templer's opinions on the practice of headhunting and the *Daily Worker* photographs.[34] Templer replied with a bold and uncompromising defence of the practice of decapitating suspected guerrillas, and accused his critics of being naïve. He also told Lyttelton that anyone who opposed Britain's decapitation of corpses in Malaya could not truly understand the reality of jungle warfare. Ironically, despite accusing his critics of being ignorant of the jungle, Templer himself had only spent a single day living in the jungle during the entirety of his time serving as a General in Malaya.[35] Templer then privately told Lyttelton that the incident shown in the *Daily Worker* decapitation photographs was the only known example of a photograph showing British forces being involved in headhunting while deployed in Malaya:

> "The incident in question, which is the only one of its kind which can be traced, took place over a year ago. It is unfortunate that the Daily Worker has now made use of it for its own purposes."[36]

Templer's claim that the *Daily Worker's* decapitation photographs depict the only known image of such an instance that he was able to trace, despite him being in charge of the British military operations in Malaya and the most powerful man in the country, exposes a flaw in his defence of headhunting. The fact that the *Daily Worker* would uncover multiple headhunting photographs and eyewitnesses suggests that Templer was potentially misleading Lyttleton about the extent to which British soldiers were indulging in the taking of photographic trophies depicting severed heads. However, assuming Templer was being honest in his response to Lyttelton, Templer may have been largely ignorant of the behaviour of his own troops. In fact awareness of the decapitations among British soldiers was so widespread that some soldiers felt bold enough to use official military communication channels to joke about creating shelves filled with jars full of decapitated heads for the amusement of the colonial police.[37] Some Commonwealth personnel were even bold enough to take photographs of soldiers posing alongside corpses and send the negatives to be developed by photo studio businesses, allowing the workers developing the photographs to witness these grizzly corpse trophy photographs.[38]

In the following decades after the Malayan Emergency, General Gerald Templar became an icon within British military circles. Much of the early literature on the Malayan Emergency sought to credit Britain's victory in Malaya to Templer's supposed genius, fermenting a quasi-cult of personality surrounding his image. Lyttelton would confess that he never truly believed in Templer's defence of headhunting.[39]

It is true however that the British military put an incredibly high emphasis on intelligence during the Malayan Emergency, which naturally included their ability to identify potential MNLA members. In one instance which demonstrates the extreme lengths British troops would go to when it came to identification, the British Army's Suffolk Regiment dug up the graves of suspected communists so that the police could publicly display their corpses. The bodies were then shown to crowds of civilians (including children) to identify potential associates, and the platoon which exhumed the graves then became known as "The Gravediggers".[40]

Churchill forbids headhunting

On the 6 May 1952, Churchill met with his government Cabinet to discuss the *Daily Worker* decapitation photographs and articles exposing Britain's use of headhunting. This meeting included a wide range of interesting characters, with some of the most notable being the future British Prime Minister Anthony Eden, former Nuremberg Trials prosecutor David Maxwell Fyfe, Conservative Party Chairman Frederick Marquis, the notorious white supremacist Robert Gascoyne-Cecil, and the architect of the final stages of the Dunkirk evacuation Harold Alexander.[41] Together these men met at No.10 Downing Street to decide the fate of the headhunting policy.

Though some of the men present at this meeting declared that they would support the continuation of headhunting in Malaya,[42] most felt that the potential propaganda value of headhunting to pro-communist and anti-colonial causes outweighed any potential military intelligence gathered via decapitations.[43] Churchill told his Cabinet that he believed that the headhunting seen in the *Daily Worker* photographs was a justifiable method to use against the MNLA. However despite having no ethical objections to using headhunting against pro-independence forces in Malaya, he still argued for the abolition of Britain's headhunting practices in Malaya. Churchill's reasoning was that he feared that the resulting photographs of decapitations in Malaya would give ammunition to communist propaganda, and this possibility outweighed any potential military intelligence that headhunting may potentially provide.[44] Following the decision of Churchill and his Cabinet to end the practice of headhunting, British military leaders in Malaya were notified that corpses were not to be mutilated under any circumstance.[45]

Government confirms the photographs are authentic

On the 7 May 1952, British politicians gather in Parliament to publicly discuss issues pressing the British Empire, including the subject of the *Daily Worker's* decapitation photographs. This is the first time that the issue of decapitating corpses in Malaya is discussed openly in Britain's Parliament. Stanley Stephen Awbery, a Labour Party MP from Bristol, requested a statement from Oliver Lyttelton on the *Daily* Worker photographs.[46] Speaking to MPs in the House of Commons, Lyttelton confesses that the decapitation photographs are authentic, explaining that the photographs published in the *Daily Worker* both depicted the aftermath of an incident that happened in April 1951 when a so-called "bandit" was killed by British soldiers and his head chopped off by an Iban "tribesman".[47] Lyttelton's use of the term "bandit" was a part of a British propaganda strategy to give the impression to outside observers that Britain was fighting against isolated criminal elements rather than facing a war of national liberation by anti-colonial freedom fighters. People resisting British colonialism in Malaya were commonly branded with unflattering labels such as "bandit" or "terrorist", both such terms were used to dehumanise the enemies of Britain's colonial and capitalist interests. One activist comments on the government's admittance that the *Daily Worker* photographs were real:

"The government, by questions raised in Parliament have been forced to admit that pictures of British soldiers playing with the severed heads of Malayans are genuine, that the army authorities are employing head-hunters to hunt down Malayan fighters who continue to resist the exploitation of their country whether by British or Japanese. The *Daily Worker* so far as I know was the only paper to publicise these horrors, but that did not make them untrue."[48]

Questions concerning the Malayan Emergency were commonly raised in the House of Commons in 1952, including many other alleged wrongdoings by the British occupation and their Commonwealth allies including crop destruction,[49] the weaponised use of chemical defoliants,[50] the collective punishment of villagers (including children),[51] and 22-hour curfews.[52] However, what makes Oliver Lyttelton's statement so important is that this was the first time that Britain's practice of headhunting in Malaya had arisen in the House of Commons. This event also signifies the moment in which the British government officially admitted to the public that the *Daily Worker's* decapitation photographs were authentic, and that previous government and newspaper claims that the photographs could be fake were incorrect.

J.R Campbell intensifies his anti-war campaign

This admission of guilt by the British government prompted the *Daily Worker* to make the headhunting scandal front-page news yet again, triumphantly publicizing the British government's confirmation that their decapitation photographs were genuine and that their reports of headhunting had been vindicated.[53] However, the *Daily Worker*, likely believing that the government was trying to downplay the issue, responded by warning the British government that they had in their possession many more headhunting atrocity photographs, some of which were far more gruesome and horrible than anything ever seen before. Several days later the *Daily Worker* would make good on this threat, but in the meantime they focused their efforts on further publicising the existence of Britain's headhunting practices in Malaya and writing commentaries on the political scandal which they had sparked:

"While admitting the authenticity of the photographs yesterday, Mr. Oliver Lyttelton, the Colonial Secretary, suggested it was an isolated incident. However, the Daily Worker has proof that the beheading of Malayan patriots is a common occurrence. We have in our possession pictures of more recent origin than those originally published. Since the first report letters have poured into this office with eye-witness accounts of atrocities in Malaya."

"The photographs with them are even more horrible than those first published. The admiralty yesterday withdrew their claim that the pictures published last week were fakes."[54]

Immediately following the government's confirmation that the decapitation photographs were genuine, the *Daily Worker* began a campaign to send Malayan headhunting photographs along with all the evidence they had collected to influential people throughout the UK. Such people included various Labour and Conservative MPs, the Archbishop of York, and multiple British national newspaper editors. The spearpoint of this campaign was a personal telegram sent to Winston Churchill by the *Daily Worker* and signed by J. R. Campbell, calling for a stop to the atrocities committed against the Malayan people by the British military.[55] Within this telegram Campbell attached several never before published headhunting atrocity photographs. One of these photographs depicting a smiling Royal Marine holding two decapitated heads, was far grizzlier and more shocking than any image of the Malayan Emergency ever published. Campbell explained to Churchill that these newly discovered photographs were proof that the decapitations were not isolated cases:

"The British public will be shocked to learn of the admission by Mr. Oliver Lyttelton in Parliament yesterday of the inhuman practice of decapitating Malayan patriot dead. In his reply Mr. Lyttelton admitted that the picture of the severed head published in the "Daily Worker" on April 28 was genuine. He tried, however, to create the impression that this was an isolated, specific incident and not a general practice. We cannot accept this. For your information I enclose more pictures of further cases, horrible evidence that this barbaric practice, a gross violation of the rules of war, is widespread."[56]

Copies of Campbell's protest letter were also sent to Anthony Eden and Oliver Lyttelton, both of which were accompanied by the same never before published atrocity photographs sent to Churchill.[57, 58] When writing his telegram to Churchill, Campbell made the intelligent decision not to appeal to Churchill's ethical concern for the victims, but rather to his fear that images of headhunting atrocities and other war crimes would potentially become powerful propaganda weapons against the British Empire. Due to both his white supremacist and anti-communist worldviews, Churchill expressed little empathy for victims who were both Asians and communists that had also been killed while resisting British colonialism. However, by appealing to Churchill's love of the British Empire and the potential threat such photographs had to its reputation, Campbell had correctly predicted Churchill's concerns and attempted to emphasise with him using his own logic.

Chapter 3

"This Horror Must End": The Scandal Reaches its Boiling Point

The war's most graphically violent images are revealed (10 May)

On the 10 May, 1952, the *Daily Worker* published four previously unseen photographs in a front page report titled **"This Horror Must End"**.[1] These four photographs, three of which Campbell had previously sent to Churchill and other government officials, were far more horrific and visceral than any images of the war ever published before.

The largest and most prominent photograph depicted a Royal Marine smiling and posing triumphantly with a female head in his right hand and a male head in his left.[2] The woman's head shows possible signs of torture, as some of her front teeth are missing. The British government never released any public response to this photograph, and has never apologised for the actions depicted in these scenes. The story behind the photographs and the exact details surrounding the Marine holding two heads remains a mystery. This gruesome photograph, which some historians have described as "the most notorious" of all the decapitation photographs,[3] has since become the most iconic photograph of the Malayan Emergency ever created.

The image of the Royal Marine holding two decapitated heads has often been used by academics and activists as a visual tool to highlight the violent and racist nature of British colonialism. It is common to see online commentators comparing Britain's headhunting in Malaya to the actions of the Islamic State (ISIS) and Al-Qaeda. Marxist activist Robert Clough used this image to help readers visualise the racist and imperialist policies of the Labour Party.[4] Former MNLA leader Chin Peng used the image to show how ironic it was that Britain called the communists "terrorists" despite the atrocities that the British Empire had committed.[5] British historian James Heartfield used the image to illustrate the betrayal of Malayan communists by the British.[6] The human rights organisation

Veterans for Peace UK (VFPUK) used this photograph to visualise the horrors of Britain's colonial wars.[7] This brutal image is often reprinted by the *Daily Worker's* modern successor the *Morning Star* in articles relating to colonialism, it occasionally appears across online forums, blogs, and social media sites discussing British colonialism. This photograph has also appeared in multiple documentaries to highlight British brutality during the war.[8] One MNLA guerrilla who had fought in the jungles for 13 years, went on to write a novel based on his experiences titled *Hunger*, a story which was likely inspired by this photograph.[9]

Previously the British government and military had often claimed that decapitating MNLA bodies was necessary for identification purposes. However the *Daily Worker's* photograph of a Marine holding two decapitated heads shocked and confused British government officials, who privately shared their fears that they could no longer use "identification" as a justification for the events depicted in the *Daily Worker's* headhunting photographs. Government officials therefore stopped issuing statements and rebuttals in respect of these atrocities. One official commented:

> "From the Propaganda angle these are in some ways worse than the previous ones and I do not see how they could possibly be justified on the grounds of identification put forward in the earlier case."[10]

The second photograph published on the front page of the *Daily Worker* on 10 May 1952, showed the same two severed heads on the floor with a dismembered hand propped between them, positioned as though the severed hand was saluting the severed heads.[11] The third photograph depicts an Iban man wearing a beret with the badge of the Royal Marine Commandos as he prepares a human scalp above a basket overflowing with severed human body parts. In the fourth photograph, the same Iban headhunter poses for the camera with a freshly cleaned human scalp.

Headhunting's final mention in Parliament

The subject of headhunting became a discussion topic within the House of Commons for the final time on the 21 May 1952, when the Minister of

State for Colonial Affairs, Henry Hopkinson, was asked by Labour Party MP Michael Stewart, whether any of the British soldiers shown in the *Daily Worker* photographs had been identified and if any of them were to be punished. Hopkinson made clear that the British government had zero intention of punishing any British soldier who partook in the decapitations, claiming that British soldiers were not explicitly forbidden from cutting people's heads off and therefore cannot be punished for any mutilation of corpses or being involved in a mutilation.[12] This attempt by Hopkinson to retrospectively justify British military atrocities provides historians with yet another example of government officials lying to hide the details of the decapitations. The mutilation of the bodies of enemy soldiers during wartime was a violation of Article 15 of the Geneva Convention of August 1949. The mutilation of corpses or treatment of bodies in any way that could be potentially considered offensive was also a violation of section 297 (F.M.S Cap.45) of the Malayan penal code. With this final defence in Parliament of Britain's decapitation atrocities, the British Malayan Headhunting Scandal of 1952 came to a slow and quiet close.

The deployment of Iban soldiers continues

Although the *Daily Worker's* decapitation atrocity articles and the political scandal which it sparked had severely damaged the reputation of Iban soldiers in Malaya, it did not hamper the British military's willingness to recruit Ibans. Only a few months after the British Malayan Headhunting Scandal, experimental Iban platoons were created with a stronger orientation towards frontline combat.[13] Then in March 1953, less than a year after the *Daily Worker* published their first decapitation photograph, a specialised Iban regiment called the Sarawak Rangers was formed which consisted almost entirely of Ibans, turning them from mercenaries into soldiers. The news of the Sarawak Rangers' creation had initially been a secret which was leaked to newspapers shortly after the British Malayan Headhunting Scandal.[14] Oliver Lyttelton was concerned about this timing, however it does not appear to have affected the creation of the regiment.[15]

One Iban called Awang Anak Rawang was even awarded the prestigious George Cross for an unbelievable story where he (allegedly) repelled almost fifty MNLA guerrilla fighters, and in the following decades was invited on numerous occasions to meet with British royalty. The British royal family, whose members openly approved of Britain's war in Malaya, sent the Duchess and Duke of Kent to Malaya to inspect British troops.[16] During their trip they met with Iban men attached to a regiment whose Ibans were known headhunters, and presented the Duke and Duchess with a parang, the same type of knife that Iban headhunters used to decapitate and scalp their victims.[17] The Duke and Duchess's meeting with Ibans in Malaya took place only a few months after the *Daily Worker* released its headhunting photographs. This was far from the only link that British royalty had to the atrocities of the Malayan Emergency. Several of the British regiments in Malaya which took part in headhunting (Coldstream Guards), massacres of civilians (Scots Guards), and served alongside Iban mercenaries (Grenadier Guards), are all considered Foot Guard regiments, meaning that they provide soldiers for protection duties in royal residences.

The end of the British Malayan Headhunting Scandal did not stop the *Daily Worker* from again discovering and leaking further proof of British atrocities, as they still held many more photographs which they intended to publish. The *Daily Worker* announced that it would compile a four-page information folder/pamphlet containing photographic evidence of British war crimes in Malaya, including their previous headhunting photographs, complete with commentary by journalist Phillip Bolsover.[18,19] On the 14 June 1952 Harry Pollitt, the leader of both the British communist movement and the British anti-war campaign calling for Britain to withdraw from Malaya, published an article containing yet another Malayan atrocity photograph. This image showed twenty British troops grinning triumphantly while standing over the bodies of anti-colonial freedom fighters whom they had killed.[20] However, just like the previously published *Daily Worker* headhunting photographs, many people were sceptical as to whether this photograph was real. One Conservative Party MP, Henry Brooke, even wrote to the Colonial Office after a concerned constituent brought the image to his attention.[21]

"This Horror Must End": The Scandal Reaches its Boiling Point

Headhunting in Malaya continues

Despite Churchill and his cabinet having officially called for an end to headhunting, this decision was widely ignored by British soldiers and the decapitation of suspected MNLA members continued regardless of orders from politicians and military leaders.

- John Chynoweth of the Malay Regiment, a man who strongly supported the headhunting policy, said that despite the removal of heads being unpopular with British troops, many Army units continued to decapitate MNLA guerrillas despite orders in 1952 from their commanders to halt the practice.[22]
- Rex Flowers of the Lincolnshire Regiment who fought in Malaya between 1955–1956 witnessed his fellow soldiers carrying the freshly decapitated heads of Malayan communists.[23]
- Dato Seri Yuen Yuet Leng, a former Special Branch Leader, told journalists that "the practice of headhunting for the purposes of identification was never officially terminated."[24]
- Adam John Quinton who fought in Malaya between 1955–1958 with the South Wales Borderers Regiment, also witnessed headhunting. During an interview with the Imperial War Museum, he revealed that he saw a brown paper bag containing a decapitated head while visiting the office of police officer Evan Davies.[25]
- NCO Jim O'Neill fought in Malaya as a member of the Royal Inniskilling Fusiliers regiment. During an interview with the Imperial War Museum he said that after the order to stop the decapitation of corpses, Ibans began using this as an excuse to instead take the ears of the people they had killed.[26]
- Ron Harper served as a private in the Queen's Royal Regiment and fought in Malaya between 1954–1957. During an interview he described an incident in 1954 when Iban mercenaries attached to his regiment murdered two civilians whom they believed to be communists and cut off their heads. Ron attended the funeral of the two civilians who the Ibans had decapitated, and noted that the incident caused the local civilians to hate British troops.[27]

Shortly after the Malayan Emergency came to an end, Britain quickly found itself fighting yet another war against communist guerrillas in the jungles of East Asia. This time however the war took place in the Iban's native land of Borneo. This war between Indonesia and Malaysia became known as the **Indonesia-Malaysia Confrontation (1963–1966)**. During this war, rumours emerged that the British were yet again using headhunting to encourage Iban warriors to fight and take heads.[28] One veteran of the British Army's Intelligence Corps, describes the decapitated heads of suspected Indonesian communists being used for intelligence purposes. He writes of an instance in early 1965 when six men belonging to Indonesian forces were decapitated by Ibans allied with British forces:

> "Six, scavenging for food, were captured by a Sarawak Police Field Force Sergeant Major on leave in his longhouse and were then decapitated by Iban headhunters. Meanwhile, Lieutenant Brian O'Flaherty, who was detached to the Border Scouts from 2/10th Gurkha Rifles, was being poled along the Rajang to visit his men. Invited to stay at the longhouse, when supper turned out to be rice topped by six heads, he arranged for them to be sent in biscuit tins by helicopter to Kuching for identification, however when this was completed, the heads became muddled with fresh rations and were dropped to B Company."[29]

The continuation of headhunting being practised by Britain's Iban allies against suspected communists is further corroborated by primatologist Dr John MacKinnon. During fieldwork with orangutans in Borneo, Dr MacKinnon spent lengthy expeditions living in the jungle among Ibans and noted that the local government would tolerate Iban headhunters decapitating people so long as their victims were communists.[30] However the most damning evidence that Britain supported (or at least tolerated) headhunting during the Indonesia-Malaysia Confrontation, comes from photographic evidence. There exists a photograph kept by London's Imperial War Museum showing a British sailor holding up the decapitated head of an Indonesian man before a crowd of people. The photograph was taken onboard a Royal Navy minesweeping ship during the conflict

"This Horror Must End": The Scandal Reaches its Boiling Point 25

between Malaysia and Indonesia. The caption says that the head had been severed by a "native tracker".[31]

However unlike the highly detailed instances of headhunting exposed during the Malayan Emergency by the *Daily Worker*, the accusations that Britain encouraged headhunting against Indonesian forces lacks the wealth of declassified government documents and published eyewitness that historians have for the Malayan Emergency. The extent to which headhunting was encouraged by Britain and its Commonwealth allies as a tool to fight against Indonesians in Borneo, has yet to be studied in depth.

Accusations that decapitations were again being used against communist guerrillas on the Malay Peninsula resurfaced after independence, when it was discovered that soldiers serving the newly independent Malaysian government's Senoi Praaq unit, an organisation originally created by the British colonial occupation and inherited by the post-independent Malay government, were using decapitations against communists near the Thai border.[32] Here the normalisation of headhunting and collecting the body parts of rebels as trophies in Malaysia, proves itself to be a part of Britain's colonial legacy. In the words of one American anti-communist writer who supported the practice of headhunting:

> "Very rarely did Senoi Praaq troopers fail to return without a nice bagful of hands to show for their trouble. Heads were also taken on occasion for identification purposes as were the occasional pair of ears as proof of a kill. Hands though were of greatest value. If a match for the finger prints could be found this would allow the Special Branch to go after the families of the individual in question."[33]

Not only did headhunting among British forces in Malaya continue, but the British military's tradition of slicing off body parts from the corpses of anti-colonial resistance fighters continued outside of Asia. Soon after Churchill and his cabinet decided to ban the taking of heads in Malaya, British soldiers yet again began using "identification" as a justification for taking body parts which often ended up becoming trophies. In Kenya during an anti-colonial rebellion known as the **Mau Mau Uprising (1952–1960)** which saw Britain fighting against yet another rural guerrilla army, it became commonplace for colonial forces to cut the hands off the people they had killed.[34][35]

The brutality and savagery of the British military in Kenya reached far greater heights than any atrocities Britain had ever committed in Malaya. In Kenya the British military was running what can very accurately be described as concentration camps, which had far more in common with Nazi concentration camps than Britain's New Villages in Malaya. Within Britain's Kenyan concentration camps, prisoners were forced to work and were routinely beaten, raped, and tortured to death. Castration and the severing of limbs were popular methods of torture used by the British against their prisoners. One photograph taken in Kenya depicting an African man having his arm sawn off was acquired by a British communist academic, whose mind was immediately drawn to memories of the *Daily Worker's* headhunting photographs.[36]

Similar to the corpse mutilations that the British performed in Malaya, many actions in Kenya such as torture and severing the limbs of corpses, were conducted citing intelligence purposes. Bodies were often mutilated in Kenya despite the widespread availability of both cameras and equipment for taking fingerprints, all without the physical and technical challenges present in Malaya's jungles. According to military historian Douglas Porch, it was common for the British to decapitate suspected Mau Mau members and stick their heads onto pikes outside Kenyan police stations.[37]

Chapter 4

The Aftermath of the Headhunting Scandal

The British Malayan Headhunting Scandal of 1952 sent Parliament into a panic, shaking the faith and confidence in the Empire for countless soldiers, politicians, and military leaders. Gruesome images published by the *Daily Worker* of some of the most visually shocking acts had succeeded in bringing the reality of colonialism to the eyes of countless people who may otherwise have trusted the endless streams of imperialist propaganda that dominated Britain's newspapers.

However despite the seemingly widespread apathy of the British public to the headhunting images and the lack of a wider media response and opposition to Britain's occupation of Malaya, there were protests and local movements outraged by the *Daily Worker's* articles on headhunting in Malaya. Most of this anger came from Britain's trade union movement and left-wing workers, but attention to the headhunting scandal didn't just stay region locked to British media. The *Daily Worker's* headhunting photographs had attracted the attention of communist media as far as China, the Soviet Union, and the United States.

This chapter will explore how British trade unions and their supporters reacted to the British Malayan Headhunting Scandal of 1952. It will also examine one recorded instance of a protest against those partially responsible for the headhunting policy, the Dunlop Rubber company. Next this chapter delves into the responses of the mainstream British newspapers to the headhunting scandal, examining British print media during this time period to answer why British newspapers widely ignored the *Daily Worker's* headhunting photographs. Finally, this chapter will examine the reaction of foreign news media to the scandal, with special attention given to publications based in both China and the Soviet Union.

Trade union reaction to the headhunting scandal

Although the decapitation scandal never reached a wide public audience, and many of those who did see the atrocity images assumed them to be forgeries, there were sections of British society outside of both the government and the communist party who felt deeply affected by the headhunting photographs. British trade union activists were the most vocal about the scandal, many of whom saw the persecution of Malayan pro-independence guerrillas and trade unionists as a parallel to their own fight for better working conditions and rights in Britain.

Workers of the Willesden Factory of British Thomson-Housten, then the largest engineering factory in all of London, circulated a petition directed to Colonial Secretary Oliver Lyttelton which denounced the use of headhunting among other colonial atrocities including the "burning of villages" and "erection of concentration camps".[12] The *Daily Worker* reported that thirty similar yet separate petitions had been created and distributed across London's docklands.[3] This was followed by a denouncement of colonial atrocities in Malaya from unionised engineers and firemen in Gateshead.[4] The Southend-on-Sea branch of the Electrical Trades Union sent a message to the Royal Navy demanding an investigation into the headhunting atrocities depicted in the *Daily Worker*.[5] After the British government had confirmed the authenticity of the decapitation photographs, seventy engineering workers at Ambrose Shardlow and Co. Sheffield, donated money to fund the *Daily Worker's* protest telegram to Churchill.[6] The *Daily Worker* also reported that Shoreditch Trades Council had condemned the practice of headhunting, that a meeting of 500 people in Hyde Park had passed a resolution condemning both headhunting and the British military occupation of Malaya, and that another telegram sent to Winston Churchill condemning headhunting was signed by 170 people in Stamford Hill.[7]

The famous British trade unionist and women's rights activist, Betty Tebbs, showed the *Daily Worker* decapitation photographs to people at her workplace. However she found that many of her fellow workers believed the photographs were fake.[8] Disgusted by the decapitations among other atrocities committed by the British military in Malaya, both she and her husband abandoned the Labour Party and joined the Communist Party of Great Britain.[9]

With memories of the Holocaust still fresh in the minds of the British public, news of British soldiers rounding up Malaya's ethnic minorities into internment camps called "New Villages" compelled many activists to compare the colonial occupation of Malaya to the Nazi occupation of Europe. The North and North East London branches of the Union of Shop Distributive and Allied Workers passed a resolution comparing British colonialism in Malaya to Nazi fascism.[10] Another resolution, unanimously passed by the London No.10 branch of the Electrical Trades Union, similarly compared the British occupation of Malaya to Nazism. "The German people claimed ignorance of the existence of Belsen-let us not blind ourselves to what is happening now in Malaya."[11] Though the wider British public felt largely unaffected by British war crimes against Asians, the little sympathy that was present came primarily from communists and their trade union allies. It was not only trade unions but also some journalists who compared Britain's treatment of Malayans to Nazism. In one instance a *Daily Worker* reporter confronted British General Gerald Templer on his oppressive and dictatorial methods, comparing them to fascism and questioning him on the levels of malnutrition in Malaya under his rule. Templer responded by threatening to have the reporter kicked out of the room.[12]

Images of British soldiers rounding up civilians into internment camps in Kenya received a similar response from the *Daily Worker* which published eyewitness accounts from British soldiers comparing prison camps in Kenya to Nazi fascism.[13]

Though few leading British people publicly spoke of the existence of the British military's headhunting policy outside of government, military, and socialist circles, there was one prominent personality outside of Parliament who was willing to publicly denounce Britain's use of headhunting in Malaya. Arthur Clegg, a popular British trade unionist, human rights activist, lifelong anti-fascist activist, and the *Daily Worker*'s expert on East Asia, was an accomplished organiser who had led successful dockworker strikes against the Japanese in protest of their treatment of Chinese civilians.[14] These protests successfully won Clegg the support of people such as Bertrand Russell, the Archbishop of York, Eric Gill, Robert Cecil, Harold Laski, Ellen Wilkinson, Tom Mann, J.B. Priestly, Herbert Morrison, Ben Tillett, and many more.[15] Clegg used his fame and reputation with British activists to lend his aid to the *Daily Worker*, becoming one of the few notable people to openly denounce British atrocities against Malayans, including the beheadings and execution of trade unionists, comparing the Malayan communists to the Tolpuddle Martyrs.[16]

The Dunlop Rubber Company protest

Despite the failure of the *Daily Worker* photographs to spark a nationwide backlash and turn mainstream public opinion against colonialism, there was at least one protest which took the realities of headhunting straight to some of the people most responsible. On the 9 June 1952, ten former British soldiers stormed into the annual shareholders meeting of the Dunlop Rubber Company in protest against the British occupation of Malaya. Two of the protesters were former prisoners of the Japanese on the infamous Siam Railway, the entire Dunlop board of directors were present to witness the protest, and leading the directors was one of the most powerful businessmen in Britain, Sir Clive Baillieu. The protestors distributed leaflets containing one of the *Daily Worker's* headhunting photographs and threw them around the meeting room. The *Daily Worker* reported on the protest:

> "They threw out leaflets showing a British Marine Commando holding the severed head of a murdered Malayan patriot, and unfurled posters saying "Stop the War in Malaya" and "Bring British Lads Home." "Millions in profits out of British boys' lives," they shouted. "Why don't you go and fight the war yourselves? "Your money is made out of British lives." Most of the shareholders were too dazed to do or say anything."[17]

Dunlop was targeted by anti-war protesters because the company was known for its extreme exploitation of Malayan rubber plantation workers, attacks against trade unionists, and for its looting of Malaya's natural resources. Dunlop fully supported the British and Commonwealth forces in their fight against Malayan communism in an attempt to protect their profits from revolutionaries. The company also owned a fleet of armoured cars which it used to dissuade its workers from any attempt at resistance or sabotage. Dunlop was opposed by the Malayan communists who fought to nationalise Malaya's industry and use their nation's natural resources to better the lives of the working class, as opposed to simply making profits for wealthy European capitalists as Dunlop intended. Despite the British public's widespread ignorance and apathy towards headhunting in Malaya, the Dunlop Rubber Company protest and the aforementioned petitions and meetings of trade unionists show that the decapitation images did indeed sully the image of colonialism in the eyes of many British people.

British media reaction to the photographs

Most of the historians who have encountered the *Daily Worker*'s headhunting images have been deeply puzzled by the lack of any mainstream media response to these atrocities, pointing out that the *Daily Worker* was the only British newspaper to publish the decapitation photographs.[18, 19, 20] How could such visually gruesome images and shocking revelations about the behaviour of British troops fail to stir up any wider media outcry? The fear of losing press privileges is one possible factor that may have influenced the decision of British newspapers to avoid reprinting the *Daily Worker* decapitation photographs. Journalists who published stories favourable to British colonialism were often rewarded with greater access to colonial and military organisations. They could also expect this access to be swiftly denied if they were to publish stories critical of British imperialism.[21,22] Any British newspaper which chose to republish the *Daily Worker* decapitation photographs could expect to potentially lose key sources of information for future stories. In this way, self-censorship played a larger role in squashing stories of headhunting atrocities in Malaya than direct censorship. In fact the relationship between the British occupation in Malaya and the mainstream British press was so strong that some newspapers even sent gifts of chocolate, booze, and cigarettes to soldiers in Malaya.[23]

Although the British government never directly censored the *Daily Worker* for publishing their Malayan headhunting photographs, the Lord Chancellor was said to have asked the Attorney General in 1952 to consider initiating proceedings against the *Daily Worker* for publishing these images.[24] There is also at least one instance of the British government implementing direct censorship within Britain to stop the knowledge of headhunting from spreading. Mona Brand's stage play titled *Strangers in the Land* featured a story set in the Malayan Emergency in which British plantation owners in Colonial Malaya were depicted as bloodthirsty racists who enjoyed torching villages and keeping severed heads as trophies.[25] In Britain the play only ran at London's tiny activist run 'Unity Theatre' because the UK government banned the play from being performed on commercial British stages.[26] Such actions served as a warning to any newspaper planning on publicising Britain's Malayan headhunting atrocities.

The *Daily Worker* was no stranger to harassment, being barred from distribution by British wholesalers for almost 12 years, temporarily outlawed by the UK government between 1941–1942, targeted by government spies, attacked by politically motivated libel suits, being banned in many British colonies for its anti-colonial articles and support for racial equality, and its journalists barred from the frontlines of WWII. Among these countless difficulties, the most significant attempts to threaten the *Daily Worker* for exposing an atrocity happened shortly before the British Malayan Headhunting Scandal. In 1950 while serving as the *Daily Worker's* far-east correspondent during the Korean War, journalist Alan Winnington reported the discovery of mass graves in Taejon containing thousands of corpses of civilians executed by the South Korean government. Winnington who was then working as one of the only two native English speaking journalists on the northern side of the Korean War, and is recognised by many modern historians as one of the most reliable journalists to have ever worked during the conflict, compiled all the evidence he could gather and published his report in a pamphlet titled *"I saw the Truth in Korea"*.[27,28] Embarrassed by the *Daily Worker's* exposure of a massacre against civilians perpetrated by British allies in South Korea, Clement Attlee's Labour Party government responded by debating whether or not Winnington should be charged with treason, a crime which carried the death penalty. However the

Attlee government decided that such a punishment would bring greater attention to his journalistic work, and instead chose to banish Winnington by refusing to renew his passport, effectively making him stateless. The threat of censorship, usually through the Official Secrets Act, was usually enough to deter potential whistleblowers from reporting abuses (including headhunting) committed by British troops in Malaya.[29]

The *Daily Worker* was strong enough to withstand such treatment, but many other British journalists and newspaper editors were likely dissuaded from republishing material such as the *Daily Worker* headhunting photographs for fear of similar government attacks. To survive the *Daily Worker* had to continuously withstand difficulties that would have crushed most other newspapers. Their strength to withstand attacks, coupled with the paper's unique socialist political affiliation, turned the *Daily Worker* into a lifeline for whistleblowers throughout the British Empire whose stories had been ignored by mainstream British news media. Although the *Daily Worker* had incorrectly predicted that the MNLA would win the war, they still proved themselves to have provided the most accurate and reliable news coverage of the Malayan Emergency available to the British public.

The exposure of headhunting photographs in Malaya was just one of many instances when the *Daily Worker* and British communists played an instrumental role in exposing the horrors of British colonialism. In 1949 the *Daily Worker* helped bring to light the infamous Batang Kali massacre of civilians committed by British troops less than a month after it happened, during a time when other British newspapers found such an incident undeserving of coverage.[30,31] Despite a government cover-up, evidence released decades later showed that the *Daily Worker's* account of the Batang Kali massacre was accurate.[32] Killing scoreboards managed by the British military in Malaya were exposed to the public by communist activist John Eber, and a few years later CPGB activists created the Kenya Committee which helped expose the torture and murder of black Africans by the British military during the Mau Mau Uprising.[33,34] Even at the height of the British Malayan Headhunting Scandal, the *Daily Worker's* journalists found the time to publicise accusations that the USA was engaging in germ warfare in Korea, detailed reports of attacks against Korean refugees, and collect eyewitness reports on POWs. Some writers have argued that the

Daily Worker decapitation photographs constituted the only major blow to British propaganda in Malaya during the war.[35] The *Daily Worker* and the British communist movement acted as a lifeline for whistle-blowers, bringing light to the uncomfortable realities of imperialism through a combination of highly skilled journalists, an unwillingness to budge in the face of government threats, and a committed grassroots readership willing to support its distribution.

It was argued by some commentators during the beginning of the British Malayan Headhunting Scandal that the *Daily Worker* could not be trusted because it was run by communists, and that this meant that the photographs must have been fake. However the paper's political affiliation can also be seen as a great benefit to the quality and accuracy of its reporting on issues within the British Empire. The Marxist ideology of the *Daily Worker*'s journalists somewhat immunised their reporting from the mainstream racial and pro-colonial lenses dominant within most mainstream British newspapers. The activist nature of the paper acted as a safety net, allowing the *Daily Worker* to post controversial stories without having to fear a sudden financial collapse from advertising sponsors withdrawing their support.

In the 21st century the *Daily Worker* decapitation photographs from 1952, along with many references to the headhunting scandal, are often republished in a newspaper called the *Morning Star*, which is a continuation of the original *Daily Worker* under a new name. The *Morning Star* newspaper is extremely proud of its predecessor's exposure of colonial-era crimes and often uses the 1952 headhunting photographs from Malaya to illustrate the brutality of the British Empire in articles critical of colonialism. In 1983 when government documents on the headhunting scandal were declassified by the British government, the *Morning Star* celebrated their role with an article commemorating this new evidence.[36] In celebration of the leading role their paper played in exposing colonial wrongdoings, the *Morning Star*'s publisher chose to include several of the paper's Malayan headhunting articles within a collection of both the *Daily Worker* and *Morning Star*'s best articles in a book titled *Is That Damned Paper Still Coming Out?*[37]

This research failed to find a British newspaper which had republished the *Daily Worker* headhunting photographs during the 20th century. However, the most infamous image of a British Marine holding two decapitated heads would eventually appear in one newspaper over half a century after its initial publication. In 2005 *The Sunday Times* reprinted the photograph within an article discussing images of war, inspired by recently uncovered photographs of British soldiers torturing civilians in Basra, Iraq.[38] It appears that news of British soldiers in Iraq photographing themselves torturing and sexually abusing their prisoners caused numerous writers to remember the *Daily Worker* photographs and the British Malayan Headhunting Scandal.[39] This article was part of a larger trend of British military failures in Iraq causing people to re-examine Britain's past counterinsurgencies, most notably the Malayan Emergency.

Foreign Media reaction to the photographs

Despite the refusal of British newspapers to republish the *Daily Worker's* decapitation photographs, they were acknowledged in communist publications overseas including the Soviet newspaper *Pravda*,[40] and the Chinese-communist English language publication *China Monthly Review*.[41] The Soviet English language journal *New Times*, describes the *Daily Worker's* publication of Malayan headhunting photographs:

> "The *Daily Worker* published a series of photos of British soldiers holding the heads of decapitated Malayan freedom-fighters. These acts of savagery, proved beyond question by photographic documents, have aroused a storm of indignation among the British public."[42]

British embassy staff noted an increase in Chinese media attention given to Malaya following the exposure of the *Daily Worker* decapitation photographs and found that the Shanghai edition of the *Ta Kung Pao* newspaper had also printed Malayan decapitation photographs.[43] It was also noted that headhunting in Malaya was mentioned within a Daily News Release by the New China News Agency, Peking.[44] Claims that British soldiers in Malaya were publicly displaying decapitated heads appeared in speeches by organisers of Malayan civilians deported to China by the British.[45] One newspaper in India reported that the images of decapitated heads from Malaya were real and had been confirmed to be genuine in Parliament.[46]

In the United States, one article mentioning the banning of headhunting in Malaya was published inside *The Washington Post*.[47] The only newspaper in America which stood against the British occupation of Malaya and denounced Britain's use of headhunting was a communist newspaper also called the *Daily Worker*, which coincidentally shared a name with the British communist newspaper of the same name. In one example, the American *Daily Worker* compares British imperialism to Nazism, while denouncing the use of headhunting by British forces:

> "The truth about the British imperialist war against the people of Malaya is one of the most shocking and revolting facts of these times. Although the British had participated in the Nuremberg and pronounced sentence on the Nazis, during the last four years they have committed crimes against the Malayans every iota as fiendishly brutal as those of the Hitlerites."
>
> "The new wrinkle introduced into warfare by the lords, dukes, earls and other honourable gentlemen of her royal majesty's ruling class – this "innovation" of these heroes of the "free world," is headhunting!"[48]

In the weeks following the *Daily Worker's* first headhunting photograph, the practice of decapitating corpses in Malaya was quietly acknowledged by several newspapers in Singapore. The *Singapore Standard* published three articles in tiny text and without images, acknowledging the *Daily Worker's* first headhunting photograph,[49] that the practice of decapitating corpses had been banned,[50] and a brief description of the events behind the *Daily Worker* headhunting photographs.[51] This was followed by *The Singapore Free Press* and *The Straits Times* publishing tiny articles acknowledging the order to end headhunting in Malaya.[52, 53] It is especially unusual that the headhunting scandal would gain any mention in the *Straits Times*, considering that this newspaper was a British propaganda organ which waged psychological warfare against the MNLA by publicising both cash bounties for murdered communists and articles containing fake news.[54] Unlike the Soviet and Chinese newspapers whose journalists could write lengthy and opinionated articles on the evils of colonialism and the desecration of corpses by British forces, newspapers in Singapore and Malaya had no such luxury, as they risked been shut down by the occupying British forces if they were to ever became too critical of British colonialism.

What these newspaper articles published in the Soviet Union, China, United States, and Singapore show is that there was indeed an interest in Britain's Malayan headhunting policy expressed within the media outside of Britain, especially in countries with communist party governments. The same also rings true for the aforementioned play *Strangers in the Land* by Mona Brand which despite being banned on UK commercial stages managed to find success in the Soviet Union and East Germany.

Chapter 5

Debate: Military Necessity and the Intelligence Gathering Theory

After the British government had openly confessed in Parliament that the *Daily Worker* photographs were genuine, there was one key question remaining that had yet to be answered. Why would British soldiers conduct these atrocities with seemingly no military gain? The official government and military justification was that beheading the corpses of suspected guerrillas was necessary for identification purposes, arguing that cameras often failed to function within humid tropical environments and that complete intact corpses could rarely be physically retrieved within the deep jungle.[1] The argument that headhunting was solely a practice for the purposes of identification, hereby referred to as the **Intelligence Gathering Theory**, became the primary justification for the British military's headhunting policy in Malaya.

This chapter will delve deeper into specific aspects of the headhunting policy to investigate whether there is any truth to the idea that headhunting was necessary for military intelligence gathering. It will examine what we know about the identities of the headhunting victims, the provenance and context of known headhunting photographs, the treatment of skulls and scalps, conflicting soldier eyewitness testimonies, the reliability of cameras, and finally the availability of successfully proven alternatives to headhunting.

Hen Yan – the only known communist victim of British headhunting

The names of all but one of the headhunting victims are unknown to historians, which is highly ironic for a policy enforced for the purpose of identifying guerrillas. The only known communist victim of the headhunting policy in Malaya whose name is known to historians was a man called Hen Yan.

Debate: Military Necessity and the Intelligence Gathering Theory

Hen Yan was a socialist revolutionary, guerrilla fighter, and a relatively high ranking local communist leader who was killed and decapitated by British soldiers in April 1952. The following paragraphs contain a reconstruction of Hen Yan's death and beheading, created for this research by piecing together multiple sources from British military archives:[2]

On the 23rd of April 1952, an experienced British officer and WW2 veteran by the name of **James Patrick Macdonald** of the British Army's Suffolk Regiment, woke up at 7am. It was a Wednesday and happened to be St George's Day.

By 7:30am he had been ordered to lead patrol of Commonwealth soldiers into the Malayan jungles. The patrol passed through a rubber estate before advancing into the "Ulu" (jungle). During their trek through the jungle the soldiers silently stopped, and Macdonald (whose eyesight was poor) noticed what appeared to be a backpack resting on a fallen tree. However the backpack was actually still attached to the back of an armed communist guerrilla who was travelling alone and was now hiding behind the fallen tree. The communist guerrilla rose up and raised his gun in self-defence, only to be quickly shot dead by the patrol. They then searched the corpse of the guerrilla and discovered a large number of important military documents written in Chinese. Though they were unable to read the documents, the patrol realised the value of what they had discovered and prepared to transport both the corpse and the documents out of the jungle.

The soldiers cut down a tree and began to craft a wooden pole with which to carry the body out of the jungle for identification. However as this was happening, a tropical storm began. Arguing that the thick rain and resulting mud would make it impossible to carry the entire corpse out of the jungle, Macdonald gave an order to have both the head and right hand of the corpse cut off. However, the young and inexperienced soldier he ordered to perform the decapitation was unsuccessful and created a bloody mess. Macdonald then finished the job and ordered the inexperienced soldier to carry both the head and hand in his backpack. Macdonald noted that many of his soldiers were outraged by the beheading, and were afraid that cutting the heads off guerrillas would make it appear as though they were butchering people. The head, hand, and valuable documents were removed from the jungle by Macdonald's patrol. It was then subsequently discovered that the communist guerrilla was a man called Hen Yan, an important local MNLA guerrilla with the rank of Branch Committee Member, who had been travelling alone from one MNLA regiment to another.[3]

Despite being in the middle of the jungle and believing they could not carry the body back intact, the patrol was less than a day's march away from civilisation, and by 6:30pm were enjoying drinks on an estate.[4]

Hen Yan's decapitated head was then photographed, and a copy was kept in a British intelligence diary alongside dozens of gruesome photographs depicting dead suspected MNLA members.[5] However, it is unknown whether it was the decapitated head and severed right hand which was used to identify Hen Yan, or whether it was the large treasure trove of important documents which he had been transporting that revealed his identity.

In 1998 a soldier from the same British Army regiment that killed Hen Yan published a book titled *The Suffolks in Malaya* which attempted to record every MNLA guerrilla that the regiment had killed during the Malayan Emergency. The author describes a very different version of events, claiming that Hen Yan was accompanied by five fellow guerrillas who all survived the encounter, and that Hen Yan was the 134th guerrilla killed by the Suffolk Regiment. The same book also misspells Hen Yan's name, insults him by calling him a "bandit", and does not contain a single mention of how British soldiers decapitated Hen Yan or any other corpses in Malaya.[6]

This is the most conclusive proof known to historians that there was at least one instance of Britain's headhunting policy in Malaya leading to the successful identification of an MNLA member. Further complicating matters, Hen Yan happened to be carrying a large number of guerrilla documents when he was killed, meaning it is possible that it was these documents and not the decapitated head that allowed the British to uncover Hen Yan's identity. Even given this extremely rare circumstance of

Debate: Military Necessity and the Intelligence Gathering Theory 41

a decapitated head being successfully identified, there remains a noticeable lack of evidence that the British colonial occupation benefitted from such knowledge.

During the onset of the British Malayan Headhunting Scandal, it would have been extremely advantageous from a public relations standpoint for the British government and military to name an instance in which decapitating a head provided information which proved useful to the British forces. Trawling through British regimental histories, biographies, newspapers, declassified government documents, personal testimonies, and other such sources to gather all known sources concerning Britain's headhunting policy in Malaya, this research has failed to find any proof to support the claim that the beheading of corpses had in any way helped the British military fight the MNLA. It could be argued that using this method to identify guerrillas may have potentially helped to paint a clearer picture of the MNLA command structure, pinpoint the approximate location of an MNLA regiment, or perhaps even use forensics to identify the MNLA's potential food sources. However there is no proof that this was the case, and this research was unable to identify any instances of such intelligence gained via headhunting proving useful, or any former soldiers, commander, police officer, or politician, ever giving an example of British forces benefitting from headhunting. Similarly it appears that despite the large body of literature covering the history of British policing and intelligence in Malaya, fellow historians of the Malayan Emergency have also failed to uncover any recorded instance in which the British benefitted from their headhunting policy. In a testimony to the extreme rarity of evidence when historians have successfully identified the victims of Britain's headhunting, there is only one other potential victim whose name this research was able to uncover, and his name was Lim Tian Shui.

Lim Tian Shui, the first decapitation victim?

Lim Tian Shui[7] was a victim of the infamous Batang Kali massacre committed by the British Army's Scots Guards who in 1948 rounded up the entire population of a small village, terrorised the civilians they captured with mock executions,[8] before performing real executions, killing almost every adult male inhabitant of the village. The British forcefully evicted the women, children and elderly from the village who were then forced to beg on the streets for food and shelter.[9] Almost a week later the survivors returned to find that the British had burned down their homes, that the corpses of their loved ones were rotting above ground, and that British allied newspapers were calling their murdered family members "communist terrorists".[10] As far as historians have been able to gather, this is the only known instance of a massacre of civilians on this scale committed by the British during the Malayan Emergency.

After the massacre, Lim Tian Shui's body was discovered by survivors who noted that his head was missing.[11, 12] The head was never recovered, although some Malaysian news outlets have reported unconfirmed rumours that Lim Tian Shui's detached head had been allegedly thrown into a nearby river where it flowed to a nearby Malay village before being thrown back into the river by a frightened woman.[13] Unlike most cases of decapitations during the Malayan Emergency it does not appear as though any Iban headhunters or police officers were involved in this particular instance, even though the same battalion that committed this massacre commonly worked alongside Iban mercenaries during the war.[14] Lim Tian Shui's son lived long enough to help forward a legal case for the families of the victims of the Batang Kali Massacre in the early 2010s which led to wider recognition of the massacre. However because the eyewitness who testified that he saw Lim Tian Shui's headless corpse was an elderly man during the legal battle with the British government, there is the possibility that his memories are the result of conjecture. It is also possible that the decapitated head he witnessed was not intentionally cut off with a knife, but rather that the body was so riddled with bullets and badly decomposed that the head became detached.

The case of Lim Tian Shui's killing was not the only instance of a civilian's head being removed by commonwealth forces during the Malayan Emergency. In one instance Iban mercenaries discovered two civilians fishing in the countryside. Falsely believing that the two civilians were communists, the Iban mercenaries murdered and decapitated them. This incident caused the local population to hate the British military. Former British Army soldier Ron Harper of the Queen's Royal Regiment, recounts his experience of attending the funeral of these two civilians killed. Below is a transcript of an oral account that he gave during a video recorded interview:

> "I can remember we had a couple of Ibans with us which were native trackers from Sarawak in Borneo and they were very agitated and when they get agitated they are head hunters and you sort of get a little bit worried."
>
> "…we had an incident when I was at that place called Laying Laying where a group of our boys, it was only a platoon so it was a section that had gone out with a couple of these trackers and they had come across in the jungle these chaps fishing and they thought that they were bandits as we called them and they went down there and chopped their heads off. Our boys stayed away. It turned out they were villagers who were in an area they should not have been and we, myself and another chap were on the gate when the funeral possession came through the gates and it was a very tense time. We had gone from being welcome in that village to being hated overnight. Basically I don't think it was as much the fact that they were dead, it was the fact that they had been decapitated which caused most of the trouble."[15]

If the British forces and their allies only conducted decapitations for intelligence gathering purposes, then why was Lim Tian Shui's head not taken to a police station for identification? Why were unarmed civilians with zero links to armed groups, decapitated? The possibility that the first recorded victim of Britain's headhunting policy was an innocent unarmed civilian with zero links to communism or the MNLA, raises the uncomfortable possibility that many more of the decapitation victims seen in preserved photographs may not have been guerrillas as the British had claimed, but rather innocent civilians. During the Malayan Emergency there were incidents of British intelligence officers planting communist literature on innocent civilians, arresting them, and then using threats of deportation and execution to coerce them into becoming spies for the British.[16] It is for these reasons that this research makes liberal use of the term "suspected" guerrillas/MNLA members when describing the victims of Britain's headhunting policy, so as not to risk incorrectly labelling murdered civilians as armed combatants. This researcher believes that there is a high likelihood that many of the victims of headhunting preserved in photographs during the Malayan Emergency, may have been civilians.

Sources, content, and treatment of both heads and photographs

Tracking where the photographs ended up after the war, analysing their content (soldiers present, lighting, quality, etc), and studying their proliferation, are all useful methods which can help researchers learn more about Britain's headhunting policy in Malaya.

Occasionally headhunting trophy photographs from Malaya found their way into family homes and were discovered by the relatives of former British soldiers. One instance of this happening was investigated in the 2007 Channel 4 documentary "Empire's Children", a show which followed the quests of notable British people from politicians to celebrities as they discover their family histories. Episode five featured British television actress and writer Jenny Éclair (aka Jenny Clare Hargreaves) whose father was a British intelligence officer with the British Army's Green Howards during the Malayan Emergency.[17] As a child, Jenny discovered Malayan headhunting trophy photographs kept in her father's bedroom.[18] After suppressing the memories of discovering these photographs for most of her life she later confronted her father and asked him to explain their context.[19] His response was entirely unrepentant, calling the MNLA "terrorists" and telling Jenny that he had no regrets. "We didn't ask questions," he said. "It was simply a case of goodies versus baddies."[20] Although Jenny's experience is the only published instance of a British child coming into contact with atrocity photographs from Malaya, it is not uncommon to find people with similar experiences within online military blogs and forums.

The *Daily Worker*, which contains the largest single collection of headhunting photographs from the Malayan Emergency currently known to historians, depict scenes of British soldiers gleefully posing with heads, and Ibans crafting scalp trophies next to baskets overflowing with body parts. The content of these photographs depicts heads serving as either sources of enjoyment for British soldiers, or as tokens of bravery taken by Ibans striving to increase their social status. The irony of soldiers claiming that heads were taken for intelligence, despite photographs arising of soldiers playing with heads and treating them like toys, has not been missed by academics. Historian Calder Walton describes his own scepticism of the claims that heads were only ever taken for intelligence purposes, and proposes an alternative explanation for the headhunting photographs published by the *Daily Worker* in 1952:

> "Some of the acts of decapitation were allegedly performed by Iban 'headhunters', though this hardly explains the pictures that emerged of British soldiers posing with the heads of decapitated enemies as trophies. It seems fair to say that on one level these acts of barbarism arose because of the nature of warfare in Malaya, which was both brutal and brutalising. Invariably, however, the immediate cause of the atrocities there was the same as it had been in Palestine: there was a vicious cycle of violence, in which incidents by and against security forces were followed by reprisals."[21]

Though fewer in number, there are Malayan decapitation photographs which were shot in a style appearing more in line with identification photographs. There are in existence four headhunting photographs all depicting the same decapitated head which were all taken in a style more suitable for identification than trophy purposes. All four images are clear, simple, and brightly lit closeup images of the same head from several angles with enough detail to capture all the facial features, and unlike the *Daily Worker* photographs there are no soldiers posing in these photographs.

Some headhunting photographs may have been created to serve as tools for intelligence gathering, however the sources for many of these images reveal them to have served as both trophies for the entertainment of British soldiers and as materials preserved by an archivist aiming to highlight the brutality of colonialism. Two of these four photographs of the same head were discovered not among official documents as would be expected from intelligence related resources, but were found sandwiched between photographs of fancy dress parties and smiling soldiers posing with a child, all held within a soldier's personal photo album which had been handed to the UK National Army Museum by the soldier's wife.[22]

The other two photographs of this same decapitated head exist only from surviving photocopies kept by the Working Class Movement Library (WCML) in Manchester.[23] The WCML was originally founded to contain the overflowing literature collections of the British bibliophile communist couple Edmund and Ruth Frow, both of whom were heavily involved with the *Daily Worker*.[24] None of these four photographs come attached to any information detailing their dates, exact location, their purposes, or the identity of the victim, which is all information which should have been recorded if these photographs had truly been created for intelligence purposes.

More insights into how the headhunting photographs and similar trophy images of corpses were treated can be found within the archives of the British Army's Suffolk Regiment. Within these archives, macabre photographs of murdered Malayans sit alongside images of partying British soldiers. These images are not held within official military files but rather a soldier's personal photo album adorned with a painting of a lingerie pin-up model.[25] Other albums belonging to soldiers of the same regiment contain images of smiling British soldiers posing over the relatively intact corpses of Malayans they had recently killed. Not all the victims in these atrocity photographs are dead. In some of them, suspected MNLA members are forced at gunpoint by British soldiers to sit and pose next to the corpses of fellow Malayans killed by the British.[26] These photographs show that such trophy photographs of soldiers posing with the bodies of suspected MNLA members was not unique to headhunting photographs.[27]

Another way of learning more about headhunting during the Malayan Emergency using photographs is to investigate their proliferation and provenance. In contrast to the British government and military's claim that headhunting photographs depicted isolated events, the news of said incidents was common knowledge within regiments. Photographs of dead Malayans were commonly traded between British soldiers, their families, and close friends.[28] Atrocity photographs from the Malayan Emergency were treated as collectables both during and after the war, much akin to the tradition of trading football cards. Eamonn McCann, one of Ireland's most famous political journalists, witnessed this post-war collecting and trading behaviour. While planting trees alongside a group of former British soldiers, the soldiers reminisced about headhunting during the Malayan Emergency and shared headhunting photographs.

McCann remembers the former soldiers he knew:

> "recalling their service in the Malayan "Emergency" when they'd cut the heads or smaller bits off "Chinese communists". I remember one fellow passing round creased pictures of himself and his mates holding their prizes aloft. These were conscript soldiers, the last intake of National Servicemen, not professionals. Generally speaking, when you pressed them, they'd admit to shame at what they'd gotten up to, but also to a certain fascination with the fact that they'd had it in them to do it. And they'd all tell you that, hell, they'd been pussy-cats when compared to the prestige outfits, the crack troops, the corps d'elite of the military machine, the SAS, the Marines, the Paras."[29]

The collecting and trading behaviour among British forces is further demonstrated by the appearance of many duplicate atrocity photographs appearing within the personal possessions of different soldiers.[30] Even British soldiers who had never seen a living MNLA guerrilla were given photographs of guerrillas by fellow British soldiers.[31] In one instance a British soldier of the South Wales Borderers Regiment had come into possession of a Malayan headhunting photograph, despite claiming to have never personally witnessed a dead MNLA member and having only served in Malaya between 1956–1957, many years after Churchill's ban on headhunting.[32] Similarly, Jenny Éclair's father also claimed to have never been directly involved in the decapitation of corpses, despite owning a Malayan headhunting photograph which he kept in his possession many years after the war. This further suggests a pattern of photographs featuring the corpses of suspected MNLA guerrillas being duplicated and traded between British soldiers. There were also many instances of British soldiers enclosing atrocity photographs from Malaya in letters that they sent home to their families.[33] This tendency for British soldiers to collect and distribute atrocity photographs between each other was a practice which made it easier for the *Daily Worker's* journalists to acquire such images.

Skulls and scalp trophies

Photographs weren't the only trophies created in Malaya as a result of Britain's headhunting policy. In 1952 the *Daily Worker* reported that Iban headhunters were smuggling human scalps out of Malaya once their military service had ended. As proof the *Daily Worker* cited an article written by Harry Willcox, a Senior Civil Liaison Officer with the rank of Major, who was in charge of recruiting Ibans to fight with the No.3 Commando Brigade of the Royal Marines.[34] According to Willcox, Ibans were permitted by their British handlers to take the scalps of their victims and return home with them after their service in Malaya. Iban communities rewarded headhunters who returned home carrying a human scalp with a four-day feast, and the proven headhunter would then be considered more sexually desirable in the eyes of Iban women. Perhaps not realising that he was publicly confessing to being an accessory to war crimes by permitting the bodies of enemy soldiers to be turned into aphrodisiacs, Major Willcox openly admitted that he permitted Ibans to take scalps within an article he wrote for *Globe and Laurel*, the official journal of the Royal Marines:

> "First, foremost and of supreme importance to all concerned is the question of whether he has brought back an enemy head or the scalp and hair which nowadays serve as a token head. If he hasn't been lucky on his patrols here [in Malaya] and goes back empty handed, the welcome is altogether cooler. But if he has, he will, of course, have sent word ahead, and at a meeting the head of the longhouse will have commissioned the most highly skilled weaver among the women to weave a special ceremonial cloth for the reception of the head. This lady, in a state of great excitement and importance, is the first to greet him, taking the head in the cloth, while the other women sing the anthem for returning warriors. The tracker will have fitted the scalp or hair on to a pumpkin, giving it the appearance of a turnip head, and this he places in the cloth with ceremony. Every boy and young

man there is green with envy, and every girl gives him the sort of look Errol Flynn is used."[35, 36]

This was far from the only time that articles published inside *Globe and Laurel* had admitted to allowing Ibans to scalp corpses. According to one article in 1951 describing a meeting between a British general and troops in Malaya:

"Afterwards, while he was talking to the officers, the two Iban trackers were produced and insisted on shaking hands with their Commandant-General. This was an honour second only to the taking of a bandit head, or rather, as officially sanctioned, "a reasonable proportion of the hair and scalp.""[37]

It was not uncommon for British commanders to allow Ibans to scalp the corpses of suspected MNLA members. This was not only done in the hope of gaining community prestige back in Borneo, but was also sometimes practised as a symbol of revenge. John Norton, a British military Lieutenant who allowed the Ibans he worked with to scalp corpses, describes taking part in this practice after approaching the site of the Ulu Caledonia Estate Ambush.[38] This guerrilla attack on a British military convoy saw the largest single loss of British soldiers in a single ambush during the entire war:

"We heard some firing, and I contributed two bursts into a bandit. Remang, an Iban, was eager to scalp him in accordance with Iban tradition. I gave him permission to do so. (The dead bodies of his fellow Ibans were still laying below us down the slope on the estate road together with the other dead and wounded, so he was keen to avenge them). Remang cut a lock of hair and skin off the scalp of the dead bandit with his parang as if he was taking the top off a coconut. Then, waving it aloft, he made a noise reminiscent of a huntsman at the kill of a fox or hare. (This lock of hair later adorned the end of Remang's best parang, and the knuckle of one of his fingers was tattooed as a sign that he claimed a kill)."[39]

The collection of human body parts was such a strong cultural staple of Britain's Iban mercenaries that some Ibans arrived in Malaya already carrying severed human body parts which they had brought from home. British soldiers of the Royal Corps of Signals describe this practice among Ibans (Ebans) during the early years of the Malayan Emergency:

> "The Ebans all wore necklaces wrapped in cloth strips, one night we were in the canteen having a beer when Cpl Monks asked one of them to show us what the wrapping covered, it was human ears of people they had killed in fights/tribal battles in Borneo."[40]

Although the majority of the decapitations during the Malayan Emergency were conducted by Iban mercenaries, they were not the only people to collect physical headhunting trophies and take them home. There has been at least one recorded case of a skull trophy collected by British soldiers during the Malayan Emergency which was prominently displayed within a UK regimental museum.[41] This is very unusual, as it is the only recorded instance that this research was able to uncover of British troops taking human remains from the Malayan Emergency back to Britain. Typically British soldiers avoided taking trophies in the form of human remains during the Malayan Emergency, preferring to instead loot the corpses of MNLA for money, watches, and even their star caps which became treasured collectables.[42]

As shown by the photographs released by the *Daily Worker* on the 10 May 1952, many of the heads taken by Iban soldiers in Malaya were scalped, a practice which holds zero intelligence value for the British (DNA forensics had not yet been invented) and only served to make war trophies. If the taking of heads by Iban headhunters was meant solely as an intelligence gathering exercise, then why were they allowed to turn these heads into trophies?

Soldier eye-witness testimonies cast doubt on the official story

There are countless testimonies of soldiers who witnessed headhunting in Malaya, however these accounts often greatly contradict both each other and the official narrative of the British government. Outside of the cases publicised by the *Daily Worker*, this research was able to uncover multiple instances of British soldiers recounting their experiences with Britain's use of headhunting during the Malayan Emergency from a wide range of ranks, regiments, and service dates.

The first of these eyewitness accounts comes from officer Herbert Andrew's memoirs, *Who Won the Malayan Emergency*. Andrew writes that a fellow British man close to him known as Police Lieutenant Barron had somehow acquired a sack containing five decapitated human heads. According to this account, an Officer Commanding Police District (OCPD) official had accused Police Lieutenant Barron of slacking off work. Barron returned weeks later and responded to these accusations by calling over a fellow soldier who then emptied the sack of human heads onto the OCPD official's desk.[43] The identities of the heads are not revealed, how they were gathered was not explained, the author does not elaborate on what happened afterwards, and no further details are given that could shed light on any possible way these heads were used. The details are left as a mystery, despite the fact the book's author was a police lieutenant specialising in anti-insurgent intelligence. Giving us further clues into the mentality of the soldiers involved in the decapitations, the same soldier who wrote this book dedicated several pages to bragging about how he was allowed to break the Geneva Convention because the British called the conflict an "emergency" and not a war.[44]

The second eyewitness account comes from Francis Gerald Green, a former Royal Marine 42 Commando who had personally witnessed an Iban headhunter decapitate an MNLA member who he and his fellow soldiers had shot dead. In an audio recorded interview held by the Imperial War Museum, Green says that the British had ordered the Iban to decapitate the suspected MNLA guerrilla, and that said Iban was overjoyed before getting into a "tussle" with his British superior after realising he was not allowed to keep the head he had taken. Green also said that he and his fellow British soldiers were not far from camp and noted that they could have easily carried the body back, but that the policy of decapitating corpses dictated that they should instead remove the head.[45]

The third eyewitness account comes from Eddie Clark, a former British soldier of the 1st Battalion of the Cameroonians (Scottish Rifles)

Regiment. During his time in Malaya a patrol of his regiment came into contact with multiple MNLA guerrillas which they fought. After the fight, the corpses of two MNLA members were then beheaded by an Iban who had accompanied the British soldiers. The Iban then proceeded to remove the brains of the two heads and take the heart out of one of the corpses, and had to be calmed down by the British soldiers he had accompanied. After the Iban had stopped mutilating the bodies, a British soldier approached with a camera and took photographs of the two heads close to where they had been killed.[46]

Andrew's account backs up the *Daily Worker* reports that decapitated heads were treated like trophies to be proudly shown off by soldiers to prove their skills and kills, although it does act as further proof that many heads were taken with intelligence in mind as they were delivered to a police officer. Green's account shows that decapitations were not only used as last resort methods but were practised even when the bodies could easily be carried back to British bases. Clarke's account demonstrates that the taking of heads was often performed with no questions of intelligence being raised and only served to indulge the bloodlust and cultural practices of Iban mercenaries.

All three of these accounts contradict the British government and General Templer's official justification that the use of Iban headhunters for decapitations was a rarely used method of last resort for intelligence gathering in the deep jungle.

The eyewitness testimonies of another two British soldiers, Walter Heaton and John Chynoweth, also provide radically different views on the decapitations conducted by Ibans by suggesting new possible incentives for soldiers to decapitate heads.

Walter Heaton was a former member of Britain's Coldstream Guards regiment, currently the oldest continuously serving regiment in the British Army. Heaton witnessed the aftermath of the Batang Kali Massacre and witnessed his fellow soldiers burning down the homes of innocent civilians. Heaton was so disgusted by what he had witnessed in Malaya that it influenced him to become a lifelong socialist and civil rights activist, eventually joining Veterans For Peace UK where he opened up about his experiences during the war. Heaton's comments on Britain's decapitation

Debate: Military Necessity and the Intelligence Gathering Theory 53

policy give a particularly nasty impression of Iban headhunting as not only a method for gathering trophies but also for monetary gain. During his time in Malaya, Heaton became aware of a case in which an Iban headhunter had been given a cash reward in exchange for a decapitated head.[47] The British colonial occupation often promised huge cash rewards for a number of actions, including handing in weapons and ammo to the police, escorting people to police stations, reporting on their neighbours, and also for murdering alleged communists. Though the cash rewards were usually awarded by the police, some British commanders were known to have promised cash rewards to men within their regiments for capturing or killing communists.[48, 49] In 1953, Gerald Templer promised villagers in Malaya's Jabor Valley an acre of land as a reward for any communists killed as a result of information they gave. This desperate and controversial attempt to bribe local people failed because none of the locals gave any information.[50] The exact details on who was allowed to claim these rewards and in what circumstances were often vague and poorly communicated, something which may have frustrated attempts by Iban headhunters to claim cash bounties and further complicated by their status as "civilians".[51]

According to historian Dr David Bonner, Ibans in Malaya often attempted to use decapitated heads to claim cash rewards, and this bounty system was ended after it proved too controversial.[52] One SAS soldier recalled that the Ibans he served alongside were unofficially paid money by Malay police to cut the ears off suspected MNLA members to prove their kills and that this practice was ended after officials in Britain learned of its existence.[53] While there may not have been an official long standing-policy to reward Ibans with money for heads, during many 20th century wars it was not unheard of for British military commanders to offer cash-in-hand rewards for soldiers who performed certain tasks with distinction. News that Iban mercenaries were being rewarded with cash bounties for providing decapitated heads was picked up by the *Daily Worker* newspaper which then asked the Colonial Office for a response. However, like many of the *Daily Worker's* articles exposing wrongdoings in Malaya, government officials gave the paper's inquiry the silent treatment. When a *Daily Worker* reporter asked a British government spokesperson whether it was true that decapitated heads were being traded for cash bounties, the spokesperson responded with a simple "No Comment."[54] The British Army's practice of providing cash rewards for these types of actions was not isolated to Malaya but was also practised in Kenya, with some British soldiers being promised by their commanders that they would receive 5 shillings per head for each black man they killed.[55] In some instances the phrase "per head" was taken literally.

Another soldier who provides a radically different account of how decapitated heads were used is John Chynoweth. As a racist, chauvinistic, and unapologetic supporter of colonialism, John Chynoweth embodied all the worst traits of a British soldier. Confessing that despite being a university graduate he could not even point to Malaya on a map before being conscripted and ordered to fight in the Malayan Emergency,[56] Chynoweth expressed a seething contempt for non-Europeans. He insisted on using racial pejoratives for aboriginals despite being warned by his commanders, describing the aboriginals as "primitive child-like people"[57] with "the intelligence of a child of ten".[58] He begins his autobiography by rallying against "political correctness",[59] calling ethnic Chinese people untrustworthy,[60,61] and goes on to describe non-Europeans as a "collection of riff-raff" who are all "smelly, filthy, and noisy" before continuing his description of Malaya's people with an unhinged misogynist rant on the supposed sagginess of African and Asian women's breasts.[62] He also openly admitted that he often visited Britain's 'New Village' internment camps because he enjoyed terrorising the civilians imprisoned within them, something he described as "putting the fear of god into the co-operating Chinese."[63]

Unsurprisingly given his aforementioned views, John Chynoweth was a strong supporter of Britain's headhunting policy and wholeheartedly believed in the government's justification that decapitations were necessary to identify MNLA guerrilla.[64] Chynoweth fully agrees with the military's Intelligence Gathering Theory. However, he also admits that the severed heads were used for a far more sinister purpose than intelligence gathering. According to Chynoweth, the decapitated heads of suspected MNLA members were used as instruments of terror, describing them as being useful tools for scaring Chinese civilians in New Villages to "discourage the inhabitants from supporting terrorists."[65]

Debate: Military Necessity and the Intelligence Gathering Theory 55

On the alternative use of corpses, there is very scant evidence to suggest that any of the headhunting victims were alive when their heads were severed. One Malayan Emergency veteran and Gurkhas specialist claimed that there was an incident where Gurkhas in Malaya "captured a guerrilla and took his head off".[66] One former MNLA guerrilla who was also a former inmate in one of Britain's New Village internment camps, recalls that her fellow inmates who tried to assist the MNLA would be decapitated as a punishment:

> "The British were very strict with the people in the New Villages. If anyone was caught assisting the Communists, they were beheaded immediately."[67]

However despite these two interesting cases, there is little evidence to prove that the British routinely decapitated suspected MNLA members while they were still alive. If there were cases then it would have been an extremely rare instance and not a part of any widespread military policy such as the practice of decapitating corpses.

This research has discovered heads turned into tools of terror to intimidate prisoners in internment camps, heads taken to receive cash bounties for personal monetary gain, and even heads turned into sexual aphrodisiacs to impress tribal women. Yet despite all these numerous recorded cases there appears to be little evidence that decapitated heads were ever successfully utilised for intelligence-gathering purposes.

The availability and reliability of cameras

One of the primary justifications used by the military to defend their headhunting policy was the claim that British troops couldn't maintain and operate camera equipment within humid jungle environments. However, British soldiers who fought in Malaya often noted that many of the MNLA guerrillas they killed had been carrying high-quality photographs of their comrades in their pockets and packs, and that these photographs taken in the jungle often depicted armed MNLA guerrillas in uniform. Many of these photographs found on the bodies of MNLA members were later published in books written by British soldiers who fought in the war.[68, 69, 70] Cases of MNLA guerrillas photographing each other in the depths of the Malayan jungle were so widespread that the British forces were able to create entire tree-shaped collages of the MNLA chain of command using photographs found in the possessions of killed, captured, and surrendered MNLA members.[71] One group of Royal Marine Commandos even discovered an MNLA jungle camp containing photographic processing equipment.[72]

Some British soldiers recall that according to the official list of Army equipment, it was mandatory for all platoons to own a camera.[73] Lieutenant Colonel J.P. Cross wrote that he was perfectly able to use cameras in the depths of the Malayan jungle to successfully capture the faces of dead MNLA guerrillas.[74] Many Gurkhas also found no difficulties in photographing the corpses of suspected MNLA members in the locations in which they had been killed.[75] The demand by military superiors for corpses was so strong that in one instance, Commonwealth soldiers were ordered to exhume the grave of a dead communist who they had already photographed and fingerprinted, even though doing so would blow their cover and likely alert nearby guerrillas to their presence, potentially allowing for them to be ambushed.[76]

Historian of Cold War propaganda and British counterinsurgencies Susan Carruthers has pointed out that in many cases cameras were readily available, a fact proven by the very existence of headhunting photographs. She also notes that amateur photography was a common hobby among British soldiers in Malaya:

> "It was ironic, then, that a practice Templer justified in the absence of photographic means of corroborating identities should have turned into a scandal precisely because of cameras' illicit presence at such scenes."[77]

The MNLA was a small and nomadic guerrilla army of impoverished peasants that could barely feed itself and often spent months or even years in isolation deep within the Malayan wilderness. If these impoverished and desperate people could acquire and maintain camera equipment while endlessly running through mountains and jungles, then it should not have been a difficult task for the professional armed forces of the world's wealthiest and most technologically advanced empire.

The availability of alternative tactics

Despite the government and military publicly insisting that decapitations were necessary to retrieve corpses from the deep jungle, there existed a myriad of proven alternatives for successfully retrieving and identifying bodies. One of the most unique methods implemented by the British was the use of helicopters to transport bodies from remote areas. The Royal Air Force first deployed Dragonfly helicopters in Malaya as early as May 1950 for casualty evacuations and these were also used to transport the corpses of suspected MNLA members.[78] This use of helicopters in Malaya predates all of the dated decapitation incidents depicted in the *Daily Worker* photographs. Despite being used for casualty evacuations, one pilot refused to allow a patrol to load his helicopter with eight decapitated heads, claiming that the weight was too much.[79] During a separate incident, another helicopter pilot became suspicious because of the weight of a soldier's bag and opened it to discover five decapitated heads.[80] It appears that using helicopters to transport decapitated heads was a common practice during the Malayan Emergency. Another British RAF official recounted that one of his helicopter pilots mournfully told him of how he flew a helicopter to transport a sack full of decapitated heads in Malaya.[81]

When patrolling the deep jungle British soldiers would keep in contact with their commanders via radio and would often extract their men by cutting down trees to create a clearing for helicopter evacuations. By 1953, helicopters were so commonly used for transporting corpses from the jungle that the British constructed special body-holding carriage underneath their helicopters to compensate for the increased numbers of MNLA guerrillas being killed.[82] According to one former SAS soldier who fought in Malaya, the availability of helicopters during the later period of the war meant that he never had to take part in any decapitations.[83]

Another use for military aircraft in identifying insurgents came in the form of airdrops from Dakota aeroplanes. British soldiers on lengthy jungle expeditions would chop down jungle trees and radio for an airdrop of supplies of food, clothes, beer, and water to be parachuted into the jungle.[84] Commonwealth soldiers would sometimes use orange inflatable balloons and smoke grenades to signal their location to supply aircraft.[85] If the troops were not carrying cameras then they could have obtained them by radioing their commander and requesting one to be included within their regular supplies.[86]

However despite these technologies which made identifying corpses possible without resorting to headhunting, in the vast majority of instances that British soldiers retrieved a corpse from the jungle they successfully managed to do so without any specialist equipment or severing of limbs. The most commonly used method was to tie the corpse's hands to the ankles, putting a sapling in-between, and carry the body out of the jungle.[87] This was often done with the body itself covered in fabric, however even these methods were often used by British soldiers as opportunities to take trophy photographs.[88, 89, 90] This was a commonly used and highly effective method of removing bodies from the jungles for police identification and was practised by virtually every British Army regiment which saw combat during the Malayan Emergency. As a result of its widespread use and effectiveness in retrieving corpses from the jungle, photographs of corpses tied to poles are extremely common in archives, books, and photographic albums created by British soldiers who fought during the Malayan Emergency.

Another method used by the British to identify corpses without needing to move them was to bring a person familiar with the guerrillas into the jungle. Often MNLA bases were discovered when a guerrilla who had surrendered to the British, known as Surrendered Enemy Personnel (SEPs), would betray their former comrades by accompanying British troops into the jungle to locate MNLA bases. Having led the British forces to their former allies, the SEP would identify the corpses exactly where they had been killed.[91] This was typically a method used during more shallow jungle patrols. This exact method of identification without moving the bodies was successfully used by the Suffolk Regiment, and there are even recorded cases of SEPs accompanying Ibans into the jungle.[92]

The Suffolk Regiment which was especially known for its heavy use of Iban mercenaries even managed to successfully identify MNLA corpses by simply leaving the bodies alone and returning later with more men

Debate: Military Necessity and the Intelligence Gathering Theory 59

to recover them. In this instance the Suffolks fought a party of MNLA guerrillas, killing three of them but also losing one of their own men. They then returned to the scene of the battle the next day with more troops to retrieve the bodies and were able to successfully identify two of the three MNLA corpses.[93]

In a testimony to the abysmal failure of the headhunting policy, this single instance in which corpses were left alone and retrieved later, resulted in more historically recorded instances of the successful identifications of MNLA than the decapitating of bodies managed to achieve during the entirety of the war.

It should be recognised that methods such as helicopter retrieval, camera airdrops, SEP guides, leaving bodies with plans to return at a later date, and carrying bodies with the wooden pole method, would not have been possible in all circumstances. However, the existence of such a wide variety of successfully tested and easily available methods of identification demonstrates that there were almost always potential alternatives to decapitating heads. This acts as further evidence against the argument that headhunting was a necessity to identify bodies and was a crucial component of intelligence gathering operations. From a dispassionate military standpoint, dedicating more time and resources into the technical challenges of body retrieval would have been a sensible choice in comparison to the public relations and logistics nightmare of recruiting over 1,000 foreign mercenaries with reputations as headhunters and risk permanently tarnishing the British military's reputation.

Intelligence Gathering Theory Conclusion

This research has uncovered numerous and diverse cases of both headhunting in Malaya and the photographs of this practice, including children coming into possession of atrocity photographs, civilians being decapitated, scalps taken as trophies and aphrodisiacs by Iban headhunters, scalps taken as a symbol of revenge, photographs of severed heads being widely collected and traded among British soldiers, heads taken for cash rewards, corpses decapitated despite the body being within walking distance of a colonial military base, heads used as tools of terror, and even cranial remains being displayed as a trophy in a British regimental museum. Despite the numerous instances of headhunting examined throughout this chapter, this research has only managed to uncover a single instance of a decapitation which may have possibly led to the successful identification of an MNLA member. However despite this one possible case of a successful identification of a decapitated head, this research has failed to find any proof that the British military benefitted from any potential information gathered through the headhunting policy.

Evidence against the Intelligence Gathering Theory includes the aforementioned *Daily Worker* articles, the existence of countless trophy photographs, the MNLA's ability to operate cameras in the jungle, the conflicting and dissenting eyewitness testimonies of British soldiers, the widespread availability of successfully proven technical alternatives, the availability of cameras, the civilian victims of headhunting, the taking of scalps, and most importantly the lack of any known cases of headhunting ever producing intelligence proven to have been useful to Britain's counterinsurgency. In stark contrast, the evidence in favour of the Intelligence Gathering Theory rests almost solely upon an appeal to common sense by the same military conducting the decapitations, and a government which attempted to obfuscate its existence. For the above reasons, the decapitations committed by Commonwealth forces and their Iban allies during the Malayan Emergency cannot be explained as a practice motivated solely by the need to gather military intelligence, as the British government has attempted to argue.

The claims by the British government and military that decapitations were only ever performed in last-resort circumstances, to gather information on guerrilla activities in the deep jungle, have been thoroughly discredited. The headhunting policy may have been originally envisioned as an intelligence-gathering activity by a colonial occupation willing to go to any lengths to achieve victory. However, in the face of the thorough dehumanisation of the enemy, the practice quickly devolved into a grizzly and gratuitous expression of colonial barbarity with little strategic value, and only served to permanently tarnish the reputation of the British military. This research was unable to uncover an instance where information about the MNLA

Debate: Military Necessity and the Intelligence Gathering Theory 61

gathered through the use of headhunting, was shown to have aided Britain's eventual victory during the Malayan Emergency.

When speaking to fellow colonial officials, Arthur Creech Jones wrote that the Ibans Britain was deploying in Malaya were not headhunters. When speaking to the public following the first *Daily Worker* headhunting photograph, an Admiralty spokesperson incorrectly claimed that the first *Daily Worker* photograph was fake, and a Colonial Office spokesperson misled the public by suggesting that the image depicted a disembodied head possibly removed by the MNLA communists themselves. Finally, speaking in the House of Commons during the British government's final acknowledgement of the headhunting policy, the Minister of State for Colonial Affairs, Henry Hopkinson, attempted to retrospectively justify Britain's headhunting policy by claiming that there were no rules forbidding decapitations in Malaya, despite the fact that Britain's headhunting policy potentially violated both the Malayan penal code and the Geneva Convention.[94]

Chapter 6

The Historiography: Questions and Comments by Researchers

As this research is the first attempt by any historian to gather all the available evidence and create a complete timeline of the British Malayan Headhunting Scandal, detailed mentions in the academic literature of Britain's headhunting policy are relatively rare. Unfortunately, of the few instances when researchers have acknowledged the beheadings, they have only lightly touched the subject and are typically only a couple of sentences in length. Many mentions of headhunting in Malaya in academic works are filled with mistakes, and very few of these acknowledgements examine the *Daily Worker* archives, which are kept in London and are both free to access and openly available to the public. One such example comes from the work of historian T.N. Harper. After taking a quote from the biography of a British soldier at face value without examining the available evidence, Harper went as far as to claim that Ibans were not responsible for the decapitations shown in the *Daily Worker* photographs.[1,2] Harper also argues that the reputation of Iban mercenaries as headhunters was "undeserved" without elaborating why he believes that.[3]

Harper is not alone when it comes to researchers only lightly touching the British Malayan Headhunting Scandal without examining the easily available primary sources. In a testament to just how few people have bothered to examine the original *Daily Worker* articles, both legal documents created in support of the victims of the Batang Kali Massacre,[4] and the official history of the CPGB,[5] both failed to correctly pinpoint the year that the *Daily Worker* debuted their headhunting atrocity photographs.

The most infamous photograph published in the *Daily Worker* of a soldier holding two decapitated heads has been spread across the internet and reprinted in various books due to its shocking nature, however they rarely acknowledge the *Daily Worker* as the source for the photograph.

One former SAS soldier wrote a book using this iconic photograph, but also neglected to mention the original source of the photograph.[6] In 2009 a mainstream British newspaper called the *Independent* uploaded one of the *Daily Worker's* decapitation photographs to their website. However in yet another example of how little writers have engaged with the available sources, the article neglected to mention where the photograph came from.[7]

Soldiers' relatives and their reactions to headhunting

Despite the widespread lack of recognition and interest shown by researchers concerning the British Malayan Headhunting Scandal, certain questions are commonly raised during the rare occasions when historians have acknowledged the *Daily Worker* photographs.
- Why did the decapitations take place and how was it that British soldiers were able to support such a practice?
- Why did seemingly all non-communist media in 20th century Britain refuse to republish the decapitation photographs?
- How did such a noteworthy story seemingly fail to gain widespread attention from the British public?

One way that researchers can speculate as to why the *Daily Worker* images failed to spark any widespread public outrage outside of left-wing political circles is to look at the reaction of British civilians to learning that a family member in Malaya was involved in the practice of headhunting. Unfortunately there is only one thoroughly recorded instance of such a reaction, and it happens to come from the aforementioned instance of Jenny Éclair and her childhood discovery of her father's atrocity photographs (as covered earlier in chapter 5). Jenny's appearance on the Channel 4 documentary Empire's Children provides an extremely rare and thoroughly documented example of a British civilian being confronted with evidence that a loved one had been involved in atrocities during the Malayan Emergency. The episode also sheds further light on the psychological factors hampering potential public opposition to British colonialism, especially in the face of the *Daily Worker's* decapitation photographs.

Despite feeling deeply disturbed by her father's photographs and being morally opposed to mutilating corpses, Jenny found it too emotionally painful to accept that he had done anything wrong. Her attempts to learn more about both the war and the headhunting atrocities only served to worsen her emotional distress and deepen her internal crisis over her national identity.[8] Jenny grew increasingly defensive when confronted with uncomfortable truths surrounding the British Empire's occupation of Malaya. Despite having claimed to be apolitical, she went as far as to begin a political debate with historian Ban Ar Kam, whose father was killed by British soldiers who then publicly displayed his corpse. During these scenes, Jenny ironically accused the historian of being too emotionally invested in the history of the Malayan Emergency to view the conflict objectively. Jenny's failure to accept information that she found uncomfortable and which contradicted her positive image of her father, was highly unpopular with the show's audience who harshly criticised Jenny's reaction.[9]

Jenny's cognitive dissonance was later used by academic researchers studying how the British public has confronted the history of British colonialism.

> "In the programme, Eclair is confronted by an ethnic Chinese man whose father had been executed by the British for his communist activities. The two descendants had completely different received (family, and in Eclair's case, national) memories of the past, and the programme format shaped and revealed this confrontation at a national, familial and personal level. In this example we can see the emergence of a memory that has been suppressed or silenced in the past family history and the uncomfortable encounter with a different version of the past. This challenged the certainty of memory and the role played by Eclair's father in the Empire, which Eclair found hard to accept."[10]

Jenny's emotional journey to uncover the history behind her father's headhunting photographs did not cause her to grow sympathetic towards communists and anti-colonial movements, nor did she feel any increased sympathy for the headhunting victims. Quite the opposite, it appears that

Jenny's emotional pain when confronted by her father's involvement in colonial atrocities caused her to become increasingly defensive. This could shed light on a potential factor which hampered potential public outrage in 1952, as the mothers and fathers of conscripted soldiers sent to Malaya for their national service would have found it emotionally unbearable to consider that their sons were involved in such horrific deeds.

Arguments and theories presented by modern researchers

One researcher who expertly touches on the Malayan headhunting photographs and the British public's reaction to similar colonial atrocities is historian Erik Linstrum. In his article *Facts About Atrocity* which examines the publicity of British colonial atrocities, Linstrum suggests a multi-faceted explanation as to why the *Daily Worker* photographs (among other British colonial atrocities of the same decade) failed to gain widespread public acknowledgement. One of the many theories he suggests is that a generation of Britons who grew up during WWII were largely unwilling to condemn British colonial atrocities because they appeared minuscule in comparison to the recent memories of far greater war crimes such as the holocaust.[11]

Another historian who also proposes a combination of factors which explain the lack of widespread response to the *Daily Worker* headhunting photographs is Wen-Qing Ngoei. Within his book *Arc of Containment*, Ngoei theorises that government pressure on newspapers, the distraction of the Korean War, Lyttelton's public relations spin, and racial apathy towards Asians, had all together succeeded in "drowning popular aversion to beheading communists with yellow faces."[12]

The argument that race played a role in the British Malayan Headhunting Scandal is also proposed by anthropologist Simon Harrison, the author of *Dark Trophies: Hunting and the Enemy Body in Modern War*. This book contains one of the largest and most detailed examinations of Britain's headhunting Malayan policy ever written. Harrison links the decapitation photographs to many other facets of the war, including the thorough dehumanisation of the enemy by British forces through extended safari metaphors, the symbolisation of the power of the British state, and

Britain's cultural image of justice being performed via the decapitated head of a rebel or king being shown to a crowd. Harrison agrees with Linstrum and Ngoei by also recognising that race played a large role in Britain's headhunting policy, and that military trophy-taking during the Emergency and similar colonial wars "related to highly racialized perceptions of the enemy, and the pervasiveness of hunting imagery in the ways these wars were represented and experienced."[13] From an anthropological perspective, Harrison describes headhunting during the Malayan Emergency as an example of a "violent form of ethnographic data collection."[14]

> "These practices reflect a conception of power as connected inextricably with knowledge. Control over something mysterious, secretive and unknown is gained only after it has been brought, perhaps violently, into the realm of the knowable – to be studied, categorized and at last displayed."[15]

Recognising the central role that racism played in the British occupation of Malaya can help researchers to better understand why images of headhunting failed to change the wider public's opinions on colonialism, and explain how many British soldiers could uphold such a policy with seemingly little guilt. From imprisoning aboriginal Orang Asli communities within internment camps, to creating the "New Villages" primarily used to imprison ethnic Chinese civilians, Britain's fight against the MNLA was predicated upon a highly racialised perception of who their enemies were. This racist worldview upheld by the British military also extended to their allies, most notably ethnic groups such as the Gurkhas and Ibans who the British believed were genetically suited for warfare.

Fighting alongside Britain during the Malayan Emergency were all-white Rhodesian SAS soldiers who were tasked with using deadly force to uphold white minority rule in Rhodesia. These SAS soldiers were commanded by the notorious white supremacist Peter Walls who used the experience he gained killing Asian communists in Malaya to massacre black people in Africa. Rhodesian soldiers used skills honed during the Malayan Emergency to create the infamous Selous Scouts, a white supremacist organisation that killed thousands of black Africans, and whose imagery has since become a staple of 21st century white supremacist iconography.[16] While British communists fought to break up the British Empire and fight for independence for all of Britain's colonies, the emerging British fascist movement in the 1940s and 1950s sought to preserve British imperialism.

White Europeans living in rural Malaya were encouraged to turn their estates into mini fortresses and with the full assistance of Commonwealth military and policing units. Meanwhile, many Asians who lived in rural Malaya had their villages burned down and forcefully removed by British forces, a treatment which was never used by the Commonwealth against white Europeans in Malaya. White European civilians were often permitted to own advanced military grade weaponry including machine guns and armoured cars. Meanwhile Asian civilians could be arrested and sentenced to be hanged for owning a single shotgun shell. White Europeans in Malaya gorged themselves on large banquets in racially segregated country clubs and luxury villas, while their Asian neighbours were subject to forced food rationing and could be sentenced to years in jail for owning more than the bare minimum amount of food needed for survival. Every aspect of Britain's counterinsurgency was steeped in racial hypocrisy, where the treatment that a person can expect to receive from the colonial administration was heavily determined by race and geography.

It can even be argued that the Malayan Emergency itself was fought because the British believed they had the right to colonise and exploit the resources of races they viewed as lesser. Modern academics are not the only people to link racial prejudice to Britain's headhunting policy in Malaya and the absence of any widespread public and media reaction to the *Daily Worker* decapitation photographs. One early commentator noted how unconfirmed claims of Arabs displaying the decapitated heads of British soldiers were given widespread mainstream media coverage followed by an immediate condemnation by the British government.[17] This reaction was in stark contrast to how the British government and media reacted to British soldiers taking heads, and how the *Daily Worker* decapitation photographs were accused of being fakes and widely ignored by British newspapers.[18]

Racist attitudes towards Asians undoubtedly hampered much of the potential sympathy that both British soldiers and the public may have felt when confronted with both headhunting and the *Daily Worker's* atrocity images.

Headhunting from the victim's perspective

One of the earliest and most detailed works to investigate the British Malayan Headhunting Scandal and the story of how the *Daily Worker* helped to expose these atrocities, comes not from any professional historian but rather from research written by the former leader of the MNLA. Chin Peng, an OBE recipient, trade union leader, and veteran anti-fascist guerrilla leader during WWII, went on to lead the Malayan Communist Party and the MNLA in their fight against the British Empire and Commonwealth during the Malayan Emergency.[19] After laying down his weapons and engaging in peace talks with his former enemies, Chin Peng visited the UK in 1998 and began researching the Malayan Emergency using sources held in British archives.[20] The result of his research was the autobiography *Alias Chin Peng: My Side of History*, published in 2003 and co-written by *Daily Telegraph* correspondent Ian Ward and his wife Norma Miraflor. Not only did *My Side of History* become one of the few English language accounts of the war from the view of the communists and arguably one of the most valuable documents in the historiography of the Malayan Emergency, but it finally shed light on the decapitation scandal from the perspective of the victims.[21]

My Side of History contained ground-breaking research into the headhunting scandal, was one of the only pieces of research to investigate the headhunting scandal, and one of the few to use declassified archives and the original *Daily Worker* articles. Despite speaking English as a second language, Chin Peng achieved a more in-depth and thorough investigation into the headhunting scandal than any professional historian had ever written. Within *My Side of History*, Chin Peng accuses the British military of decapitating the corpses of his soldiers, and displaying the bodies of his fallen soldiers in public spaces to intimidate people.[22] Commenting on the British military's killing and beheading of his comrades, Chin Peng had the following to say:

Figure 1: Cartoon drawn by the socialist artist James Friell (Gabriel) criticising the British government's deployment of Iban headhunters in Malaya, *Daily Worker*, 1948.

Figure 2: Soldiers of the Malayan People's Anti-Japanese Army (MPAJA), 1945. Funded by Britain to resist Japan, their veterans would regroup in 1948 to fight the British colonial occupation.

Figure 3: A village in Johore being burned down by the British military during Operation Rugger, 1948.

Figure 4: Malcolm MacDonald, the son of Britain's first Labour Party prime minister, welcomes newly recruited Iban mercenaries to Malaya in 1950. On the far right is Penghulu (headman) Jinggut who was allegedly 17 years old when Malcolm recruited him to lead the first Iban recruits during the Malayan Emergency.

Figure 5: The first ever published headhunting photograph from Malaya, published by the *Daily Worker*, 28 April 1952.

Figure 6: The second headhunting photograph published by the *Daily Worker*, released in response to accusations by the government and military that the first photograph was fake, 30 April 1952.

Figure 7: Cartoon published by the *Daily Worker* mocking General Gerald Templer and his attempts to crush the MNLA, *Daily Worker*, 1952.

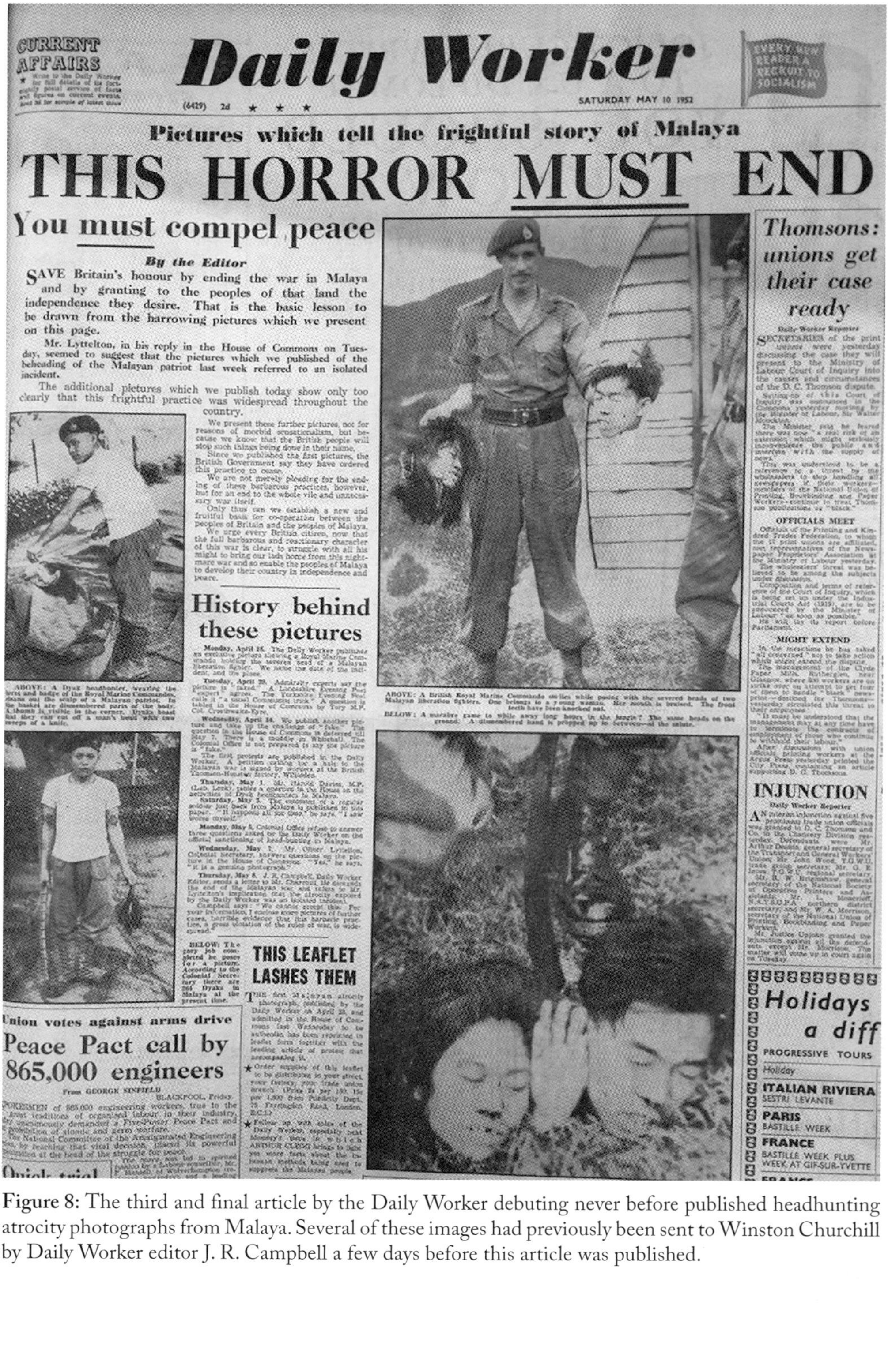

CURRENT AFFAIRS

Daily Worker

(6429) 2d ★ ★ ★

SATURDAY MAY 10 1952

EVERY NEW READER A RECRUIT TO SOCIALISM

Pictures which tell the frightful story of Malaya

THIS HORROR MUST END

You must compel peace

By the Editor

SAVE Britain's honour by ending the war in Malaya and by granting to the peoples of that land the independence they desire. That is the basic lesson to be drawn from the harrowing pictures which we present on this page.

Mr. Lyttelton, in his reply in the House of Commons on Tuesday, seemed to suggest that the pictures which we published of the beheading of the Malayan patriot last week referred to an isolated incident.

The additional pictures which we publish today show only too clearly that this frightful practice was widespread throughout the country.

We present these further pictures, not for reasons of morbid sensationalism, but because we know that the British people will stop such things being done in their name.

Since we published the first pictures, the British Government say they have ordered this practice to cease.

We are not merely pleading for the ending of these barbarous practices, however, but for an end to the whole vile and unnecessary war itself.

Only thus can we establish a new and fruitful basis for co-operation between the peoples of Britain and the peoples of Malaya.

We urge every British citizen, now that the full barbarous and reactionary character of this war is clear, to struggle with all his might to bring our lads home from this nightmare war and so enable the peoples of Malaya to develop their country in independence and peace.

ABOVE: A Dyak headhunter, wearing the beret and badge of the Royal Marine Commandos, cleans out the scalp of a Malayan patriot. In the basket are dismembered parts of the body. A thumb is visible in the corner. Dyaks boast that they can cut off a man's head with two sweeps of a knife.

History behind these pictures

Monday, April 28. The Daily Worker publishes an exclusive picture showing a Royal Marine Commando holding the severed head of a Malayan liberation fighter. We name the date of the incident, and the place.

Tuesday, April 29. Admiralty experts say the picture is "faked." A Lancashire Evening Post "expert" agrees. The Yorkshire Evening Post calls it "a usual Communist trick." A question is tabled in the House of Commons by Tory M.P. Col. Crosthwaite-Eyre.

Wednesday, April 30. We publish another picture and take up the challenge of "fake." The question in the House of Commons is deferred till May 7. There is a muddle in Whitehall. The Colonial Office is not prepared to say the picture is "fake."

The first protests are published in the Daily Worker. A petition calling for a halt to the Malayan war is signed by workers at the British Thomson-Houston factory, Willesden.

Thursday, May 1. Mr. Harold Davies, M.P. (Lab. Leek), tables a question in the House on the activities of Dyak headhunters in Malaya.

Saturday, May 3. The comment of a regular soldier just back from Malaya is published in this paper. "It happens all the time," he says, "I saw worse myself."

Monday, May 5. Colonial Office refuse to answer three questions asked by the Daily Worker on the official sanctioning of head-hunting in Malaya.

Wednesday, May 7. Mr. Oliver Lyttelton, Colonial Secretary, answers questions on the picture in the House of Commons. "Yes," he says, "it is a genuine photograph."

Thursday, May 8. J. R. Campbell, Daily Worker Editor, sends a letter to Mr. Churchill. He demands the end of the Malayan war and refers to Mr. Lyttelton's implication that the atrocity exposed by the Daily Worker was an isolated incident.

Campbell says: "We cannot accept this. For your information, I enclose more pictures of further cases, horrible evidence that this barbaric practice, a gross violation of the rules of war, is widespread."

BELOW: The gory job completed he poses for a picture. According to the Colonial Secretary there are 264 Dyaks in Malaya at the present time.

THIS LEAFLET LASHES THEM

THE first Malayan atrocity photograph, published by the Daily Worker on April 28, and admitted in the House of Commons last Wednesday to be authentic, has been reprinted in leaflet form together with the leading article of protest that accompanied it.

★ Order supplies of this leaflet to be distributed in your street, your factory, your trade union branch. (Price 2s per 100, 15s per 1,000 from Publicity Dept., 75 Farringdon Road, London, E.C.1.)

★ Follow up with sales of the Daily Worker, especially next Monday's issue in which ARTHUR CLEGG brings to light yet more facts about the inhuman methods being used to suppress the Malayan people.

Union votes against arms drive

Peace Pact call by 865,000 engineers

From GEORGE SINFIELD

BLACKPOOL, Friday.

SPOKESMEN of 865,000 engineering workers, true to the great traditions of organised labour in their industry, today unanimously demanded a Five-Power Peace Pact and prohibition of atomic and germ warfare.

The National Committee of the Amalgamated Engineering Union, by reaching that vital decision, placed its powerful organisation at the head of the struggle for peace.

The move was led in spirited fashion by a Labour councillor, Mr. F. Massell, of Wolverhampton ...

ABOVE: A British Royal Marine Commando smiles while posing with the severed heads of two Malayan liberation fighters. One belongs to a young woman. Her mouth is bruised. The front teeth have been knocked out.

BELOW: A macabre game to while away long hours in the jungle? The same heads on the ground. A dismembered hand is propped up in between—at the salute.

Thomsons: unions get their case ready

Daily Worker Reporter

SECRETARIES of the print unions were yesterday discussing the case they will present to the Ministry of Labour Court of Inquiry into the causes and circumstances of the D. C. Thomson dispute.

Setting-up of this Court of Inquiry was announced in the Commons yesterday morning by the Minister of Labour, Sir Walter Monckton.

The Minister said he feared there was now "a real risk of an extension which might seriously inconvenience the public and interfere with the supply of news."

This was understood to be a reference to a threat by the wholesalers to stop handling all newspapers if their workers—members of the National Union of Printing, Bookbinding and Paper Workers—continue to treat Thomson publications as "black."

OFFICIALS MEET

Officials of the Printing and Kindred Trades Federation, to which the 17 print unions are affiliated, met representatives of the Newspaper Proprietors' Association at the Ministry of Labour yesterday.

The wholesalers' threat was believed to be among the subjects under discussion.

Composition and terms of reference of the Court of Inquiry, which is being set up under the Industrial Courts Act (1919), are to be announced by the Minister of Labour "as soon as possible."

He will lay its report before Parliament.

MIGHT EXTEND

In the meantime he has asked "all concerned" not to take action which might extend the dispute.

The management of the Clyde Paper Mills, Rutherglen, near Glasgow, where 800 workers are on strike over an attempt to get four of them to handle "black" newsprint—destined for Thomsons—yesterday circulated this threat to their employees:

"It must be understood that the management may at any time have to terminate the contracts of employment of those who continue to withhold their labour."

After discussions with union officials, printing workers at the Argus Press yesterday printed the City Press, containing an article supporting D. C. Thomsons.

INJUNCTION

Daily Worker Reporter

AN interim injunction against five prominent trade union officials was granted to D. C. Thomson and Co. in the Chancery Division yesterday. Defendants were Mr. Arthur Deakin, general secretary of the Transport and General Workers' Union; Mr John Wood, T.G.W.U. trade group secretary; Mr. G. E. Iston, T.G.W.U. regional secretary; Mr. R. W. Briginshaw, general secretary of the National Society of Operative Printers and Assistants; Mr. L. Moncrieff, N.A.T.S.O.P.A. northern district secretary; and Mr. W. A. Morrison, secretary of the National Union of Printing, Bookbinding and Paper Workers.

Mr. Justice Upjohn granted the injunction against all the defendants except Mr. Morrison. The matter will come up in court again on Tuesday.

Holidays a diff

PROGRESSIVE TOURS

Holiday

ITALIAN RIVIERA SESTRI LEVANTE

PARIS BASTILLE WEEK

FRANCE BASTILLE WEEK PLUS WEEK AT GIF-SUR-YVETTE

Figure 8: The third and final article by the Daily Worker debuting never before published headhunting atrocity photographs from Malaya. Several of these images had previously been sent to Winston Churchill by Daily Worker editor J. R. Campbell a few days before this article was published.

Figure 9: Photo sent to Churchill by Campbell of an Iban headhunter using a knife to prepare a human scalp with baskets overflowing with body parts.

Figure 10: Photo sent to Churchill by Campbell of an Iban headhunter with a knife and a human scalp. Note the Royal Marines beret.

Figure 11: Photo sent to Churchill by Campbell of a British Royal Marine posing with the decapitated heads of two suspected MNLA members. This image would go onto become the most iconic and widely known image of the Malayan Emergency ever published.

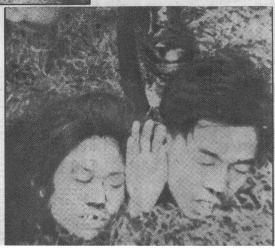

Figure 12: *Stop This Horror in Malaya*, an anti-war booklet designed and created by the British communist movement to turn public opinion against colonialism, May 1952.

£30,000 REWARD FOR BETRAYAL NOBODY HAS CLAIMED IT

The deeds of the head-hunters are appalling ... but t are only part of the policy of terror that is being carr out in Malaya in our name ... ON THE RIGHT is rep duced a police notice printed in five languages.

It offers 80,000 Straits dollars for the "bringing in al of Chan Peng, secretary of the Malayan Communist Pa That was six months ago. Now the reward has been rai to $250,000, worth about £30,000.

The sum of $125,000 is offered for information lead to Chan Peng's killing.

Since a Malayan worker or peasant earns only ab 2s. 6d. a day, the reward in our terms would be as a prize to a Malayan as £250,000 would be to a v moderately paid British worker.

Chan Peng has not been betrayed even for so enorm a fortune. That is because he is a national hero in Mal —because the Malayan people support the Malayan I eration Movement and its army.

Huge rewards are offered also for the betrayal of ot Malayan leaders.

LOOK AT THE PICTURE BELOW RIGHT . Here are some of the men on whose heads the Brit Malayan Government has put a price. They took th place in the Victory March, in London in 1945, as pr allies of Britain who had taken up the fight after Japanese had swept through Malaya.

Many were honoured by Britain ... Chan Peng him was awarded an O.B.E.

This picture was taken by a British soldier recently returned from Malaya. The severed head was of a Malayan patriot shot in the jungle. "It was not an uncommon experience", said the soldier. It happened late last year in the village of Kuala Kesan (known to troops as K.K.).

Standing beside a British soldier are two Asian soldiers recruited by the British, one of whom wears a crucifix. Other soldiers can be seen behind. In the background is a hut with the sign: "40 Commando R.M."

The soldier who took this photograph said: "We can never win in Malaya. The guerillas are too well organised. The people are with them. The morale of our lads is low." Below, right, another picture at the same spot.

A Dyak head-hunter, wearing the badge and beret of the Royal Marine Commandos, cleans out the scalp of a Malayan patriot. In his basket are dismembered parts of the body ... The job completed he poses for his picture ... These photographs dispose of the Government's excuse that heads are severed for "identification purposes"

WIPE OUT BR

HIS FRIENDS: MEN WHO HUNT FOR HEADS

Mr. Malcolm MacDonald, British Commissioner-General, receives Dyak head-hunters on their arrival in Malaya in 1950 ... According to Mr. Lyttelton, the Colonial Secretary, there are 264 Dyaks in Malaya now ... The responsibility

[Continued from page 1] papers. For they are a blot on our national honour; they reveal the true character of the Malayan war.

So the *Daily Worker* published these pictures. Here is a brief record of what happened.

April 28. The picture showing two men holding a head and the third pointing a rifle was published. It came from a soldier in Malaya.

April 29. An Admiralty spokesman said: "To Admiralty minds the picture is a fake." "Fake" was the description used by several national newspapers.

April 30. The *Daily Worker* replied by printing a second picture showing two Asian soldiers holding a head (page 2 of this pamphlet), and challenging anybody to prove the

Heavy Weapons Group Office; MMG Section; Sniper Section; 3rd Mortar Section.

May 1. More photographs began to reach the *Daily Worker* — and this continued for many days. All were from men who had served in Malaya.

May 2. A soldier walked into the *Daily Worker* office to say that during his three years' service in Malaya he had seen Gurkhas coming back from patrol and emptying severed heads from their packs.

"I saw that late in 1950 in the village of Bentong," he said. "It's happening all the time."

May 5. The Colonial Office refused to answer questions about the activities of Dyak head-hunters in Malaya, or to say whether head-hunting was

half of the C the original genuine, sayin been decapita man last year

Instructions given, said M this should no future.

The Admir allegation tha was a "fake".

On the sam *Worker* sent c tures to natio Mr. Winston Archbishop o number of M.

May 10. A statement im original photo ture of an isol *Daily Worker* ber of others, on the front p

Figure 13: *Stop This Horror in Malaya*, page 2/4.

Why has the British Government thrown over heroic allies such as Chan Peng? ... The picture above tells you. Here is the manager of Dublin Estate, thirty miles east of Penang ... He is setting out with members of the Malay Regiment to inspect "guard posts". This estate is one of six owned by Malayan American Plantations ... We have thrown over the Malayan people, for the rich planters and tin mine owners.

... And here are plantation employees of an American rubber company who we taught to use U.S. arms to shoot down their own people ...

...ITAIN'S SHAME!

Shootings, head-huntings, the offer of blood money shock us ... but the terror takes other forms and goes on all the time ... Here is an everyday incident ... Troops have raided Mengkarak and the women are rounded up and marched past a wall. Hidden behind slits in the wall is a spy. Or M...

...overnment, that photograph was g that a body had ed by a tribes-

were being Lyttelton, that be permitted in

lty withdrew its the photograph

e day the *Daily* pies of other pic- nal newspapers, Churchill, the York and a P.s.

Mr. Lyttelton's lied that the raph was a pic- ed incident, the published a num- ncluding the one age of this pam-

has been made, Government or

these pictures are not authentic.
May 21. Mr. H. Hopkinson, Minister of State for the Colonies, said in the House of Commons that one of the men in the first photograph had been identified. But there would be no disciplinary action in any of the cases that had appeared.
The Dyak head-hunters arrived in Malaya as long ago as 1948, when Reuter's agency described how they had been brought from Borneo and Sarawak. In the words of Reuter's, the head-hunters arrived "armed with head-hunting knives decorated with tufts of human hair and howling their jungle war-cry."
Not one of the pictures sent to the millionaire Press has been published. For the purpose of the millionaire Press in such affairs as this is to suppress, not to reveal, the truth.
Yet the truth is there. Truth in the end is known. It is the

spread the truth.
These savage barbarities corrupt the men by whom they are committed. This war causes our men to act like savages. These atrocities befoul our national name.
The Malayan people are fighting for independence — as many other colonial peoples have done for centuries past. They seek a Malayan People's Democratic Republic free from foreign interference, but maintaining friendly relations with all countries, including Britain. That is what they want.
No fair-minded British man or woman is opposed to such aims. No ordinary British soldier will look with anything but revulsion on the horrors depicted in this pamphlet.
And no civilised person in all Britain can do anything but demand an end to this war. And act to make sure it shall end. That is the only way to

Figure 14: *Stop This Horror in Malaya*, page 3/4.

DICTATOR GENERAL STEPS UP TERROR

Shootings, killings, arrests, spraying of crops with chemicals... and the burning down of villages. This picture shows an incident in "Operation Rugger", a sporting name for one of the most unsportsmanlike jobs British troops have been called upon to perform. But the Malayan people hold out... In January General Sir Gerald Templer was appointed—on American insistence—as High Commissioner for Malaya. His job is to increase the terror... Looking at his picture, below, you might think he is the very man for the work... He tries a gun fitted with a silencer... But for our credit's sake, we Britons cannot pass over in silence the terror in Malaya

WAR CRIME AGAINST VILLAGERS

Who are these people? "Bandits"? No. They are the adult population of Tanjong Malim, a village collectively "punished" by General Templer in defiance of International Law... They are people like you. And you should help them and help yourselves by ending the disgraceful war in Malaya

NOW

that you have seen for yourself something that all the other papers sought to hide from you, doesn't that make you want to change to the *Daily Worker*? Yes!

READ THE DAILY WORKER EVERY DAY

This is no isolated example. In the last few weeks the *Daily Worker* has published many stories the other papers have suppressed including—

★ Interviews with American Airmen who admit to dropping Germ Bombs in N. Korea.

★ Eye-witness accounts and photographs of British P.O.W.s in Korea.

★ Red Cross Investigation Commission's evidence of American brutality on the notorious Koje Island.

WHY

has the Daily Worker alone been unafraid to publish these facts and photos?

BECAUSE

of all the daily papers, the *Daily Worker* is the only one which does not depend on Press Lords or Big Business for finance.

And, therefore, it is not under the control of Press Lords or Big Business.

The *Daily Worker* is financed and controlled by over 12,000 workers through a Co-operative Society. Anyone can join —and join in the control of the paper. Why not join them and

READ the newspaper that is owned by the workers.

OWN the newspaper that you need every day.

If you have difficulty in getting a copy from your newsagent or want to know more about the *Daily Worker*, write today to the DAILY WORKER, 75 Farringdon Road, London, E.C.1.

Published by the "Daily Worker" Co-operative Society Ltd., 75 Farringdon Road, London, E.C.1, and printed by Farleigh Press Ltd. (T.U. all depts.), Beechwood Rise, Watford.

Figure 15: *Stop This Horror in Malaya*, page 4/4.

Figure 16: Anti-war article by British communist leader Harry Pollitt exposing yet another never-before-seen British corpse trophy photograph taken in Malaya, *Daily Worker*, 14 June 1952.

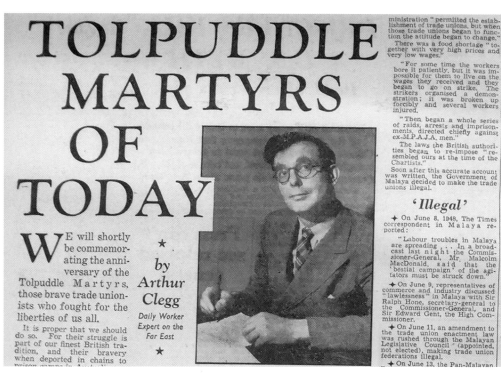

Figure 17: Arthur Clegg compares the MNLA to the Tolpuddle Martyrs, *Daily Worker*, 12 May 1952.

Figure 18: A photograph of the Dunlop Rubber Company Protest which saw Malayan headhunting photographs shown to Dunlop's shareholders, *Daily Worker*, 10 June 1952.

Figure 19: The decapitated head of socialist revolutionary Hen Yan, a Branch Committee Member (BCM) of the MNLA in Sungei Tinggi. Hen Yan is currently the only victim of British headhunting in Malaya whose name is known to historians.

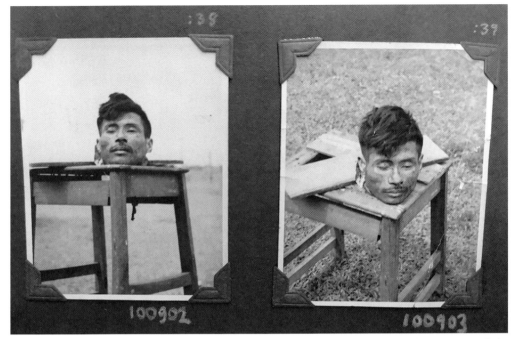

Figure 20: Headhunting photographs found within the personal photo album of a member of the Coldstream Guards regiment, National Army Museum.

Figure 21: A photocopied collection of Malayan atrocity photographs including five headhunting photographs. Two of these headhunting photographs are the only known copies in existence. They were discovered and provided to the author of this book by a librarian of Manchester's Working Class Movement Library (WCML)

Figure 22: A trophy photograph showing British soldiers of the Suffolk Regiment grinning while standing over the corpses of Malayans whom they had murdered. According to British author Mike Forsdike, the man standing on the left is a man called Corporal Hambling and on the right was Corporal Brown.

Figure 23: Suspected MNLA members are forced at gunpoint to sit next to corpses for trophy photographs with British soldiers of the Suffolk Regiment.

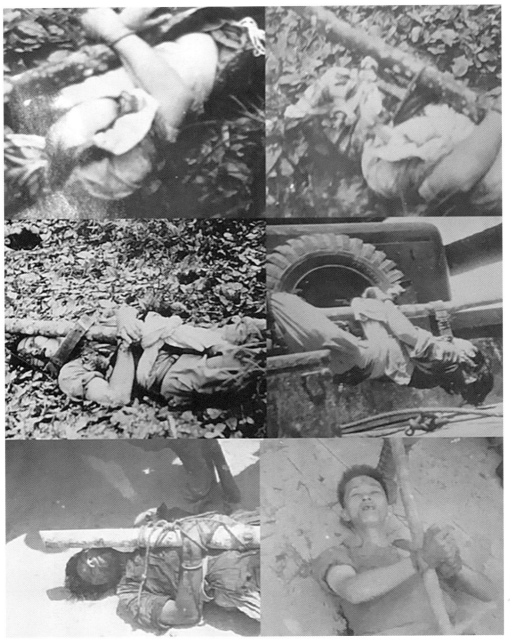

Figure 24: Using wooden poles to transport corpses was a common method used to transport corpses and presented popular opportunities for British soldiers to take trophy photographs, Suffolk Regiment.

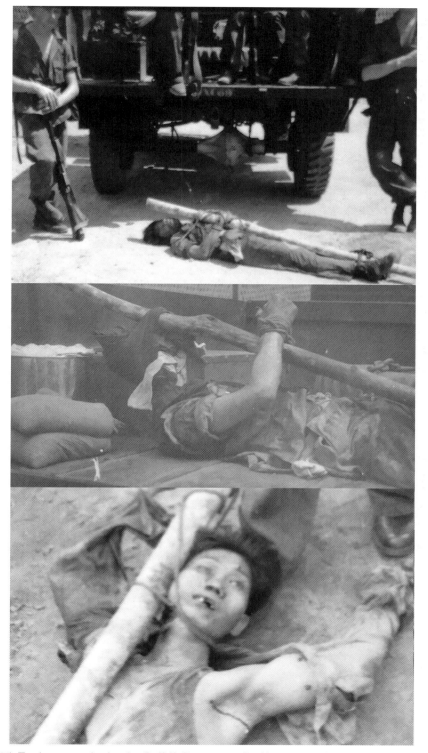

Figure 25: Further examples by the Suffolk Regiment of soldiers using the wooden pole method of transporting corpses, Suffolk Regiment.

Figure 26: A Malayan decapitation photograph of unknown date and location, published in the book *A People's History Of Malaya*, by Asoka Guikon.

Figure 27: A trophy photograph taken by The Queen's Own Royal West Kent Regiment, depicting the wooden pole method used on two corpses and the severed human head of a third corpse.

The Historiography: Questions and Comments by Researchers 69

"At no time as a liberation commander – first against the Japanese and then against the British – did I ever order the mutilation of enemy bodies for any reason whatever. Nor did I quietly condone such excesses. I have often pondered what the colonial propagandists would have said had intelligence reports indicated I was seeking from, say, my Politburo colleagues, the same sort of permission Templer sought from his superiors in London to enable an ongoing headhunting programme."[23]

"From my standpoint, the ranking civil servant advising the Colonial Office's top echelons in this instance was far more concerned with British decorum than the horror of a severed head. He missed, completely, or conveniently, the moral position on the mutilation issue."[24]

Although there are rare cases of MNLA guerrillas mutilating the corpses of their victims, there do not appear to be any cases of Malayan communist guerrillas turning enemy heads into trophies, and there is zero evidence that they took trophy photographs of corpses similar to those collected by British soldiers. The closest instance was when several former communist guerrillas allegedly decapitated their squad leader, then used his head to flag down a train and defect to the British so they could claim a cash reward of $75,000.[25] The British colonial authorities tried searching for photographic evidence of communist atrocities but found that none of the photos they could procure matched the brutality of their own killings.[26] This has led to some commentators noting that the Malayan guerrillas were rather tame in comparison to similar guerrilla armies across the globe.[27]

Still ever haunting the British Malayan Headhunting Scandal is the question as to why news of such atrocities never reached a wider audience and failed to generate any noticeable protest from the British public. Perhaps one explanation was the failure of the MNLA to produce effective means of spreading their own viewpoints and version of events when confronted with the vast information capabilities of the British Empire. Chin Peng ponders this question and comments on his army's inability to counter Britain's propaganda narratives;

"...we were not shackled to desks housed in grand buildings. My army was constantly moving and reorganising and facing food shortages. You could say idealism was the biggest weapon in our stockpile. We had neither the skill nor the sophistication to phase columns upon columns of elegant prose meant to mislead."[28]

Historian Erik Linstrum puts forward a similar theory, arguing that a lack of resources in the hands of anti-colonial rebels had a direct consequence on their ability to counter imperialist propaganda and highlight colonial wrongdoings.

"Whether spuriously or not, sources from within the state bureaucracy could speak with the authority of a comprehensive knowledge which insurgents in the field had no hope of matching. Officials offered facts; rebels, whistleblowers and witnesses could reply only with anecdotes."[29]

Access to media and educational resources was certainly an issue which allowed Britain to dominate the news media's narrative of the war and drown the voices of its opposition. While British officers enjoyed being railroaded into the world's top universities, MNLA members were often poor and working-class people who lacked the same educational opportunities as their British counterparts. This was especially true for women, many of whom joined the communists as a way to escape abuse and servitude in their communities. Women in the MNLA were given full equality and expected to fight as soldiers just as the male members were, often gaining far higher levels of self-esteem and freedom than their non-communist counterparts.[30] The fact that women fought as soldiers in the MNLA was a fact that fascinated British troops, with one platoon of the Suffolk Regiment renaming themselves "The Ladykillers" after killing several women suspected of being communists.[31] Women in many communities throughout British Malaya were harshly discriminated against, which meant they were often denied educational opportunities. For this reason, a large percentage of the MNLA's membership was effectively illiterate and had to learn to read while living in the jungle as guerrillas fighting the British occupation.[32] Long after the war had ended this lack of equal opportunities made it extremely difficult for female MNLA veterans to write their own histories.[33]

Despite lacking grand writing halls, wireless communication hardware, and all the same powerful information instruments that the British enjoyed, the MNLA was successful in perfecting oral communication through the use of trusted couriers, plays, and speeches, which were successful in spreading its messages throughout urban locations through posters erected in public spaces.[34] However, none of these methods used by the Malayan communists enjoyed the same longevity and reliability as the physical books and newspaper articles that the British published in their thousands. The Malayan communists were forced to rely on barely functional underground newspapers, spreading their news through spoken words, and temporary posters secretly slapped onto buildings. Meanwhile the British enjoyed some of the most powerful media apparatus to ever exist, bolstered by grand archives, world-class museums, and sprawling libraries, all of which served to preserve their view of history. These factors coupled with the language barrier meant that English-speaking writers were largely cut off from learning the MNLA's version of events in the immediate decades following the Malayan Emergency. It has been no wonder that histories which depicted the British military in a favourable light while demonising the communists have managed to dominate the public's perception of the Malayan Emergency for so long.

Chapter 7

The Public Display of Corpses

Headhunting was far from the only controversial issue concerning Britain's mistreatment of corpses during the Malayan Emergency. Another hotly debated topic was the practice of publicly displaying the bodies of suspected communists whom they had killed.[1]

The British military often publicly displayed the corpses of suspected MNLA guerrillas and communist sympathisers in town centres, markets, and outside police stations.[2] These displays were sometimes accompanied by signs which mocked the victims with loudspeakers broadcasting British propaganda and were a relatively common sight during the Malayan Emergency. Many of the corpse displays were both temporary and mobile, with the corpse of the suspected MNLA member often being tied to a vehicle. Another practice closely related to the corpse displays was photographing the corpses of people the British soldiers had killed, printing their faces onto 100,000s of leaflets, which were often distributed by being thrown from aeroplanes.[3] These practices of distributing highly graphic images and erecting physical displays to exhibit dead communists were common sights during the first half of the Malayan Emergency. Come the mid-1950s, British officials became concerned that such graphically violent methods were counterproductive and risked triggering heightened sympathy for the communists among civilians, disincentivise communist guerrillas from surrendering, and igniting within many people a stronger desire to fight against British colonialism.

So why would the British military and their Commonwealth allies openly engage in such brutal and visually disturbing behaviour? Below are the key reasons why British forces believed that publicly displaying the corpses of suspected communists would help them fight the MNLA, all of which this chapter will explore in depth.

The public corpse displays were intended to serve three key purposes:

1. **Tools of terror:** The corpse displays were intended to terrify rural people away from supporting the MNLA by acting as a warning to show what the British will do to people who are sympathetic to socialism.
2. **Tools of reassurance:** The corpse displays were created to provide physical proof to (largely illiterate and sceptical) civilian populations that Britain was winning the war. The British theorised that this would encourage pro-British and anti-communist civilians to take a more proactive role in resisting the MNLA by providing more information to the police.
3. **Tools of intelligence:** The corpse displays were used by the police to identify dead guerrillas whom the colonial occupation could not identify. The police would gather local civilians to view a corpse and ask them if they knew the identity of the suspected guerrilla. The corpse displays were also used to identify potential supporters of the MNLA by monitoring the emotional reactions of onlookers for signs of distress and fear.

This chapter will examine all the intended effects of the British occupation's public corpse displays and judge whether the desired effects of the displays match the results. This chapter also investigates the victims of the public corpse displays whose identities are known to historians and will describe the British media's reaction to the corpse displays.

Corpse displays as tools of terror

The MNLA commanded a vast undercover civilian support network known as the Min Yuen who were charged with supplying the MNLA's guerrillas with food, medicine, clothing, information, and anything else they needed. The Commonwealth forces understood that behind every guerrilla, there were local people supporting them. For this reason, the British publicly displayed the corpses of the guerrillas to warn civilians and supporters of the Min Yuen what the British would do to people who sympathised with the MNLA.

Unsurprisingly, communist leader Chin Peng described the public displays featuring the corpses of his soldiers as a "terror tactic" which was "geared specifically to terrifying the rural population into compliance".[4] This viewpoint is held by many Malayan communists and opponents of imperialism, who argue that the public corpse displays increased their hatred for the British Empire. However, criticism of the corpse displays was not relegated solely to the communists. Many British soldiers also disapproved of the practice of putting the corpses of guerrillas on public display.[5] Some British soldiers shared the view of the communists, arguing that the public display of corpses in Malaya was designed to deter local people from joining or supporting the communists.

Peter Woodhouse, an NCO with the 13th/18th Royal Hussars, told an interviewer that the objective of the corpse displays was to act as a deterrent, scaring the local population away from supporting the MNLA:

> **Woodhouse:** Anybody killed urm in those days were put outside the police station, and stuck on the pavement. And when the ...
>
> **Interviewer:** Why?
>
> **Woodhouse:** Well that was a deterrent. You, you know you see somebody ... sprawled out on the pavement with the flies all buzzing round ya, it's quite a deterrent.[6]

Another man who served the British military during the Malayan Emergency, Paul Richards, corroborates that the corpse displays were intended as a form of psychological warfare to scare people away from supporting the MNLA. In his memoirs, Richards describes the nature of the public corpse displays:

> "If the patrol was two or three days or more from the pickup point on a road, where the patrol would be collected, the body should be photographed and buried, as a patrol usually carried a small lightweight spade. If on the other hand, the patrol was only a day's trek from a main road, then the body would be tied to a bamboo pole, and carried back.
>
> It would then sometimes be displayed outside a police station for a couple of days, with a notice above it, stating that this is what happens to would be bandits, or words to that effect!"[7]

The Public Display of Corpses 75

One British soldier, Roy Follows, who joined the Malay police force, gives a far more graphic account of participating in the public corpse display of four communist guerrillas that he had personally helped to kill. He even describes using the corpse of a guerrilla leader with the rank of District Committee Member, to personally threaten the dead guerrilla's brother:

> "On our arrival at Cha'ah police station, the four dead men were soon identified as being the District Committee Member and some of his outfit."
>
> "All the village seemed to turn out to stare at the corpses. Amongst the crowd I noticed the late District Committee Member's brother, so I made my way to where he was standing. 'Apparently your brother paid no heed to my message,' I said. He didn't answer. I then told him that if he was thinking of joining the Communists to seek revenge he had better think again. 'If you do,' I went on, 'these local people will be viewing *your* dead body, so remember my warning.' With that I left him to think it over."[8]

Not only do former MNLA guerrillas and many British soldiers agree that the primary purpose of the corpse displays was to inspire terror and to act as a warning, but academics and authors specialising in Chinese cultural studies have universally agreed with this interpretation. Peter Nolan, a professor of Chinese studies at the University of Cambridge, notes that corpses were "routinely placed on public display to cow local people."[9] Souchou Yao, a senior lecturer at the University of Sidney and an anthropologist specialising in Chinese culture, agrees that the purpose of the public corpse displays was to act as a warning to the public, showing them what happens to people who are sympathetic to the MNLA.[10]

One expert in Chinese studies who actually witnessed the corpse displays with her own eyes was Catherine Lim, a Singaporean author of traditional Chinese culture. In her book *Romancing the Language*, she briefly describes her childhood experience of encountering one of Britain's public corpse displays in the town of Kulim:

"We sometimes saw the dead bodies of the enemies brought out from their hiding places deep in the jungle, and exhibited in the town's open marketplace, as a stern warning to all. Malayan and British soldiers would stand guard, suspiciously scanning the faces of those who came to watch, as if they were secret Communist sympathisers.

"One day, I must have been about ten years old, I accompanied a maidservant who was eager to see one of these bodies, laid out on the ground. We stood among the circle of onlookers gazing silently, gravely at it. The corpse with its close cropped hair and rough khaki trousers and shirt, looked to be male. Suddenly a young British officer, wearing heavy army boots, raised his right foot and held it over the dead body. I gave a little scream, thinking the rather brutal-looking soldier was going to stomp on the corpse. But no. With an arrogant smile, he used his heavy-booted foot to flip over the corpse's unbuttoned shirt, exposing a woman's bare breast, bloodied by bullets. There was a collective gasp from the crowd."[11]

Although Catherine Lim disliked communism, this experience inspired her to begin plans to write a fictional story based on the woman the corpse belonged to when she was alive. However, Lim found that she could not commit to writing this story, finding that her experience of witnessing one of Britain's public corpse displays was too emotionally painful to write about.[12] It was a common strategy for British troops to allow children of all ages to witness the public corpse displays, as children could not conceal their emotions and so British troops would use their reaction as an indicator of whether the child was related to the dead guerrilla.

Another academic called Eddie Wong, a computational artist at Goldsmiths university in London, recounts his family history and how his grandfather's body was featured in a public corpse display during the Malayan Emergency:

"In 1949, my grandfather left his family and joined the Malayan Communist Party (MCP) in a guerrilla armed struggle against the British Malaya colonial government. Three years into jungle warfare, the British ambushed and killed the MCP's chief propagandist and two of his bodyguards. My grandfather was one of the bodyguards. The colonial authority publicly displayed their corpses in the town square to instil fear in the masses. My grandmother and her five children who witnessed the scene from afar had to suppress their tears. Following that incident, the British began to hound and persecute the family members of the Communist fighters. They interrogated my grandmother at gunpoint about her connection to my grandfather. An admission would lead to retribution on the entire family. She refused to cooperate and denied that she knew of such a person. Soon after, she fled the village with her children, and they were declared fugitives of the law."[13]

The experience that Eddie Wong's family suffered at the hands of Britain's public corpse displays was so traumatic that it destroyed their lives, and the pain of this experience was felt over half a century later. To survive, Eddie Wong's parents were forced to become servants to the very same colonial occupation that murdered his grandfather. This family story would then inspire Eddie Wong to create a short film and art instillation on the subject of surveillance at Goldsmiths, titled *the Unknown Person* (2019).[14]

Tan Teng Phee, one of the world's leading experts on the Malayan Emergency, agrees that the public corpse displays served to both terrify and intimidate onlookers. However he also suggests that the displays were also intended to provide reassurance to anti-communist and pro-British members of the public. In his seminal work *Behind Barbed Wire,* Tan Teng Phee describes the public corpse displays:

"The display of corpses always drew a flock of onlookers. The police sometimes also sought help from residents to identify the corpses and their families. Some villagers would gasp when they saw the corpses. Many just remained silent bystanders. The message behind the public display of dead communists was clear to the local people: the government was winning the 'shooting war'.[15]

"The British usually displayed the corpses on a military truck, or simply left them lying in front of the police station. They wanted to intimidate the villagers, to show them the consequences of joining the communists."[16]

After interviewing civilians who had witnessed Britain's public corpse displays, Tan Teng Phee found that most witnesses were not as happy and reassured as the British had hoped. Instead of the relieved and overjoyed civilian onlookers that the British military had wished for, Tan Teng Phee discovered that the witnesses he interviewed were fixated on how young many of the corpse display victims looked, while others were too afraid to look at the faces of the bodies.[17] The results of Tan Teng Phee's extensive investigation into the New Villages paints a grim and dystopian picture of the public displays. Intended as both a tool of terror and intelligence gathering, the reasons behind the creation of the corpse displays are multi-layered, however the end result was a traumatic experience for many people in Malaya's Chinese communities. This interpretation of the public corpse displays as tools of terror is shared by archivists of the UK National Army Museum, who note that there were "cases of bodies being exhibited in public as a way of frightening any Communist sympathisers in the local population."[18]

Corpse displays as tools of reassurance and intelligence

Aside from acting as tools of terror to be used against the MNLA's supporters, another intended use for the corpse displays was to reassure civilians who were pro-British and anti-communist, conveying the message that the Commonwealth's forces were winning the war. The British believed that providing physical proof in the form of corpses would convince rural civilians, many of whom were illiterate, sceptical of government claims, or fearful that acting as a collaborator could get them killed, that the Commonwealth was able to protect informants from guerrilla reprisals. Commonwealth forces argued that this would then lead to an increase in civilian cooperation with the police, as more people can come forward with information without fear of guerrillas assassinating them for collaborating with the colonial occupation. This was believed to be the first step in convincing rural villagers to provide information to the police, therefore reassurance and intelligence went hand in hand. Although the MNLA often assassinated people they believed to be collaborating with the British colonial occupation, the MNLA's use of intimidation has often been exaggerated by British authors to avoid portraying the communists as though they were a popular grassroots movement.

Some British soldiers believed that MNLA guerrillas had brainwashed entire civilian populations of rural civilians into believing that their communist guerrillas possessed supernatural powers of protection. One example of such a myth was prevalent within the British Army's Suffolk Regiment, a British Army regiment which was infamous for its widespread use of headhunting, deployment of Ibans, and public corpse displays. Many soldiers of the regiment believed that a famous communist leader known as the "Bearded Bandit", whose actual name was Liew Kon Kim, had tricked rural villagers into believing that his pocket compass was a magical device that granted him supernatural protection powers.[19] However this research was unable to uncover any proof to corroborate the Suffolk Regiment's spurious claims that civilians in Malaya believed that communists possessed magical powers. Such stories were likely the product of colonial propaganda which sought to provide British troops with an explanation for why so many civilians were enthusiastically supporting the communist. According to supporters of the public corpse displays, the supposed mental grip that the MNLA held over rural villagers could only be broken by proving beyond any doubt that a local guerrilla leader was indeed dead, something which Commonwealth forces believed could only be achieved by producing undeniable physical proof in the form of publicly displayed corpses.

As previously explored, many British soldiers recounted that the corpse displays were used to scare local people in the hopes of deterring them away from aiding the MNLA. In contrast, some British soldiers recall the corpse displays being positively received by civilians. One member of the Somerset Light Infantry recalls taking part in a public corpse display featuring MNLA guerrillas that he had helped to kill:

> "At the road the bodies seemed to create a remarkable impression: a grinning Chinese Police Inspector made me dictate and sign a report as I handed them over, and grinning Malays crowded round the truck in which they were dumped. Everyone was grinning, and perhaps for different reasons. Everyone except us – we had lived with these corpses long enough, and now we never wanted to see them again."[20]

During the Malayan Emergency the communist forces of the MNLA fought with the goal of turning Malaya into a democratic socialist republic, which would have included the abolition of Malay royalty (Sultans) and the nationalisation of major industries. For these reasons many native people, especially those who were wealthy, upper class, anti-communist, and held pro-monarchist and conservative worldviews, were eager to help Commonwealth forces crush the communists. One such man was a leading police officer and native Malayan called J.J. Raj (JR), who was the Officer Commanding Police District Pagoh (north Johore) in 1949.[21] Officer Raj ordered his fellow police officers to publicly display the bodies of every Communist they killed. Raj called these communists "CTs", a propaganda slogan meaning 'Communist Terrorists' which was invented by the British to dehumanise people who fought for Malayan independence. In his autobiography, Raj claimed that the public corpse displays that he authorised inspired confidence in many civilians and emboldened them to give information to the police without fear of guerrilla revenge attacks:

> "The villagers in the rural areas were terrified, and Police Special Branch received very little information. This was the situation in Pagoh. Some of the villagers informed very discreetly to our Special Branch officers, that the villagers would have more confidence if they could see for themselves the CTs who were killed by the Police. Consequently, I ordered that the body of every CT shot dead be displayed in the Police compound."
>
> "Whole villages would turn up when we displayed dead terrorists in the Police Station compound. This was good for morale. In those days, some of the communist terrorists were local people from the village. Once in the jungle, some of them turned out to be very ferocious and inhuman and had no hesitation in eliminating anyone even relatives who crossed their path. As a result of these "exhibitions", villagers had more confidence in the Police, morale improved and Special Branch began received more information on CT movements. This went on well for some-time."[22]

The Public Display of Corpses   81

The above paragraphs quoted from Officer Raj describes the earliest known public corpse displays in Malaya. However the issue of the corpse displays was not contained locally. As both British activists and the *Daily Worker* began publishing evidence of atrocities during the Malayan Emergency, interest in these issues rose among left-wing British politicians. Raj continues his eyewitness account of how he ordered the public display of corpses and the criticisms he received from British politicians who were made aware of the practice:

> "Some British MPs from London were on a study tour of Malaya were brought on a visit to my district. The display of dead bodies was objected to by these British MPs. They were "horrified" at my methods and considered them "uncivilised" and barbaric, and I was ordered to stop the practice."
>
> "In those days, when we were almost daily ambushed by terrorists, we certainly could not afford to be "civilised". Desperate situations, needed desperate remedies. Hardly had the British MPs left the airport bound for the United Kingdom, I resumed the method of eliciting information by displaying the dead terrorists."[23]

The information given to the police by rural villagers was not the only source of intelligence which was gained from the public corpse displays. The emotional reactions of onlookers were also considered to be an intelligence asset to be exploited by the police. Once a corpse was put on public display, police and soldiers would carefully watch the crowds of onlookers for signs of distressed friends, family, and loved ones. This would alert the police and soldiers to a person who had close links to the dead guerrilla, who would then be arrested and interrogated for information on communist activities.

In one example of this method, an officer of the Suffolk Regiment describes how the public corpse displays were used to identify communist sympathisers:

> "Some would slink away, some would look away, and others would come bouncing up saying 'ahh you got him you got him', and similar words. It might be worth returning or just reporting that the people

who lived in the house next to the mosque or whatever it was, seemed to be rather reluctant to come look at the bodies."[24]

Civilians who did not come out to witness the corpse displays or appeared to be upset upon witnessing the bodies were treated with suspicion by the police. This forced many civilians to fake their emotions and pretend to support the corpse displays, to avoid becoming the victim of a terrifying and potentially deadly police raid, with the possibility of being imprisoned, deported, or even hanged for being sympathetic to the MNLA. For this reason, many families of slain MNLA guerrillas were too afraid to claim the bodies of their loved ones, and so many of the corpses were dumped in unmarked graves.[25]

Such incidents explain why so many British soldiers and their Commonwealth allies reported seeing overwhelming positive responses from civilian onlookers. Rural villagers who smiled and thanked the British were seen as loyal allies, whereas civilians who appeared distraught at the sight of dead communists dumped around their villages were treated with suspicion. This further incentivised civilians to conceal their true emotions under the threat of having their lives destroyed by the colonial occupation.

Warzones and colonial occupations are not places where freedom of speech can be practised safely. There was no way for civilians living in Malaya who opposed the public corpse displays to freely speak out against them, thereby giving British soldiers the impression that everybody they met supported the corpse displays. One retired reporter described witnessing British soldiers carrying a dead suspected MNLA member wearing only underwear and tied to a pole like a wild boar. He then saw the corpse publicly displayed outside a police station based inside a New Village internment camp. Although he found the public corpse display morally wrong, he did not believe that he had the freedom to speak out against it. He concluded by saying "it was inhumane, but you couldn't say anything about this during the Emergency period!"[26] Had he openly spoken out against the practice of corpse displays, he would have risked being seen as a communist sympathiser in the eyes of the colonial occupation, putting both himself and his family in danger.

The Public Display of Corpses 83

However not everybody in Malaya's rural villages was capable of disguising their emotional response to the corpse displays. Unlike adults, young children were far less capable of concealing their emotions, a fact that Britain and their Commonwealth allies insidiously exploited. The public display of dead communist revolutionaries was often performed in full view of young children of all ages, even in front of infants barely old enough to walk.[27] Photographs of children standing over the feat of murdered communists do exist and have been preserved, however there has not yet been any research into how the public corpse displays affected children.[28]

Despite arguing that the public displaying of corpses was done for the benefit of civilians, the practice angered and traumatised many of the witnesses to these gruesome displays, many of whom likely knew the victims. According to veterans of the MNLA, the public corpse displays increased their hatred for the British and inspired them to fight harder. For people who were already ardently anti-communist, the displays appear to have raised their confidence in the police. Far from winning the "hearts and minds" of the Malayan people, such actions only intensified the existing convictions of those who witnessed the displays.

It is understandable how many British troops came to believe that they enjoyed the overwhelming support of rural populations. Typically, British troops in Malaya were either teenagers or conscripts, were unable to speak any Asian languages, and had no understanding of Asian cultural and social norms. For most of these men, their military service in Malaya was the first time they had ever interacted with an Asian person.

The claims by British troops and their Commonwealth allies during the Malayan Emergency that everybody loved their corpse displays, can be accurately described as an instance of survivorship bias. The happy anti-communist civilians celebrating the sight of a dead guerrilla are easily visible, whereas the unhappy and traumatised civilians are not, giving Commonwealth forces the false impression that all Malayan civilians loved to view the corpses of murdered communists. For every civilian who willingly came to see a public corpse display, there were invisible civilians who chose to avoid them, giving Commonwealth soldiers and police a warped perception of how popular their public corpse displays truly were.

Known victims of the public corpse displays

Unlike the victims of Britain's headhunting policy, there is far more information available on the identities of the victims of public corpse display. Of the victims that have been identified, the vast majority were veterans of the MPAJA, the communist guerrilla army that was trained and funded by Britain to resist the Japanese occupation of Malaya during WWII. Many of the names of guerrillas whose dead bodies were put on public display have been preserved by writers sympathetic to the MNLA.

The following examples include people who were alleged to have become victims of the public corpse displays:

- Wan Qiao Ying, a socialist revolutionary and young teenage supporter of the resistance against Japan, was 19 years old when the British shot her in the face and displayed her corpse at a roadside in 1950.[29]
- Xiao Li was another MNLA member and MPAJA veteran of the anti-Japanese resistance struggle. During the Malayan Emergency he drowned while fleeing the British who then recovered his body and publicly displayed it in a town called Ampang in 1956. The gruesome display of his body angered many people who knew him personally and further motivated guerrillas to resist the British occupation.[30]
- Ye Guan Xi was a student activist leader and anti-fascist who resisted the Japanese as a guerrilla commander. He later resisted the British occupation until he was killed by British forces in 1950 who then publicly displayed his corpse.[31]
- Ye Shi Min was a labour activist and socialist revolutionary who had taken part in successful ambushes against Japanese forces in Malaya during WWII. During the Malayan Emergency he was killed by the British and his corpse was publicly displayed on a lawn opposite a police station.[32]

The most infamous case of a corpse being publicly displayed was the body of Liew Kon Kim, a leading MNLA guerrilla often dubbed the "Bearded Bandit" by British soldiers.[33] Liew Kon Kim was an orphan and refugee from China who travelled to Malaya and became an anti-colonial guerrilla, fighting against the Japanese occupation during WWII and later serving as a guerrilla commander resisting the British occupation.[34] He became famous not only for his charisma and large beard, a rare physical trait for a Chinese man in Malaya, but also for being one of the most effective guerrilla commanders in the MNLA. After the British Army's Suffolk Regiment killed him, they paraded his corpse around New Village internment camps on the back of a lorry with loudspeakers blasting British propaganda.[35] This grizzly corpse-displaying parade lasted several days. One British soldier called Tony Rogers, who drove the truck displaying Liew Kon Kim's corpse around towns and villages, recalls those days:

> "After formal identification, his body was lifted onto the back of a very high GMC truck for the journey around the kampongs. Liew was still tied to a pole and I and another man who like me was rather short had difficulty in lifting him as his head was dangling. As we went forward his head struck the back of the GMC with a sickening 'thwack'. The colonel who was watching this was heard to remark 'Well, if he wasn't dead, he is now!'"[36]

The British then displayed Liew Kon Kim's body in Kajang marketplace for the public to view. His corpse was then photographed and the images were printed on propaganda leaflets and thrown out of aeroplanes above Malayan towns.[37] For decades after the Malayan Emergency had ended, veterans of the Suffolk Regiment recounted the public displaying of Liew Kon Kim's corpse as something to be proud of.

Liu Guan Geng, a "blood brother" of the aforementioned Liew Kon Kim, was also an anti-Japanese resistance fighter during WWII. Just like his brother he was killed by the British during the Malayan Emergency and his corpse was put on public display.[38] Demonstrating just how common it was for the British army to create gruesome corpse displays to both terrify locals and identify the families of MNLA members, the Suffolk Regiment yet again conducted another public corpse display of a famous guerrilla commander, this time of a man called Loh Pin whose brother was also killed by the Suffolk Regiment.[39] According to one soldier of the Suffolk Regiment, it was a common practice within their regiment to attach the corpses of people they had killed onto the bonnets of their vehicles, something they did before driving into towns.[40]

The earliest known newspaper article describing a public corpse display during the Malayan Emergency that this research was able to uncover, dates to June 1951.[41] There were two infamous instances of public corpse displays in Malaya which garnered the most media controversy in Britain:

1. **The Telok Anson Tragedy.** The display of two corpses outside Telok Anson police station in Perak, mid-August 1952. Both were killed by the Green Howards regiment of the British Army.
2. **The Kulim Tragedy.** The public display of two corpses outside Kulim police station on the 15th and 16th of September 1953. One corpse was that of a Tamil man called Subramanian and the second corpse was that of a 17 year old Chinese girl called Lim Saw Hoon.[42]

The Telok Anson Tragedy, August 1952

In mid-August 1952, outside Telok Anson police station, a large crowd gathered to witness the two corpses of suspected MNLA guerrillas. The two guerrillas had been killed by the Green Howards outside Selaba Estate, four and a half miles from Anson.[43] Despite the public display of corpses being practiced for at least over a year, this incident would make the corpse displays common knowledge in Britain.

The incident, hereby known as the **Telok Anson Tragedy**, was nonchalantly reported on by a newspaper in Singapore. This brought the incident to the attention of British newspapers, politicians, and activists. The British colonial occupation released an official statement on August 19, 1952, confirming that two corpses were publicly displayed outside Telok Anson police station, while stressing the need to identify the bodies for intelligence purposes. The official statement went on to state that public corpse displays were used for identification purposes, to allow members of the public to identify the guerrilla corpses:

"In such a case the body is photographed and may be exposed for a period for identification by a member of the public."

"Naturally such visible evidence that public enemies have been eliminated from the area they have been terrorising arouses considerable public interest and satisfaction, especially among the Chinese. It is not normal, however, to display bodies of dead terrorists for this reason. No hard and fast rule has been laid down, but it can be said that such public exposure is not authorised unless there is a specific intelligence or operational advantage to be derived from it."[44]

The British occupation's presence in Telok Anson had already been controversial before the Telok Anson Tragedy. Previously, British soldiers had allegedly murdered innocent civilians in the town. British troops fired their guns on a row of shops, killing two civilians and leaving 100 bullet marks. The British troops claimed that they were fired on and that a grenade was thrown at them from the town's shops. However a subsequent forensic investigation failed to find shell casings, weapons, or evidence of a grenade, and local people said that they did not hear any gunfire coming from within the shops.[45] The town also had a troubled and violent history during the Japanese occupation, where Japanese troops at Telok Anson's police station had received decapitated heads.[46]

While most non-communist news media that commented on the Telok Anson Tragedy attempted to downplay its significance, some openly defended the practice of publicly displaying the corpses of dead communists. One writer for *The Scotsman* newspaper openly defended the public corpse displays, praising them as a useful method for convincing "Simple minded peasants" that communists were not invincible.[47]

British communists and trade unionists brought greater media and political attention to the gruesome acts involving corpses committed by British troops in Malaya, but so did the bloodlust of the Commonwealth's civilian allies. Amid the rising awareness of Britain's public corpse displays following the Telok Anson Tragedy, the Incorporated Society of Planters, a professional body representing the interests of the wealthy capitalist owners of Malaya's private rubber plantations, called for even more public corpse displays.[48] The Incorporated Society of Planters knew that their wealth relied upon the continued colonial occupation and exploitation of Malaya's resources, and so threw their full weight behind supporting the British

Empire. Their relationship with British troops was so strong that they even sent cash gifts to the British Army, including $1,100 dollars to a British regiment which allowed Iban headhunters to take scalps.[49] Published inside their official journal, *The Planter*, they claimed that increasing the number of public corpse displays would be an effective method of propaganda to use against illiterate peasants.[50] The belief that illiteracy made the public corpse displays necessary tools to defeating communism was a common argument made by people and organisations that profited from the colonial looting of Malaya's resources.

Unlike the Headhunting Scandal earlier the same year, the public display of corpses in Malaya was opposed by writers in several mainstream British newspapers. One of Britain's largest liberal newspapers, *The Manchester Guardian*, hit back against *The Planter* by comparing the public display of corpses in Malaya to Nazi atrocities in Europe, while also arguing that such displays of savagery would create more communists:

> "A planters' periodical in Malaya has been advocating the public exhibition of executed communists. This suggestion conjures up the kind of sickening scenes which became all too familiar in Europe during the days of the German occupation."
>
> "In fact, ordinary Chinese folk have a very clear sense of what is decent and dignified, and the sort of medievalism advocated by "The Planter" would make as many Communist sympathisers as it would deter."[51]

The *Manchester Guardian* was joined by *The Daily Worker* in denouncing the use of public corpse displays.[52]

The Kulim Tragedy, September 1953

One of the bodies belonged to a Tamil man called Subramaniam and was displayed on the 15 September. However the other corpse, which was given far more media attention and caused a far greater reaction from onlookers, belonged to a 17 year old Chinese girl called Lim Saw Hoon. Her corpse was strapped upright to a plank and exhibited outside Kulim police station on the 16 September. Although the ranks of Malayan communists were filled with women, some of whom even became commanders in the MNLA, many British people could not conceive that a woman would be capable of fighting as a soldier in a warzone.[53] Both her young age and the fact she was a woman, shocked people in a way that the displays featuring young and middle-aged men could not. These characteristics awarded her with a presumed innocence and an aura of helplessness in the eyes of many British journalists, activists, and politicians, sparking controversy over the decision of British soldiers and their allies to publicly display her corpse. The very next day on the 17 September, the *Times of Malaya* newspaper announced the Kulim Tragedy to the world, bringing the incident to the attention of journalists and politicians in Britain.

Despite the Labour Party leadership officially supporting the British occupation of Malaya along with both the public corpse displays and decapitation of corpses, one Labour MP worked tirelessly to expose and fight against these atrocities. **Leslie Plummer (1901–1963)** was a Labour Party politician who used his position of power to challenge British colonialism and expose Britain's brutal actions in Malaya.

Leslie Plummer prepared a question to be read in Parliament concerning the Kulim Tragedy and the British occupation's practice of displaying corpses in public throughout Malaya. Learning of Plummer's planned questions, the Federation of Malaya pre-released an official statement on corpse displays, claiming that it was not a common practice.[54, 55] On November 25, 1953, Leslie Plummer's questions concerning the Kulim Tragedy were read in Parliament:

Leslie Plummer: "asked the Secretary of State for the Colonies (1) why the dead body of a Chinese woman bandit, shot and killed by Malayan security forces, was brought down from the jungle, then strapped to an upright plank and put on exhibition outside the police station at Kulim on 16th September;(2) why the body of an Indian bandit, shot and killed by Malayan security forces, was put on exhibition outside the Kulim police station in mid-September."

Colonial secretary Oliver Lyttelton, who the previous year had attempted to downplay and justify Britain's headhunting policy in Malaya, gave Plummer an answer:

> **Oliver Lyttelton:** "The bodies of these terrorists were not put on exhibition at Kulim police station. They were photographed, as is essential for criminal record and identification purposes. Owing to the siting and structure of the police station it was not possible to screen this operation completely from public sight. The High Commissioner is considering what action should be taken in future to exclude the public."[56]

Leslie Plummer's inquiry was met with weak excuses which contradicted earlier media reports. Lyttelton claimed that the bodies were only displayed outside Kulim police station because the indoor lighting was not suitable for photography. Just like the British Malayan Headhunting Scandal the previous year, the public corpse displays in Kulim saw General Gerald Templer defending his brutal counterinsurgency methods to politicians in London.[57] Just like the earlier controversy over the use of headhunting, Templer attempted to downplay the true extent of the practice of public corpse displays. Templer attempted to convince Oliver Lyttelton that the public corpse displays in Kulim were an accident, and claimed that there was no truth to the idea that the corpses of dead communists were put on public display. The dozens of eyewitness testimonies cited earlier in this work show that Templer was either lying or ignorant of the methods his own troops were using when it came to the treatment of corpses.

With Parliament giving him a weak answer on the issue of corpse displays, Leslie Plummer went to the media. As told by Leslie Plummer:

> "The official explanation that was given to me when I raised this in the House of Commons was that the bodies were being photographed for the purposes of record and identification and that owing to the siting and structure of the police station it was not possible to screen this operation from public sight. This explanation is clearly in conflict with the newspaper report. The fact is that in Malaya as well as in

Kenya we are showing to the native population what little respect we have for the dead."[58]

The above quote was published in *The Times*, one of Britain's largest conservative newspapers. Here we see that unlike the *Daily Worker's* images of headhunting, the public corpse displays found themselves being openly discussed and sometimes even challenged in many of Britain's largest mainstream newspapers.

The harder that Leslie Plummer tried to publicise the Kulim Tragedy, the harder he found himself being attacked by writers in British newspapers. Plummer's arguments against corpse displays were met with criticism from wealthy conservative men, all of whom had both collaborated with the colonial occupation and had direct financial interests in supporting British imperialism and fighting against communism. One of these men was a wealthy British-educated Malay called Ghazali Shafie, who had collaborated with the British Empire against Malayan communists and would later become Malaysia's Minister of Foreign Affairs. Shafie supported the British military's practice of publicly displaying corpses, claiming that Communists had brainwashed people into believing they possessed magical powers. In a show of contempt for Malaya's Chinese population, Shafie claimed that only killing and displaying the corpses of communists could convince "timid, illiterate, and superstitious yokels" to stop supporting the MNLA.[59]

Shafie's defence of the public corpse displays was supported by another wealthy right wing collaborator of the British occupation with financial interests in Malaya's natural resources. Nigel Hunt, a wealthy British man who had lived in Malay for several years, claimed that it was not a routine practice to display the bodies of dead communists in Malaya. However he also defended the practice of publicly displaying dead communists, citing the illiteracy of rural people as a justification for publicly displaying corpses.[60] Raja Uda, a member of Malayan royalty who had been awarded an OBE for his service to the British Empire, also attacked Leslie Plummer and claimed that the corpse displays Plummer had cited were all accidents and that the bodies were not intentionally shown to the public.[61]

Of all the people this research uncovered who defended the corpse displays on the grounds of widespread illiteracy, none of them appeared to have questioned why illiteracy was so widespread under British colonial rule, nor did they recognise any connection between the poverty Malaya suffered and the super exploitation of Malaya's resources by wealthy capitalists. It is ironic that the people most responsible for Malaya's high illiteracy rates would use the poverty which they themselves had fuelled to justify publicly displaying the corpses of people who rebelled against them.

Just as the *Daily Worker* staff had helped to expose headhunting by British and Commonwealth forces in Malaya, they also put their weight behind exposing the public corpse displays. Arthur Clegg wrote in the *Daily Worker* to denounce the Kulim tragedy where a 17 year old girl's corpse had been displayed by British forces, and attacked commentators in *The Times* newspaper who supported such practices.[62]

Conclusion on the public corpse displays

It should be recognised that methods such as headhunting and corpse displays were not used by the British in all of its post-WWII conflicts. The British military fought against two armies of European guerrillas within its Empire after the Second World War, including the Irish Republican Army (IRA) between 1968–1998 during The Troubles, and the National Organisation of Cypriot Fighters (EOKA) between 1955–1959 during the Cyprus Emergency. However never did British military leaders during these conflicts openly and routinely practice the public display of the corpses of their enemies to "reassure" the local population and to collect intelligence. The most visceral and terrifying aspects of British counterinsurgencies, most notably headhunting and public corpse displays, were exclusively targeted towards populations of non-white people in Asia and Africa. The more alien a nation's culture and ethnic makeup in comparison to white British society, the more likely it would be that the British military would use the most violent and oppressive methods available. If the anti-colonial guerrillas of the MNLA had been predominantly made up of white Europeans, then Britain would never have dreamed of using headhunting and corpse displays as a method to fight against them.

This research was unable to find eyewitness accounts by civilians who enjoyed a positive experience witnessing Britain's corpse displays in Malaya. Virtually all the evidence suggesting that many civilians were reassured by the corpse displays happens to originate from the same people who created them, or had some financial incentive in combating communism. Some of this may also have been an attempt to retrospectively justify actions they felt could show them in a bad light.

Whatever the intended message of Britain's public corpse displays, the image that they conveyed was one of terror and barbarity, acting as a warning to any Asian who would dare resist British colonialism and threaten the profits of wealthy capitalists. At best the public corpse displays in Malaya, erected by Commonwealth forces, were a gruesome display and insensitive practice which shocked onlookers. At worst they were an insidious method of psychological torture, traumatising the family, friends, children, and spouses, forced to witness the bloodied corpses of their loved ones stretched out in public and shoved in their faces by the same men who had murdered them. It is currently unknown when the British and their Commonwealth allies ended the practice of publicly displaying corpses in Malaya, or whether they continued the practice right up until the end of the war. Actions such as headhunting and displaying murdered corpses in front of their surviving relatives, are more reminiscent of the Nazi occupation of Europe than any serious attempt to win the "hearts and minds", as the British military liked to claim, of colonised people.

Conclusion

The treatment of dead anti-colonial guerrillas by the British military in Malaya provides many interesting insights into facets of British imperial history that continue to foment strong debates between researchers today. Many relatively recent developments such as the British military shortcomings and failures in Iraq and Afghanistan, coupled with the publication of multiple high-profile pieces of research detailing British colonial atrocities in Kenya and legal battles forwarded by the victims of British atrocities in Kenya and Malaya, have caused interesting changes in the historiography of British colonialism. Notably in the past twenty years there has been a sharp increase in scepticism among researchers concerning Britain's status as a self-proclaimed master of counterinsurgency strategies. This heightened scepticism has challenged the long-held notion that Britain's military had mastered the art of heats-and-minds while refraining from indulging in the unnecessary and gratuitous violence conducted by the French, Japanese, and United States during their counterinsurgencies.

This research concludes that there is little truth to the British government's claim that their headhunting policy in Malaya was a military necessity needed to identify insurgents. This research has also failed to find any evidence to demonstrate that the British military ever gained any valuable intelligence from these decapitations which could have been used to defeat the MNLA. British officials repeatedly lied about many aspects of the Ibans and their enforcement of Britain's headhunting policy in Malaya as an attempt to obfuscate potential war crimes, in what can reasonably be considered a cover-up. The Ibans, far from being a useful asset to the colonial occupation during the Malayan Emergency, proved to be a liability whose most useful contribution was raising the morale of inexperienced national servicemen. Their service in Malaya and subsequent role in the headhunting scandal has left a permanent stain on the British military, providing some of the most effective visual material for anti-imperialist causes ever created in the history of the British Empire. The decapitations committed by the British military against revolutionaries in Malaya, as exposed by the *Daily Worker* in 1952, are among the most visually graphic examples of anti-Asian violence perpetrated by any European Empire in the 20th century.

The combination of both anti-communist hysteria and anti-Asian racism in British society had dehumanised Malayan socialists and pro-independence fighters to such an extent that it fostered a culture which allowed atrocities such as headhunting and public corpse displays to flourish. The Malayan Emergency itself stemmed from the British Empire's worldview that white British colonialists had the inalienable right to exploit the natural resources of peoples they viewed as backwards. Armed with this imperialist worldview, anyone who resisted the Empire such as the Malayan communist guerrillas of the MNLA were treated as irredeemably evil to the point where the normal rules of war no longer applied, slapping them with propagandist labels such as "bandits" and "terrorists". Within the ranks of the British military, this level of dehumanisation acted to facilitate atrocities which would have been deemed utterly unacceptable according to the sensibilities of mainstream British society. Meanwhile in Britain this same dehumanisation of the enemy derailed much of the potential sympathy for the headhunting victims that the British public may have potentially expressed. The only exception to this being British socialists and trade unionists, with their anti-colonial and pro-socialist beliefs giving them both a greater immunity to Britain's pro-colonial propaganda and a higher degree of sympathy for MNLA. The Communist Party of Great Britain and the *Daily Worker* can be credited for exposing the practice of headhunting in Malay and raising awareness about the British military's practice of publicly displaying bodies.

The threat of both censorship and loss of journalistic privileges by the British government, the dedication of Britain's largest newspapers in demonising the Empire's enemies, together with the material shortcomings and failure of Malayan Communists to publicise their narrative of events, all contributed to silencing much of the potential outrage the *Daily Worker* photographs could potentially have inspired.

Despite the large number of books that have been written on the Malayan Emergency and the stream of new titles which are published every year, it is puzzling that so few experts in British colonial history have attempted to investigate the headhunting scandal. One possible factor is that the available literature on the Malayan Emergency has for decades been dominated by authors who were highly sympathetic to British colonialism. The vast majority of English language books published on the Malayan Emergency have been written by authors who are unapologetically pro-imperialist and are highly favourable towards the British Empire in their writings. These authors had little motivation to conduct in-depth research into issues that could have shown the British military in a bad light. Histories with openly anti-colonial authors whose works are sympathetic to the MNLA are much harder for English speaking audiences to find, they were often printed in very limited copies, and many are on the verge of becoming lost media. Professional academic literature on the Malayan Emergency is prohibitively expensive and only practically accessible to dedicated and educated academic readers in Britain's largest cities and university towns. On the other hand, books with pro-colonial authors who vilify the MNLA and paint the British military as heroes are much cheaper, dominate search engine results, and are numerous and widely available.

This research has been the first ever attempt to fully investigate the British Malayan Headhunting Scandal, a topic so thoroughly understudied that this very book had to choose a name to describe it. This research also includes one of the most up to date English language descriptions of Iban military service during the Emergency. However despite the colossal amount of time and effort it took to create this research, there is still much more which can be done to investigate the practice of headhunting during the Malayan Emergency. The next step is for academics based in Singapore and Malaysia to thoroughly comb through the non-English language historiography for information which has been missed by English speaking academics.

Additional Information

If you are a casual reader then here is where the book ends.

The upcoming chapter is intended to explain to specialists how this research was created and how they themselves can conduct research into this area. This chapter also includes information on the challenges of studying the headhunting scandal, acknowledgements for the academics & institutions which made this research possible, and a discussion on the ethics of using such disturbingly violent images as headhunting photographs in historical research. There are also some examples of interesting and unique sources which were rejected by this research for various reasons.

The ethics of publishing headhunting photographs in research

When early drafts of this research were shown to experts in British imperial history, several of them criticised my decision to include the most gruesome headhunting photographs in this book. They felt that if there is a possibility that the families of some of the victims might see these images, then this book would risk causing distress to the surviving families. This section will address these concerns and explain my reasons for deciding to include some of the most brutal headhunting photographs in this research.

The headhunting images have been included for the following reasons:

1. The subject of this research focuses heavily on the publishing of images which were infamous because of their shocking content. This makes viewing the images necessary for researchers to fully understand why they were so controversial.
2. Many government spokespersons and writers alleged that such images were fake and have denied the existence of the actions they depict. Publishing the original photographs reduces the chance of any further denial.

3. The author of this research believes that there is a real threat that after the publication of this book, much of the archival evidence it cites may vanish under suspicious circumstances. Publishing copies of these photographs is necessary to preserve evidence of war crimes.
4. Many of these images have never before been published and travelling to find them was extremely costly. Publishing these images in this book will save researchers time and money, thereby making this area of research more accessible and open to further investigation by academics who lack the time and money needed to travel the country.
5. If the British government one day considerers paying reparations to the families of the victims and the communities effected by headhunting, such images will act as important evidence of crimes which have since gone unpunished.

Before consulting academics of imperial history, I had never considered that anyone would oppose the republishing of these images. In response to their concerns I sought out examples of how atrocity photographs from other fields of history have been presented by British historians. With this purpose in mind I visited the holocaust exhibit at the London branch of the Imperial War Museum. There I saw a wide number of atrocity photographs far more gruesome and heart-breaking than anything published in this book. This was a museum display deemed suitable for school aged children, and in which the survivors of the holocaust were likely to view these images. The displays implied a consensus among holocaust academics that displaying horrific photographs of atrocities, most notably those including corpses, is necessary to ensure that such crimes are not repeated. I wholeheartedly agree with their methods and was inspired by the Imperial War Museum's holocaust exhibits to uncover as many headhunting photographs as possible.

Photographs from the Vietnam war were also consulted while deciding how such shocking images should be treated. One of which was the photograph taken by Nick Ut depicting Phan Thi Kim Phuc, a young Vietnamese girl who had survived a South Vietnamese napalm strike. Another set of images which inspired my search for Malayan headhunting images were the photographs taken of the My Lai massacre by military photographer Ronald L. Haeberle, whose mission to shine a light on wrongdoings is parallel to my own personal reasons for writing this book.

The Malayan Emergency has been largely forgotten by the British and Malaysian public, with most of those who are aware of the war's existence being historians, activists, and the families of those involved. However the Malayan Emergency continues to be the subject of intense study by military practitioners across the world, especially those seeking inspiration for anti-insurgent strategies. With the literature surrounding the Malayan Emergency being overwhelmingly pro-Empire, these generals of future wars are being given a rose-tinted version of the Malayan Emergency, with the atrocities and their victims conveniently pushed aside in favour of an idealised version of the past. The fact that the historiography of this specific conflict is of intense interest to such dangerous people, gives an urgent need to fight against imperial nostalgia. Publishing these images will force such people to confront the reality of armed conflict, and think twice before duplicating the supposedly flawless counterinsurgency strategies they read about the Malayan Emergency.

It is also worth stating that Malayan communists, the primary victims of the headhunting policy and public corpse displays, have widely used grizzly images in their own histories. Most Malayan communists appear to find these images very useful in highlighting the oppression that they faced, and are thus eager for as many people to see them as possible. In the most prominent example Chin Peng, the leader of the MNLA, republished and highlighted the *Daily Worker* image of a Marine posing with two heads in his own autobiography. Some descendants of slain communists have also chosen to include graphic examples of headhunting images in media they created to demonstrate the brutality of the Malayan Emergency, a key example being the documentary *Absent Without Leave* (2016). The *Morning Star*, the rebranded version of the original *Daily Worker*, has similarly republished the headhunting images. Not only have the comrades and families of the victims of these atrocities chosen to republish the images, but so have many British veterans and their supporters. Examples include *A King's Shilling* (2012), *War School* (2019), and *The Malayan Emergency: The Crucial Years* (2022). There appears to be consensus among those who fought in the Malayan Emergency, along with both their genetic and ideological descendants, that graphic and shocking images from the war should be republished.

This book was created with a desire to shed light on the terrible realities of colonialism, and to demonstrate the result of rabid anti-Asian racism when combined with mindless anti-communist hysteria. It is my hope that this research can serve to help avoid such atrocities in future conflicts by warning military practitioners of the harm to their own faction's reputations if they were to engage in needless and gratuitous displays of violence. To this end I believe that publishing these images is the morally correct thing to do.

Methodology: How was this research created?

This research is the first ever attempt by any historian to fully examine the practice of headhunting during the Malayan Emergency and also the first attempt to fully examine the political scandal that followed, which this research has dubbed the **British Malayan Headhunting Scandal of 1952**. This research is also the first attempt to create a complete timeline of events surrounding the scandal, and the first to engage with all the available primary sources including photographs, eyewitness testimonies, government documents, newspapers, etc.

I first became aware of the existence of the headhunting scandal as a teenager after speaking to my grandfather, a veteran of the British Army who had heard stories about the Malayan Emergency from fellow soldiers within his regiment. He told me there had been cases of soldiers cutting people's heads off in Malaya and that the decapitations had caught the attention of British politicians. After hearing this seemingly unbelievable story I began gathering books and articles on the Malayan Emergency and managed to find traces mentioning headhunting and the articles in the *Daily Worker*, but rarely discovered anything more than a couple of sentences.

After graduating with a Master's degree from Oxford Brookes University in 2020, I fully dedicated myself to collecting all the evidence I could find on the practice of headhunting in Malaya. I began collecting digital copies of hundreds of history books and articles related to the British military, colonialism, media, and the Malayan Emergency, most of which were either soldier memoirs or academic monographs. I then used the CTRL+F keyboard command to comb for mentions of headhunting, decapitations, the *Daily Worker*, and Ibans, among many other key terms and countless different spelling variations. Once I found a match I would learn what I could and search the footnotes for new possible sources. If these books included photographs then I would use the reverse image search options on web services such as Google Images and Tineye to find websites with information on the headhunting scandal. Running variations of keywords through Google Books revealed countless publications from newspapers to monographs which contained evidence on the headhunting scandal, which I would then order from libraries.

The majority of this research relies upon evidence collected from British archives. I combed physical archives across England in Oxford, London, Bury St Edmunds, and Manchester, to find evidence in the form of diaries, memoirs, photographs, newspapers, and declassified military/government reports. This was an extremely tedious and expensive undertaking due to the high costs of travel and accommodation, the lengthy waiting periods of many archives, and multiple return journeys. No grants or bursaries were ever awarded to conduct this research.

In London the Marx Memorial Library provided me with full access to physical copies of the *Daily Worker* which formed the bedrock of this research. Due to the *Daily Worker's* coverage of activists, protests, and episodes in British history which were often ignored by most other British newspapers, the *Daily Worker* archives held by the Marx Memorial Library have become a priceless and unique look into Britain's domestic and colonial history. Without the dedication of the Marx Memorial Library and its volunteers, this research may not have been possible. It is highly recommended that any historian looking to conduct fresh and original research into British history, that they search the *Daily Worker* archives for important issues which were ignored by the mainstream British press. The British Library provided newspapers from the digital collections of the 'British Newspaper Archive'. The UK National Archives in Kew held a treasure trove of priceless declassified colonial office, cabinet, and military documents covering almost every aspect of the British Malayan

Headhunting Scandal. The Templer Study Centre inside the National Army Museum provided two never-before-published headhunting photographs. Lastly the most important archive in London was the Imperial War Museum, which provided sound archives containing eyewitness reports from British soldiers, rare military publications, another headhunting photograph, and diaries.

In Oxford the Bodleian Library's special collections held in the Weston Library provided documents from colonial officials, and the Bodleian's Law Library provided physical access to copies of *Hansard* which recorded the debates in the House of Commons concerning the *Daily Worker* photographs. The Bodleian Library provided many more important books which had not been digitised, were out of print, or were rarely sold online.

In Manchester the Working Class Movement Library (WCML) provided archival materials related to the *Daily Worker* including leaflets, booklets, and photographs. One staff member of the WCML even rediscovered and provided me with never before published headhunting photographs from Malaya.

Finally the Suffolk Archives in Bury St Edmunds provided me with a large number of Malayan atrocity photographs and another never-before-published headhunting photograph.

I contacted multiple historians and researchers interested in both the Malayan Emergency and the history of British publishing, asking for their opinions on the scandal and inquiring about possible new sources of information. For historians looking for further evidence of headhunting during the Emergency, it is recommended that they begin with examining the museum archives of British military regiments known to have fought in the Malayan Emergency. Due to budget and time restraints, this research was conducted almost solely using sources which are available in the UK, with the only exceptions being inter-library loan requests and resources accessible online.

Several weaknesses have hampered this research and should be acknowledged by readers. The first weakness is that I the author can only speak English which means I may have potentially missed evidence recorded in other languages. As a consequence I have chosen to primarily focus on the reaction of the British media and public, only referencing to foreign reactions when translations or English language commentaries are available. The second major weakness of this research is that much of the evidence that could have been used by historians to potentially shed light on the headhunting scandal has likely been intentionally hidden or destroyed by the British government. The Operation Legacy programme run by both the Colonial Office and the Foreign Office sought to destroy archival files from British colonies such as Malaya which contained evidence of atrocities committed during the colonial occupations. In some cases the British government instead chose to simply lock away and hide archives that were too big to vet that could have potentially embarrassed the British government. This was revealed due to the recent discovery of the "migrated archives", secret government records from over 37 former British colonies including Malaya which were hidden by the Foreign Office. There is at least one instance of files pertaining to headhunting during the Malayan Emergency going missing from British archives. One researcher from the University of British Columbia looking for material for his PhD thesis, noted that he wanted to access materials in the UK National Archives including a letter believed to have contained quotes by General Gerald Templer in support of using Ibans in their traditional role as headhunters. However, when he attempted to access these documents he found that the letter he wanted had been removed from the archival file for no apparent reason.[1] Although plenty of evidence shining light on the headhunting scandal has been preserved, we may never know how much has been lost to time, intentionally destroyed, and how much potential evidence may still be concealed in secret government archives.

Despite these weaknesses, I hope that the contents of this research could one day be used as evidence to help secure compensation for the families whose loved ones were the victims of Britain's headhunting policy and the public corpse displays. In recent years the victims of war crimes by the British government have won legal battles to secure compensation with the help of historians whose work has shed light on historic wrongdoings. Multiple victims of rape and torture at the hands of British soldiers during the Mau Mau Uprising (1952–1960) and the Cyprus Emergency (1955–1959) have in recent years successfully won compensation. It is my hope that one day the evidence compiled in this book will play a role in winning similar compensation to the families of the headhunting victims, whose lives were destroyed by the murder and mutilation of their loved ones.

Sources rejected from this research

Because this book is based on research found primarily in British and online archives, many potentially useful sources kept overseas could not be found for use in this research.[2] Other sources however have been omitted from this research because the reliability of their claims and sometimes their creators is questionable.

One example can be found in Noel Barber's book *The Natives Were Friendly*. In this book, Barber claimed to have witnessed two Ibans kill and decapitate an MNLA member before jokingly implying that the Ibans took meat from the corpse and fed it to him.[3] This claim has not been included in this research because the author was likely either joking or making up a fake story to help sell his book. Despite rumours circulating between British soldiers that Ibans were cannibals, there is no proof that Ibans in Malaya ever consumed human flesh. Noel Barber's stories should not be treated as reliable sources of information on the Malayan Emergency. His books on the Malayan Emergency, notably *War of the Running Dogs*, quotes people he had never met and without citations, in a style more akin to a novel then a genuine eyewitness account. He spent much of his career working for the Daily Mail, a right-wing British newspaper infamous for promoting the British Union of Fascists, anti-Asian racism, supporting British imperialism, and fabricating stories. It is possible that Noel Barber's connections with such a newspaper may have coloured his writings on the Malayan Emergency.[4]

Another book on the Malayan Emergency written by a questionable author is Vincent Hancock's self-published *Legends of the Dragonfly: Fighting the Communists During the Malayan Emergency, 1947–1960*. The author is the son of a British soldier who fought in Malaya and claims to have discovered his father's diaries and published them in the form of a book. The writing style makes the book feel more like a novel, many of the events within it appear to have been heavily dramatized, if not fictional. The writing style is a confusing mess and reads as though it were imperialist fanfiction. The book makes the unprovable claim that the MNLA beheaded British soldiers before the Commonwealth forces ever decapitated anyone. The book then tells an absurd story that the MNLA chose to stop beheading British soldiers immediately after the author's father personally cut the heads off two MNLA members and publicly displayed them in a village alongside a warning note.[5] Despite posing as though it were a personal eyewitness account of the war, it reads as though it was written by an amateur military enthusiast struggling to imagine a war they know very little about. Attempts by both myself and fellow historians to contact the author have failed, and he does not appear to have shared these diaries with researchers. The contents of the book are likely fiction disguised as non-fiction and therefore have not been used as evidence in this research.

Tariq Ali, a famous left-wing academic and British author, provides one of the most shocking (yet believable) claims. According to Ali, under Clement Attlee's Labour Party government the British war minister John Strachey travelled to Malaya and was photographed alongside a colleague posing with decapitated heads.[6] According to Ali, this caused quite an outrage:

> "Strachey's final act of treachery, I recall, created a great deal of anger. As a minister in the Attlee Government he was photographed in Malaya with a colleague, standing triumphantly, while at his feet lay the decapitated heads of executed communist guerrillas. It was a sorry epitaph for one of the great popularizers of socialism during the thirties."[7]

Another anti-imperialist writer described Tariq's claim that Strachey posed with decapitated heads as "another episode of a British statesman barbarically glorifying in imperialist war on the darker shades of humanity."[8] It is not entirely out of the question that this could have happened. John Strachey was a former fascist and admirer of Oswald Mosley, and he did travel to Malaya in 1950, armed himself with a rifle, and patrolled the jungle alongside British soldiers looking for communists. However this research was unable to find any evidence to corroborate this story. It could be that the outrage stayed behind closed doors within the Labour Party, an organisation within which Tariq Ali had strong connections. It is also possible that Tariq is misremembering the *Daily Worker* headhunting scandal. Due to the lack of corroborating evidence, this claim has not been included in this research.

There are plenty of books about the Malayan Emergency written from the perspective of British soldiers, however many come with such little information that it is unclear whether they are supposed to be memoirs of a soldier's time in Malaya or fictional novels. One such book is *No Drums to Beat No Flags to Fly* by E. B. Parkes, an account of the Malayan Emergency written in a style as though each chapter were dated diary entries. This book provides a detailed and lengthy description of British soldiers exhuming the grave of a suspected MNLA member for an Iban to decapitate its badly decomposed head and retrieve it for identification.[9] This interesting story was rejected from this book due to the possibility that the events he describes may be fiction.

As for the reliability of these sources, memoirs and diaries created by British soldiers have been frequently used in this research for first-hand sources on headhunting, however this should not be taken as confirmation that all the content of said sources are reliable and accurate. Of the hundreds of eyewitness accounts, diaries, memoirs, and other sources created by Commonwealth soldiers who fought against Communist guerrillas in Malaya, not one could accurately explain the context behind the war and few had any idea who they were fighting or why. The British military valued politically ignorant soldiers who were unlikely to question the ethics of their actions, a preference which is reflected in the books said soldiers wrote later in life.

There is an interesting story concerning William Carbinell (Carbonell), the head of the Criminal Investigation Department during the British occupation of Malaya, allegedly and temporarily placing a decapitated human head and two hands in his refrigerator while he left his house to find a camera. While he was away his wife discovered the severed human head and collapsed from stress. Once she awoke, her husband gaslit her into believing that she simply had a bad dream and that the decapitated human head was only a figment of her imagination:

"It was 3 o'clock on a holiday and Carbinell had to go and fetch the official photographer. He put the head and the hands in the refrigerator and left the house. His wife was having a siesta in the bedroom. While he was away his wife woke up and, wanting a cold drink, went downstairs to get one from the fridge. On seeing the grisly remains she fell into a dead faint. Her husband found her unconscious and took her upstairs before getting rid of skull and hands. When his wife awoke and asked about those dreadful things in the fridge, her husband could not believe such a story. He took her downstairs and showed her that there was nothing untoward in the fridge at all. She had been the victim of a horrible nightmare."[10]

As interesting a story that this is, it has not been included in this research due to concerns that it sounds too unbelievable and entertaining. Perhaps one day evidence will be found to corroborate it. Since this research could not find any corroborating evidence, it stays in this rejection section.

Acknowledgements

Many thanks to the staff at London's Marx Memorial Library for providing me with *Daily Worker* material concerning decapitations during the Malayan Emergency. I am also grateful to Professor Karl Hack who took the time to advise me on questions concerning the Malayan Emergency and aided my search for new evidence. Credit is also due to retired Sergeant Daniel Davis of the British Army whose reminiscence of conversations with British soldiers in his regiment brought the existence of the headhunting scandal to my attention. Finally I would like to thank the extremely helpful and lovely staff of Manchester's Working Class Movement Library (WCML) for rediscovering and providing me with several newly discovered decapitation photographs. Gratitude is also due to the archivists of Manchester's People's History Museum whose CPGB archives helped expand my understanding of the Malayan Emergency.

Tips for Researchers

G rizzly trophy photographs taken in Malaya depicting corpses and decapitated heads have appeared in a variety of places, including eBay sellers, online forums, regiment histories, and the families of deceased soldiers. One photograph depicting troops posing with a corpse in Malaya was discovered inside a book purchased from a second-hand bookshop.[1] If you wish to search for new evidence concerning the practice of headhunting and the treatment of corpses in Malaya, then here are some tips:

- Try to focus your search on the years between 1948–1953. Between these years the Malayan Emergency was at its bloodiest. Consequently instances of headhunting were at their higher during this time.
- Consider focusing your search on British regiments that were known for their high kill counts. For instance, the Suffolks and the Cameroonians were known for having both a very heavy Iban presence and for claiming high kill counts.
- In historical archives, photographic albums created by soldiers who fought in the Malayan Emergency are brilliant potential sources for information on Britain's headhunting policy in Malaya. Regimental museums across the UK are common sources for such albums. It is always worth checking these albums for headhunting photographs, as gruesome images of corpses became popular collectables for many British soldiers in Malaya.
- The word "Iban" is pronounced 'ee-ban'. Many British soldiers never saw the word Iban written down, so many transcripts of interviews and memoirs use a variety of spellings for the word Iban. Try searching variations like Eban, Ebam, Ehban, and so on.

For any researcher who wishes to look at some of the original sources cited in this book, there are several issues they should be aware of:

- The *Daily Worker* often released early and late editions of the same newspaper issues to accommodate breaking news. For this reason, articles cited in the *Daily Worker* may not appear in the first, second or third issue published on the same day. The issues are indicated by the number of stars below the word *"Daily"* in the front page title. All the *Daily Worker* materials cited in this research can be found in the Marx Memorial Library.
- Many of the newspapers cited in this research have changed their names multiple times throughout their publication history. For this reason the title of the newspaper used in the citations is the same name as when the article was published.
- Until recently many historical documents held by the Rhodes House Library in Oxford were transferred to the Bodleian Library's Special Collections at the Weston Library, a several minute walk away. Many history books cite Rhodes House as the source for documents which are today kept at the nearby Weston Library.

Notes

Introduction
1. Evan Smith, "For Socialist Revolution or National Liberation? Anti-Colonialism and the Communist Parties of Great Britain, Australia and South Africa in the Era of Decolonisation," in *Workers of the Empire, Unite: Radical and Popular Challenges to British Imperialism, 1910s-1960s*, ed. Yann Béliard & Neville Kirk, (Liverpool: Liverpool University Press, 2021) 256.
2. Janina Struk, *Private Pictures: Soldiers' Inside View of War*, (London: I. B. Tauris & Co Ltd, 2011) 20.
3. John Newsinger, *British Counterinsurgency 2nd Edition*, (Basingstoke: Palgrave Macmillan, 2015) 34–35.
4. Adrian Walker, Ron Harper, Paul Riches, *A County Regiment: 1st Battalion of the Queen's Own Royal West Regiment Malaya 1951–1954*, (Brockley Press, 2001) 7.
5. John Newsinger, *British Counterinsurgency 2nd Edition*, (Basingstoke: Palgrave Macmillan, 2015) 41.
6. John Newsinger, *British Counterinsurgency 2nd Edition*, (Basingstoke: Palgrave Macmillan, 2015) 39.
7. Asoka Guikon, *A People's History of Malaya: The New Emergency*, (Oldham, England: Bersatu Press, 1980) 92.
8. John Newsinger, *British Counterinsurgency 2nd Edition*, (Basingstoke: Palgrave Macmillan, 2015) 42.
9. John Newsinger, *British Counterinsurgency 2nd Edition*, (Basingstoke: Palgrave Macmillan, 2015) 44.
10. Many writers believe that the term "Emergency" was used to protect the interests of British capitalists by keeping them covered by British insurance companies which would not pay out during wartime, however this is a myth which likely originated from the writings of a *Daily Mail* employee called Noel Barber.
11. Mark Curtis, *Web of Deceit: Britain's Real Role in the World*, (London: Vintage Books, 2003) 343.
12. John Newsinger, *British Counterinsurgency 2nd Edition*, (Basingstoke: Palgrave Macmillan, 2015) 40.
13. Hua Wu Yin, *Class and Communalism in Malaysia: Politics in a Dependent Capitalist State*, (London: Zed Books/Marram Books, 1983) 96.
14. John D. Leary, *Violence and the Dream People: The Orang Asli in the Malayan Emergency, 1948–1960* (Athens: Ohio University Center for International Studies, 1995) 43–44.
15. Mark Curtis, *Web of Deceit: Britain's Real Role in the World*, (London: Vintage Books, 2003) 342–343.
16. RAF minutes for the Director of Operations' Committee discussing use of railway flamethrowers, 28 May 1952, National Archives, AIR 20/8926, file IIJ53/16/2/15 Part 2, appendix A.

17. Contains an eyewitness account of the Malayan Emergency by Neil Ascherson of an instance where he encouraged the use of a flamethrower which then malfunctioned and burnt two civilians to death. Adrian Walker, *Six Campaigns: National Servicemen on Active Service 1948–1960*, (London: Leo Cooper, 1993) 7.
18. Karl Hack, *The Malayan Emergency: Revolution and Counterinsurgency at the End of Empire*, (Cambridge: Cambridge University Press, 2022) 320–321.
19. Mark Curtis, *Web of Deceit: Britain's Real Role in the World*, (London: Vintage Books, 2003) 339.
20. James Vernon, *Modern Britain, 1750 to the Present*, (Cambridge University Press, 2017) 419.
21. Agnes Khoo, *Life as the River Flows: Women in the Malayan Anti-Colonial Struggle*, (Monmouth, Wales: Merlin Press, 2007) 13.
22. Some prominent examples can be found here. Mark Curtis, *Web of Deceit: Britain's Real Role in the World*, (London: Vintage Books, 2003) 340–342.
23. Much of the torture carried out by Commonwealth forces during the Malayan Emergency was performed by British soldiers who had been stationed in Palestine. Interview with British Trooper of the 1st King's Dragoon Guards, 1986, Imperial War Museum Sound Archive, Accession No. 10107, reel 2.
24. S.A. Ganapathy was hanged by the British in May 1949. John Newsinger, *The Blood Never Dried: A People's History of the British Empire, 2nd edition* (London: Bookmarks Publications, 2013) 218.
25. John Newsinger, *British Counterinsurgency 2nd Edition*, (Basingstoke: Palgrave Macmillan, 2015) 50.
26. Many facets of Britain's war in Malaya were later used by the United States, including the practice of introducing self-exploding ammunition to guerrillas, the use of flamethrowers, the use of helicopters, internment camps, and the mass spraying of chemical defoliants,
27. Mark Curtis, *Web of Deceit: Britain's Real Role in the World*, (London: Vintage Books, 2003) 342.
28. Dyak and Dayak are different spellings to describe the same people. Both spellings are used by historians, journalists and government officials to refer to the Ibans hired by the British military and deployed in Malaya. British government officials preferred to use their official job title and refer to them as "trackers".
29. Calder Walton, *Empire of Secrets: British Intelligence, The Cold War and The Twilight of Empire*, (London: Harper Press, 2013) 205.
30. Ooi Keat Gin, *The Historical Dictionary of Malaysia* (Plymouth: The Scarecrow Press, 2009) 115–116.
31. Ooi Keat Gin, *The Historical Dictionary of Malaysia* (Plymouth: The Scarecrow Press, 2009) 116.
32. See here for lengthy and detailed account of headhunting against Japanese troops in Borneo during WWII. Montgomery McFate, *Military Anthropology: Soldiers, Scholars and Subjects at the Margins of Empire*, (London: Hurst & Company, 2018) 192–193.
33. Interview with Australian soldier Ian Geddes, 2004, Australians at War Film Archive, Archive number 2431, timestamp 15:00–16:00. https://australiansatwarfilmarchive.unsw.edu.au/archive/2431 (accessed 5 July 2022).
34. Ooi Keat Gin, *The Historical Dictionary of Malaysia* (Plymouth: The Scarecrow Press, 2009) 115.

35. Michael Heppell, Limbang anak Melaka, Enyan anak Usen, *Iban Art: Sexual Selection and Severed Heads*, (Amsterdam: KIT Publishers, 2005) 23.
36. Michael Heppell, Limbang anak Melaka, Enyan anak Usen, *Iban Art: Sexual Selection and Severed Heads*, (Amsterdam: KIT Publishers, 2005) 21.
37. Trophies made from human corpses, such as those taken from Japanese soldiers by Americans during WWII, were often treated with horror and disgust by the families of anglophone soldiers. Simon Harrison, *Dark Trophies: Hunting and the Enemy Body in Modern War* (Oxford: Berghahn Books, 2012) 182.
38. Michael Heppell, Limbang anak Melaka, Enyan anak Usen, *Iban Art: Sexual Selection and Severed Heads*, (Amsterdam: KIT Publishers, 2005) 46.
39. Photographs taken by British soldiers of Ibans in Malaya with collections of large tattoos. Mike Forsdike, *The Malayan Emergency: The Crucial Years 1949–52*, (Barnsley, England: Pen & Sword, 2022) 114–115.
40. Pengaroh charms (sometimes spelt "pengaruhs") were usually made from hair, skin and bone, and were believed by many Ibans to provide protection/assistance. Karl Hack, *The Malayan Emergency: Revolution and Counterinsurgency at the End of Empire*, (Cambridge: Cambridge University Press, 2022) 319.
41. The eyewitness accounts of two soldiers who were given tattoos by Ibans can be read on these pages. Adrian Walker, *Six Campaigns: National Servicemen on Active Service 1948–1960*, (London: Leo Cooper, 1993) pages 5, 124, 125.
42. Harry Miller, *Jungle War in Malaya: The Campaign Against Communism 1948–1960*, (London: Arthur Barker Limited, 1972) 47.
43. Anthony Short, *The Communist Insurrection in Malaya 1948–1960*, (London: Frederick Muller LTD, 1975) 132.
44. David French, *The British Way in Counter-Insurgency* (Oxford: Oxford University Press, 2011) 152.
45. Gregory Blaxland, *The Regiments Depart: A History of the British Army, 1945–1970*, (London: William Kimber, 1971) 81.
46. Benjamin Grob-Fitzgibbon, *Imperial Endgame: Britain's Dirty Wars and the End of Empire* (Basingstoke: Palgrave Macmillan, 2001) 112.
47. Major J. B. Oldfield, *The Green Howards in Malaya (1949–1952): The Story of a Post-war Tour of Duty by a Battalion of the Line* (Aldershot: Gale and Polden Ltd, 1953) Xxii.
48. Major J. B. Oldfield, *The Green Howards in Malaya (1949–1952): The Story of a Post-war Tour of Duty by a Battalion of the Line* (Aldershot: Gale and Polden Ltd, 1953) Xxiii.
49. Awang anak Raweng won the George Cross, and Menggong anak Panggit won the George Medal.
50. Later in the war Ibans were awarded with General Service medals. Mike Forsdike, *The Malayan Emergency: The Crucial Years 1949–52*, (Barnsley, England: Pen & Sword, 2022) 78.
51. It would have been impossible to spot and identify fifty experienced guerrillas in the depths of a jungle, and it is even more fantastical that a single man with severe arm and leg injuries could successfully fight fifty armed guerrillas on his own. It is likely that the story is the product of British propaganda.
52. Robert Rizal Abdullah, *The Iban Trackers and the Sarawak Rangers 1948–1963*, (Kota Samarahan: UNIMAS, 2019) 37–39.

53. Edgar O'Ballance, *Malaya: The Communist Insurgent War, 1948–1960* (London: Faber and Faber, 1966) 87.
54. Harry Miller, *Jungle War in Malaya: The Campaign Against Communism 1948–1960*, (London: Arthur Barker Limited, 1972) 23–24.
55. Christopher Pugsley, *From Emergency to Confrontation: The New Zealand Armed Forces in Malaya and Borneo 1949–1966*, (Victoria, Australia: Oxford University Press, 2003) 144–145.
56. Robert Rizal Abdullah, *The Iban Trackers and the Sarawak Rangers 1948–1963*, (Kota Samarahan: UNIMAS, 2019) 10.
57. According to F. A. Godfrey of the Suffolk Regiment who trained one of the first experimental Iban platoons, there were originally two Iban platoons, one attached to the Suffolk Regiment and the other with the Cameronians, aka Scottish Rifles. F. A Godfrey, *The History of the Suffolk Regiment 1946–1959*, (London: Leo Cooper Ltd, 1988) 89.
58. Christopher James Baird OBE 1895–1973, commanded the Sarawak Rangers from 1953–1960. Robert Rizal Abdullah, *The Iban Trackers and the Sarawak Rangers 1948–1963*, (Kota Samarahan: UNIMAS, 2019) 20–21.
59. Maureen Kim Lian Sioh, "Fractured Reflections: Rainforests, Plantations and the Malaysian Nation-State," PhD Dissertation (The University of British Columbia, April 2000) 113. https://open.library.ubc.ca/soa/cIRcle/collections/ubctheses/831/items/1.0089657 (accessed 27 October 2021).
60. Karl Hack, *The Malayan Emergency: Revolution and Counterinsurgency at the End of Empire*, (Cambridge: Cambridge University Press, 2022) 318–319.
61. Page contains the recollections of a British soldier who fought in Malaya recounting how the belief that Ibans were cannibals was used to tease inexperienced British soldiers. Adrian Walker, *Six Campaigns: National Servicemen on Active Service 1948–1960*, (London: Leo Cooper, 1993) 76.
62. One example of an Iban mercenary being referred to by British soldiers as the platoon's "pet head-hunter" can be found here. Adrian Walker, Ron Harper, Paul Riches, *A County Regiment: 1st Battalion of the Queen's Own Royal West Regiment Malaya 1951–1954*, (Brockley Press, 2001) 26.
63. An example can be found here. Len Spicer, *The Suffolks in Malaya*, (Peterborough: Lawson Phelps Publishing, 1998) 37.
64. Gregory Blaxland, *The Regiment's Department: A History of the British Army, 1945–1970*, (London: William Kimber, 1971) 113.
65. This was also the case during WWII. Montgomery McFate, *Military Anthropology: Soldiers, Scholars and Subjects at the Margins of Empire*, (London: Hurst & Company, 2018) 189.
66. Interview with British officer of the 1st Battalion of the Lincolnshire Regiment Darby Robert Follett Houlton-Hart, 1995, Imperial War Museum Sound Archive, Accession No. 15355, reel 4.
67. Photograph of an Iban with the Suffolk Regiment who was said to have looted a watch, shown in the photograph, from the corpse of an MNLA member during the Malayan Emergency. Mike Forsdike, *The Malayan Emergency: The Crucial Years 1949–52*, (Barnsley, England: Pen & Sword, 2022) 116–117.
68. An article on Ibans published by a Lieutenant of the 45 Royal Marine Commando. D. A. Oakley, "Ibans," *Globe and Laurel*, Vol. LVIII, No. 10 (October 1950): 260. Imperial War Museum archive, LBY E.5/125.

69. This article contains a wealth of descriptions of Iban in Malaya. P. J. Dixon, "Headhunters In Hospital," *The Spectator*, Vol. 189, No 6480 (September 5 1952): 293.
70. J.P. Cross, *Jungle Warfare: Experiences and Encounters*, (London: Guild Publishing, 1989) 157–158.
71. Interview with British officer Adrian Robert Evill of the 3rd Battalion of the King's African Rifles, 1987, Imperial War Museum Sound Archive, Accession No. 9854, reel 3. https://www.iwm.org.uk/collections/item/object/80009637 (accessed 30 June 2020).
72. Interview with British officer of the 1st Battalion of the Lincolnshire Regiment Darby Robert Follett Houlton-Hart, 1995, Imperial War Museum Sound Archive, Accession No. 15355, reel 3.
73. Donald Mackay, *The Malayan Emergency 1948–60: The Domino That Stood*, (London: Brassey's, 1997) 74.
74. Interview with British NCO Thomas Chadwick of the 1st Battalion of the King's Own Yorkshire Light Infantry, 1996, Imperial War Museum Sound Archive, Accession No. 16593, reel 18. https://www.iwm.org.uk/collections/item/object/80016061 (accessed 30 June 2022).
75. While on patrol in the jungles, Ibans in Malaya were often accompanied by a translator with the position of Junior Civilian Liaison Officer. The need for such translators made communication slow and difficult. H. D. Chaplin, *The Queen's Own Royal West Kent Regiment 1951–1961*, (Maidstone: Queen's Own Museum Committee, 1964) 26.
76. Eyewitness account of a British man who befriended an Iban during the Malayan Emergency. Adrian Walker, *Six Campaigns: National Servicemen on Active Service 1948–1960*, (London: Leo Cooper, 1993) 94.
77. An eyewitness account from a soldier in Kuala Lampur who spoke with Ibans who had refused to leave their camp after a bad dream. Adrian Walker, Ron Harper, Paul Riches, *A County Regiment: 1st Battalion of the Queen's Own Royal West Regiment Malaya 1951–1954*, (Brockley Press, 2001) 178.
78. Interview with former SAS soldier Arpad Bacskai, 2004, Australians at War Film Archive, Archive Number 2029, timestamp 27:32–29:00. https://australiansatwarfilmarchive.unsw.edu.au/archive/2029 (accessed 5 July 2022).
79. Private Kumpang Anak Tinngi was an Iban tracker who in October 1959 was killed in a friendly fire incident by a New Zealand military patrol led by Corporal Peter Rutledge during Operation BAMBOO. Christopher Pugsley, *From Emergency to Confrontation: The New Zealand Armed Forces in Malaya and Borneo 1949–1966*, (Victoria, Australia: Oxford University Press, 2003) 160.
80. On March 12, 1951, an unnamed Iban was shot dead near Ampang after allegedly being mistaken for a communist. Unknown, "Ipoh-Batu Gajah," *Commando News*, March 19, 1951.
81. Adrian Walker, *Six Campaigns: National Servicemen on Active Service 1948–1960*, (London: Leo Cooper, 1993) 73.
82. The special constable belonged to the 40 Royal Marine Commando. Robert Rizal Abdullah, *The Iban Trackers and the Sarawak Rangers 1948–1963*, (Kota Samarahan: UNIMAS, 2019) 30, 40.
83. Despite referring to headhunting in the titles to catch audience attention, the main body of these articles often claimed that the Ibans no longer practised headhunting.

84. Unknown, "Head-Hunters Prepare for Jungle War in Malaya," *The Evening Telegraph and Post*, August 11, 1948, 1. https://www.britishnewspaperarchive.co.uk/viewer/bl/0000563/19480811/001/0001 (accessed 25 October 2021).

85. Unknown, "Headhunters Train to Fight Terrorists," *Daily Mirror*, August 12, 1948, 1. https://www.britishnewspaperarchive.co.uk/viewer/bl/0000560/19480812/006/0001 (accessed 25 October 2021).

86. Unknown, "Head-Hunter Troops for Malaya," *Manchester Evening News*, August 7, 1948, 1. https://www.britishnewspaperarchive.co.uk/viewer/bl/0000272/19480807/011/0001 (accessed 25 October 2021).

87. Unknown, "Headhunters to Terrorise Terrorists," *Herald Express*, August 11, 1948, 1. https://www.britishnewspaperarchive.co.uk/viewer/bl/0001329/19480811/007/0001 (accessed 25 October 2021).

88. Unknown, "Headhunters After Terrorist Scalps," *Gloucestershire Echo*, August 11, 1948, 1. https://www.britishnewspaperarchive.co.uk/viewer/bl/0000320/19480811/020/0001 (accessed 25 October 2021).

89. Dickson Brown, "Head-Hunters Called in to Track Rebels," *News Chronicle*, August 12, 1948, 1. https://www.britishnewspaperarchive.co.uk/viewer/BL/0003214/19480812/089/0001?browse=true (accessed 25 October 2021).

90. C. K. K., "My Friends the Dyaks," *Evening Telegraph and Post*, August 18, 1948, 2. https://www.britishnewspaperarchive.co.uk/viewer/BL/0000563/19480818/019/0002?browse=true (accessed 25 October 2021).

91. Unknown, "Tuan, we Await Blowpipe," *The Press and Journal*, August 13, 1948, 1. https://www.britishnewspaperarchive.co.uk/viewer/bl/0000578/19480813/004/0001 (accessed 25 October 2021).

92. Unknown, "Dyaks bring death darts," *News Chronicle*, August 13, 1948, 1. https://www.britishnewspaperarchive.co.uk/viewer/bl/0003214/19480813/084/0001 (accessed 25 October 2021).

93. Outward telegram from Secretary of State for the Colonies Arthur Creech Jones to Sir Gerald Greasy the Governor of the Gold Coast, 24 November 1948, Oxford, Bodleian Libraries, Papers of Arthur Creech Jones, Box 26, File 9, MSS. Brit. Emp. s. 332. 9.

94. Federal Government Press Statement, March 16, 1952, National Archives, box CO 1022/57, File SEA 10/417/01, page 7.

95. Ritchie Calder, "Confused head-hunters," *News Chronicle*, August 14, 1948, 3. https://www.britishnewspaperarchive.co.uk/viewer/BL/0003214/19480814/050/0003?browse=true (accessed 25 October 2021).

96. Unknown, "A Use for Head-Hunters," *Truth*, August 20, 1948, 2. https://www.britishnewspaperarchive.co.uk/viewer/BL/0002961/19480820/004/0002?browse=true (accessed 25 October 2021).

97. Harry Willcox, "The Ibans Go Home," *Commando News*, January 15, 1951.

98. Unknown, "Tribesmen Want Guerrilla Scalps," *The Townsville Daily Bulletin*, February 16, 1951, 1. https://trove.nla.gov.au/newspaper/article/63138206 (accessed 9 October 2022).

99. Reuter Correspondent, "Descendants of Head-Hunters Fight in Malaya," *The Mercury*, February 17, 1951, 3. https://trove.nla.gov.au/newspaper/article/27023346 (accessed 9 October 2022).

100. Unknown, "This is the Dirtiest War in History," *The People*, March 18, 1951, 4. https://www.britishnewspaperarchive.co.uk/viewer/BL/0000729/19510318/096/0004?browse=true (accessed 25 October 2021).

101. Transcribed extract from *The People*, 18 March 1951, National Archives, box FCO 141/12403, file CSO S/142/2, page 125A.
102. Telegram from Acting Chief Secretary of Sarawak J. H. Ellis to Deputy Commissioner General for Colonial Affairs, Singapore, William Addis, 12 April 1951, National Archives, box FCO 141/12403, file CSO S/142/2, page 125.
103. Telegram from William Addis the Deputy Commissioner General for Colonial Affairs addressed to Acting Chief Secretary of Sarawak J. H. Ellis, 8 May 1951, National Archives, box FCO 141/12403, file CSO S/142/2, page 126.
104. Peter Munn, "With the Green Howards in Malaya," *The Yorkshire Post and Leeds Mercury*, December 19, 1951, 2. https://www.britishnewspaperarchive.co.uk/viewer/bl/0000687/19511219/035/0002# (accessed 25 October 2021).
105. Harry Pollitt, *Malaya: Stop the War!* (London: Communist Party of Great Britain, January 1952) 3.
106. Comparisons between Nazi atrocities throughout Europe and British colonial atrocities in Malaya are a common theme throughout literature published by British communist activists, most notably by Harry Pollitt, J.R. Campbell, and Rajani Palme Dutt. Cited here is an example. R. Palme Dutt, *The Crisis of Britain and the British Empire*, (London: Lawrence & Wishart LTD, 1953) 10.
107. The title of Randall Swingler's poem is The Ballad of Herod Templer which was written in 1952. Andy Croft, *Comrade Heart: A Life of Randall Swingler*, (Manchester: Manchester University Press, 2003) 217.
108. The full version of the poem can be found here. Randall Swingler, *Randall Swingler: Selected Poems*, ed. Andy Croft, (Nottingham: Trent Editions, 2000) 93–94.
109. This article by the *Daily Worker* exposing British headhunting in Burma was published on 17 June 1931. Thomas R. Mockaitis, *British counterinsurgency 1919–1960* (London: The Macmillan Press LTD, 1990) 39.
110. The author cites a letter from Churchill to Sir Orme Sargent, 31 October 1947, cited as from FO371/67010, R14857, UK National Archives. Gioula Koutsopanagou, *The British Press and the Greek Crisis, 1943–1949: Orchestrating the Cold-War 'Consensus' in Britain*, (London: Palgrave Macmillan, 2020) 263.

Chapter 1
1. One example is *Globe and Laurel*, the official journal of the Royal Marines.
2. Editor, "This is the War in Malaya," *Daily Worker*, April 28, 1952, 1.
3. The original photographs obtained by the *Daily Worker* were higher quality images than the versions published in the *Daily Worker*, hence why some of the finer details of the photographs not visible to the readers are explained in the article's text. Higher quality copies of future headhunting photographs were sent to British government officials by J. R. Campbell and were preserved by the National Archives in boxes CO1022/45 and FO 371/101228.
4. The article incorrectly identified the base near Kuala Kangsar as being located near "Kuala Kesan" and corrected this mistake in a later issue. Soldiers often called the base "K.K.".
5. Lieutenant James Barry Coop and Corporal Raymond T. Ryder both belonged to the Royal Marine Commando 40 and were killed on the 2nd April 1951. Both are buried in Kamunting Road Christian Cemetery, Perak.
6. Memorandum by the First Lord of the Admiralty delivered to Winston Churchill's Cabinet concerning the *Daily Worker* photograph, 2 May 1952, National Archives,

CAB 129/52/42, file C(52) 142. Internet Archive Wayback Machine: https://web.archive.org/web/20220217124729/https://discovery.nationalarchives.gov.uk/details/r/D7656624 (Accessed 17 February 2022).
7. Makram Khoury-Machool, "Kidnap Videos: Setting the Power Relations of New Media," in *Communicating War: Memory, Media and Military*, ed. Sarah Maltby & Richard Keeble, (Suffolk: Arima Publishing, 2007) 164.
8. Thomas Probert, "The Impact of Participating in British Counterinsurgency Campaigns on British Armed Forces Personnel: The Malayan Emergency as a Case-Study," PhD Dissertation (The Open University, 2020) 147.
9. Correspondent, "A gruesome picture," *The Yorkshire Post and Leeds Mercury*, April 29, 1952, 4. https://www.britishnewspaperarchive.co.uk/viewer/BL/0000687/19520429/080/0004?browse=true (accessed 25 October 2021).
10. *Daily Worker* Reporter, "Pictures Muddle Whitehall," *Daily Worker*, May 1, 1952, 1.
11. William Sternberg, "An 'atrocity' picture: Whitehall inquiries," *Yorkshire Evening Post*, April 28, 1952, 1. https://www.britishnewspaperarchive.co.uk/viewer/BL/0000273/19520428/006/0001?browse=true (accessed 25 October 2021).
12. Colonial Office correspondence from T. C. Jerrom to Mr Higham confirming the Admiralty's investigation of the *Daily Worker*'s 28th April decapitation photograph, 29 April 1952, National Archives, box CO1022/45, file SEA 10/162/02, page 3.
13. Draft paper for Churchill's Cabinet titled "*Daily Worker*" photograph of Marine holding the severed head of a Bandit Draft Paper for Cabinet", 2 May 1952, National Archives, ADM 1/25861, file ADM 149/52.
14. Examples include FCO 141/12403, CO 1022/45, and FO 371/101228 in the UK National Archives, and the Papers of Arthur Creech Jones, Box 26, File 9, MSS. Brit. Emp. s. 332. 9, in Oxford's Bodleian library.
15. This research contains many examples. Thomas Probert, "The Impact of Participating in British Counterinsurgency Campaigns on British Armed Forces Personnel: The Malayan Emergency as a Case-Study," PhD Dissertation (The Open University, 2020) 148.
16. Minutes of a meeting held on the 30 April to discuss "'*Daily Worker*' photograph of Marine holding the severed head of a bandit", 1 May 1952, National Archives, ADM 1/25861, file ADM 149/52.
17. Minutes of a meeting held on the 30 April to discuss "'*Daily Worker*' photograph of Marine holding the severed head of a bandit", 1 May 1952, National Archives, ADM 1/25861, file ADM 149/52.
18. Minutes of a meeting held on the 30 April to discuss "'*Daily Worker*' photograph of Marine holding the severed head of a bandit", 1 May 1952, National Archives, ADM 1/25861, file ADM 149/52.

Chapter 2

1. Frank Gullett, "These are no Fakes: How head-hunting photographs came to *Daily Worker*," *Daily Worker*, April 30, 1952, 1.
2. *Daily Worker* Reporter, "The Wild Men of Borneo," *Daily Worker*, April 30, 1952, 1.
3. The image published in 1952 the *Daily Worker* of Malcolm McDonald with headhunters was cropped to save space on the frontpage. A full version of the image was republished here. Gladys Brooks, editor, "The Terror Begins," *Comment: A Communist Weekly Review* 8, no.7 (February 14 1970): 105.

Notes 119

4. Malcolm MacDonald later wrote a book titled Borneo People in which he recorded his experiences with the Iban people. Malcolm MacDonald, *Borneo People*, (London: Jonathan Cape, 1956).
5. Clyde Sanger, *Malcolm MacDonald: Bringing an End to Empire* (London: McGill-Queen's University Press, 1995) 323.
6. Clyde Sanger, *Malcolm MacDonald: Bringing an End to Empire* (London: McGill-Queen's University Press, 1995) 324.
7. According to Lieutenant Colonel Rizal Robert Abdullah of the Sarawak Rangers, the 17 year old Iban boy who led the first batch of Iban recruits to Malaya was called Penghulu (headman) Jinggut. Robert Rizal Abdullah, *The Iban Trackers and the Sarawak Rangers 1948–1963*, (Kota Samarahan: UNIMAS, 2019) 53.
8. F. A Godfrey, *The History of the Suffolk Regiment 1946–1959*, (London: Leo Cooper Ltd, 1988) 72.
9. Colonial Office memorandum by T. C. Jerrom recording the opinions of British agents on the legality of decapitating anti-colonial fighters in Malaya, 30 April 1952, National Archives, box CO 1022/45, file SEA 10/162/02, page 4.
10. Thomas Barfield, *War Photography: Images of Conflict from Frontline Photographers* (Bath: Magpie Books, 2006) 246.
11. This page contains the eyewitness testimony of a soldier called M. Engel and his experience of carrying a severed head and two hands after a combined military operation. Brian Stewart, *Smashing Terrorism in Malayan Emergency: The Vital Contribution of the Police Force*, (Subang Jaya, Malaysia: Pelanduk Publications, 2004) 24.
12. Hutton's written statement was read aloud at Fulham Town Hall by chairman Sir Gerald Hargreaves. *Daily Worker* Reporter, "Not for this-Z man shows that picture," *Daily Worker*, April 30, 1952, 1.
13. Editor, "'It happens all the time-I saw worse'," *Daily Worker*, May 3, 1952, 1.
14. Editor, "'It happens all the time-I saw worse'," *Daily Worker*, May 3, 1952, 1.
15. Fabian Klose attributes the practice of the beheading of corpses by Gurkhas in Malaya as "excessive force", citing John Springhall. Fabian Klose, *Human Rights in the Shadow of Colonial Violence: The Wars of Independence in Kenya and Algeria*, (Philadelphia: University of Pennsylvania Press, 2013) 60.
16. John Springhall, *Decolonization since 1945: The Collapse of European Overseas Empires*, (Basingstoke: Palgrave, 2001) 55.
17. Extract from a letter from the British embassy in Nepal, 12 June 1952, National Archives, box CO1022/45, file SEA 10/162/02, page 50.
18. Paul Richards, *Better a Friend than Foe: Life with the Gurkhas*, (London: Austin Macauley Publishers, 2014) 99.
19. In one example journalist Neal Ascherson who was conscripted to fight for the 42 RM commando also says that headhunting was standard practice. Christopher Hale, *Massacre in Malaya: Exposing Britain's My Lai* (Stroud: The History Press, 2013) 360.
20. Photographs of mock wooden heads made by the Suffolk Regiment can be seen here. Mike Forsdike, *The Malayan Emergency: The Crucial Years 1949–52*, (Barnsley, England: Pen & Sword, 2022) 99.
21. Herbert Andrew, *Who Won the Malayan Emergency?* (Singapore: Graham Brash, 1995) 46.
22. Adrian Walker, *Six Campaigns: National Servicemen on Active Service 1948–1960*, (London: Leo Cooper, 1993) 57–58.

23. Two famous examples of British soldiers who became socialists and anti-imperialist activists after witnessing British atrocities in Malaya include the journalist and former 42 Royal Marine Commando veteran Neil Ascherson, and the socialist activist and Coldstream Guards veteran Walter Heaton.
24. One example is included within this work. James Edmiston, *The Sterling Years: Small-arms and the Men*, (London: Leo Cooper, 1992) 23.
25. Editor, "It happens all the time-I saw worse'," *Daily Worker*, May 3, 1952, 1.
26. Editor, "It happens all the time-I saw worse'," *Daily Worker*, May 3, 1952, 1.
27. Unknown, "Our Malaya leaflet-have you ordered?," *Daily Worker*, May 6, 1952, 3.
28. Leaflet written by the *Daily Worker*'s editor titled Stop This War! and published by the People's Printing Press Society, 1952, Working Class Movement Library, box 1 Colonies, subs/colonies.
29. *Daily Worker* Reporter, "Severed heads: We ask three questions," *Daily Worker*, May 6, 1952, 1.
30. Letter from First Lord of the Admiralty J. P. L. Thomas to Prime Minister Winston Churchill discussing Britain's use of decapitations in Malaya, 1 May 1952, National Archives, box CO1022/45, file SEA 10/162/02, pages 109–110.
31. Draft of a press statement on the decapitations in Malaya presented by the First Lord of the Admiralty J. P. L. Thomas to Winston Churchill, 1 May 1952, National Archives, box CO1022/45, file SEA 10/162/02, pages 111–112.
32. One such example was MP Tom Driberg who used his political position to raise the alarm over the conditions of British internment camps in Malaya. R. Palme Dutt, *The Crisis of Britain and the British Empire*, (London: Lawrence & Wishart LTD, 1953) 113.
33. The photograph of Oliver Lyttelton and an Iban taken in December 1951 can be found here. Mike Forsdike, *The Malayan Emergency: The Crucial Years 1949–52*, (Barnsley, England: Pen & Sword, 2022) 184.
34. Oliver Lyttelton telegram to Gerald Templer asking for clarification on his soldier's use of decapitations, 2 May 1952, National Archives, box CO1022/45, file SEA 10/162/02, page 102.
35. The details of Templer's short stay in the jungle can be found within his biography. John Cloake, *Templer Tiger of Malaya: The Life of Field Marshal Sir Gerald Templer*, (London: Harrap, 1985) 242.
36. Gerald Templer's telegram to Oliver Lyttelton elaborating on the use of decapitations against MNLA members, 6 May 1952, National Archives, box CO1022/45, file SEA 10/162/02, page 95.
37. Weekly intelligence summary containing message by an anonymous author sent to the Gurkha Rifles containing joking suggestions for the treatment of decapitated heads and hands, 1950, National Archives, co 717/198/2, file 52849/8/4 Pt II, page 241.
38. Envelope from a photo studio in Ipoh, Malaya, containing the negative of a photograph depicting soldiers posing with a corpse, 2013-08-09, Imperial War Museum.
39. Information taken from Templer's private papers. Karl Hack, *The Malayan Emergency: Revolution and Counterinsurgency at the End of Empire*, (Cambridge: Cambridge University Press, 2022) 317.
40. A photograph of this incident can be found here. Mike Forsdike, *The Malayan Emergency: The Crucial Years 1949–52*, (Barnsley, England: Pen & Sword, 2022) 62, 131.

41. Conclusion of a meeting of Winston Churchill's Cabinet, 6 May 1952, National Archives, CAB 128/24/49, file CC (52) 49. Internet Archive Wayback Machine: https://web.archive.org/web/20220217124511/https://discovery.nationalarchives.gov.uk/details/r/D7663503 (Accessed 17 February 2022).
42. The Secretary of State for War Antony Head argued that General Templer should be allowed to continue the headhunting policy. Internet Archive Wayback Machine: https://web.archive.org/web/20211215045457/https://cdn.nationalarchives.gov.uk/documents/transcript-cab195-10.pdf (Accessed 15 December 2021).
43. Karl Hack, *The Malayan Emergency: Revolution and Counterinsurgency at the End of Empire*, (Cambridge: Cambridge University Press, 2022) 318.
44. Minutes of a Cabinet meeting discussion of the *Daily Worker* photographs, 6 May 1952, National Archives, CAB 195/10/63, pages 229–230. Internet Archive Wayback Machine: https://web.archive.org/web/20211215045457/https://cdn.nationalarchives.gov.uk/documents/transcript-cab195-10.pdf (Accessed 15 December 2021).
45. RAF memorandum on the "identification of killed bandits", 10 May 1952, National Archives, AIR 20/8926, file IIJ53/16/2/15 Part 2, page 28.
46. Unknown, "Decapitated Bandit in Malaya: Action of a Tracker," *The Manchester Guardian*, May 8, 1952, 9.
47. Malaya (Decapitation), House of Commons debate, 7 May 1952. Hansard Parliamentary Debates Volume 500: House of Commons Official Report (London: Her Majesty's Stationary Office, 1952) 388. Internet Archive Wayback Machine: https://web.archive.org/web/20211214024249/https://hansard.parliament.uk/Commons/1952-05-07/debates/aca7f25e-9c4b-448d-8a72-619a23cda44f/Malaya%28Decapitation%29
48. Gertrude Carling, "Letters to the Editor: Modern Warfare," *Socialist Leader*, May 31, 1952, 7.
49. Crop Destruction, House of Commons debate, 23 April 1952. Hansard Parliamentary Debates Volume 499: House of Commons Official Report (London: Her Majesty's Stationary Office, 1952) 394–395. Internet Archive Wayback Machine: https://web.archive.org/web/20211214024128/https://hansard.parliament.uk/Commons/1952-04-23/debates/292934e5-63c7-4ed6-85a3-b9665ae95581/CropDestruction
50. Jungle Defoliation, House of Commons debate, 23 April 1952. Hansard Parliamentary Debates Volume 499: House of Commons Official Report (London: Her Majesty's Stationary Office, 1952), 395–396. Internet Archive Wayback Machine: https://web.archive.org/web/20211214024448/https://hansard.parliament.uk/Commons/1952-04-23/debates/353f7e98-81f3-4b39-8738-ebd42bd7074e/JungleDefoliation
51. Collective Punishments (Children), House of Commons debate, 28 May 1952. Hansard Parliamentary Debates Volume 501: House of Commons Official Report (London: Her Majesty's Stationary Office, 1952), 1345–1347. Internet Archive Wayback Machine: https://web.archive.org/web/20211214013028/https://hansard.parliament.uk/Commons/1952-05-28/debates/cdca4496-e7ec-47d4-b6ca-199540cbe403/CollectivePunishments(Children)
52. Malaya (Anti-Terrorist Measures), House of Commons Debate, 2 April 1952. Hansard Parliamentary Debates Volume 498: House of Commons Official Report (London: Her Majesty's Stationary Office, 1952), 1668–1671. Internet Archive

Wayback Machine: https://web.archive.org/web/20211214024605/https://hansard.parliament.uk/Commons/1952-04-02/debates/5a25f6a5-1b30-4331-b5f5-e4f9f27df315/Malaya%28Anti-TerroristMeasures%29

53. Malcolm MacEwen, "Govt. Admits Malaya Atrocity, *Daily Worker* Pictures Genuine: Lyttelton," *Daily Worker*, May 8, 1952, 1.
54. *Daily Worker* Reporter, "No isolated incident," *Daily Worker*, May 8, 1952, 1.
55. Editor, "Call to Churchill: 'Stop atrocities'," *Daily Worker*. May 9, 1952, 1
56. Message from J.R. Campbell to Winston Churchill protesting against British headhunting atrocities in Malaya, 8 May 1952, National Archives, box CO 1022/45, file SEA 10/162/02, page 81.
57. Message from J.R. Campbell to Anthony Eden with three atrocity photographs attached, 8 May 1952, National Archives, box FO 371/101228, file FZ10110/62.
58. Message from J.R. Campbell to Oliver Lyttelton with three atrocity photographs, 8 May 1952, National Archives, box CO 1022/45, file SEA 10/162/02, page 78.

Chapter 3

1. Editor, "This Horror Must End: You must compel peace," *Daily Worker*, May 10, 1952, 1.
2. Kevin Rooney and James Heartfield, *The Blood-Stained Poppy*, (Winchester: Zero Books, 2019) 125.
3. Piers Brendon, *The Decline and Fall of the British Empire 1781–1997* (London: Vintage, 2008) 457.
4. Robert Clough, *Labour: A Party Fit For Imperialism*, (London: Larkin Publications, 1992) 75.
5. Chin Peng, *My Side of History* (Singapore: Media Masters, 2013) 303.
6. James Heartfield, *An Unpatriotic History of the Second World War*, (Winchester: Zero Books, 2012) 350.
7. Aly Renwick, "Problems on Civvy Street," VFPUK, August 10, 2021. Internet Archive Wayback Machine: https://web.archive.org/web/20220125161924/https://vfpuk.org/posts/problems-in-civvy-street-by-aly-renwick/
8. The infamous image published by the *Daily Worker* on May 10 1952 showing a Royal Marine holding two decapitated heads, is easily the most iconic and widely recognised photograph from the entire war. It has also appeared in multiple documentaries, including the BBC's *Malaya: The Undeclared War* (1998), episode 5 of Channel 4's documentary series *Empire's Children* (2007), Kek-huat Lau's documentary *Absent Without Leave* (2016), and Mic Dixon's documentary *War School* (2019), to name a few examples.
9. Jin Zhimang 1912–1988 (given name Chen Shuyang) wrote the novel *Hunger* which according to scholars of Chinese studies was "based on an incident that occurred in April 1952, when British Marines were photographed holding the decapitated heads of two MCP insurgents." Chong Fah Hing and Kyle Shernuk, "Hunger and the Chinese Malaysian Leftist Narrative" in *A New Literary History of Modern China*, ed. David Der-Wei Wang, (London: The Belknap Press of Harvard University Press, 2017) 635–640.
10. Message by T. C. Jerrom to Mr Higham discussing fears of the anti-colonial propaganda value that the *Daily Worker* photographs possess, 12 May 1952, National Archives, box CO 1022/45, file SEA 10/162/02, page 9.

11. Thomas R. Mockaitis, *British counterinsurgency, 1919–1960* (London: The Macmillan Press LTD, 1990) 53.
12. Malaya (Decapitation of Corpses), House of Commons debate, 21 May 1952. Hansard Parliamentary Debates Volume 501: House of Commons Official Report (London: Her Majesty's Stationary Office, 1952) 460. Internet Archive Wayback Machine: https://web.archive.org/web/20211214024715/https://hansard.parliament.uk/Commons/1952-05-21/debates/4c22333c-0243-4d10-8445-e1e75571b48a/Malaya%28DecapitationOfCorpses
13. These pages contain accounts of an experimental Iban platoon fighting MNLA guerrillas. Len Spicer, *The Suffolks in Malaya* (Peterborough: Lawson Phelps Publishing, 1998) 119–120.
14. Telegraph by Gerald Templer confirming that a Malayan newspapers leaked classified info about the upcoming creation of a regiment of Ibans, 22 May 1952, National Archives, box CO1022/45, file SEA 10/162/02, page 69.
15. Telegram by Secretary of State for the Colonies Oliver Lyttelton to Gerald Templer expressing concerns unfortunate timing considering the daily worker headhunting articles in relation to the creation of the Sarawak Rangers, 23 May 1952, CO 1022-45, page 68.
16. An account of their visit along with photographs can be found here. H. D. Chaplin, *The Queen's Own Royal West Kent Regiment 1951–1961*, (Maidstone: Queen's Own Museum Committee, 1964) 40.
17. The Duke and Duchess of Kent met with Iban mercenaries attached to the 1st Battalion of the Royal West Kent Regiment. Reuter, "Bandit Killed on Royal Route: Parade in the Jungle," *The Manchester Guardian*, October 8, 1952, 5.
18. Editor, "Dirty War Exposed: Malaya Folder," *Daily Worker*, May 24, 1952, 3.
19. Leaflet written by the *Daily Worker*'s editor titled Stop This Horror in Malaya! and published by the *Daily Worker* Cooperative Society, 1952, Working Class Movement Library, SLING/FAREAST/6.
20. Harry Pollitt, "We Cannot Plead Ignorance: Act to Restore Britain's Honour," *Daily Worker*, June 14, 1952, 2.
21. Letter written by Henry Brooke to Oliver Lyttelton concerning Harry Pollitt's article in the *Daily Worker* containing an atrocity photograph from Malaya, 23 June 1952, National Archives, box CO1022/45, file SEA 10/162/02, page 53.
22. John Chynoweth, *Hunting Terrorists in the Jungle*, (Stroud: Tempus Publishing Limited, 2005) 120.
23. The account of his time in Malaya can be found here. Adrian Walker, *Six Campaigns: National Servicemen on Active Service 1948–1960*, (London: Leo Cooper, 1993) 54–60.
24. The Channel 4 documentary series that he was being interviewed for was "Empire's Children", aired in 2007. His response was published within a companion book to the series which was also titled Empire's Children. Anton Gill, *Empire's Children: Tracing Your Family History Across the World*, (London: Harper Press, 2007) 144.
25. Interview with British officer John Quinton Adams of the 1st Battalion of the South Wales Borderers, 1987, Imperial War Museum Sound Archive, Accession No. 9707, reel 1. https://www.iwm.org.uk/collections/item/object/80009493 (accessed 30 June 2022).
26. Interview with NCO Jim O'Neill of the 1st Battalion of the Royal Inniskilling Fusiliers, 2009, Imperial War Museum Sound Archive, Accession No. 32388, reel 7. https://www.iwm.org.uk/collections/item/object/80031209 (accessed 30 June 2022).

124   Head Hunters in the Malayan Emergency

27. Transcript of an interview with Private Ron Harper of the Queen's Royal Regiment who fought in Malaya between 1954–1957, The Queen's Royal Surrey Regimental Association. https://web.archive.org/web/20220724025524/https://www.queensroyalsurreys.org.uk/video/07_1945to59/ron_harper_02_03-trans.html (accessed July 24, 2022).
28. Ian Pfennigwerth, *Tiger Territory: The Untold Story of the Royal Australian Navy from 1948 to 1971*, (Dural, New South Whales: Rosenberg Publishing, 2008) 306.
29. According to the author, this incident happened in Borneo in 1964 sometime between January and May. Nick Van Der Bijl, *Confrontation: The War with Indonesia 1962–1966*, (Barnsley: Pen & Sword, 2014) 118.
30. John MacKinnon, *In Search of the Red Ape*, (London: William Collins Sons & Co Ltd, 1974) 27–28.
31. The caption reads "THE SERVICE OF ABLE SEAMAN RICHARD GLEED-OWEN ON BOARD THE MINESWEEPER HMS WILKIESTON DURING THE INDONESIAN CRISIS, 1963 – 1965. A British soldier holds aloft the severed head of an Indonesian infiltrator killed by native scouts (and decapitated by them). Date and location unknown." Photograph taken by Richard Gleed-Owen, unknown date between 1963–1965, HU 70290, Gleed-Owen Collection, Imperial War Museum, London.
32. Author cites Roy Davis Linville Jumper. Ong Weichong, *Malaysia's Defeat of Armed Communism: The Second Emergency, 1968–89*, (Abingdon: Routledge, 2015)
33. Roy Davis Linville Jumper, *Death Waits in the Dark: The Senoi Praaq, Malaysia's Killer Elite*, (London: Greenwood Press, 2001) 169.
34. David French, *The British Way in Counter-Insurgency 1945–1967* (Oxford: Oxford University Press, 2011) 153
35. Shiraz Durrani, *Never Be Silent: Publishing & Imperialism in Kenya 1884–1963*, (London: Vita Books, 2006) 103.
36. Peter Worsley, *An Academic Skating on Thin Ice*, (Berghahn Books, 2008) 120.
37. Douglas Porch, *Counterinsurgency: Exposing the Myths of the New Way of War*, (Cambridge: Cambridge University Press, 2013) 260.

Chapter 4

1. *Daily Worker* Reporter, "Malaya head-hunt 'barbaric'," *Daily Worker*, April 29, 1952, 1.
2. Maria Creech, "All Too Graphic," *History Today* 71, no. 12 (December 2021). Internet Archive Wayback Machine: https://web.archive.org/web/20220912184412/https://www.historytoday.com/archive/history-matters/all-too-graphic
3. *Daily Worker* Reporter, "Pictures Muddle Whitehall," *Daily Worker*, May 1, 1952, 1.
4. Forum, "The Rich Men's War," *Daily Worker*, May 2, 1952, 2.
5. Message from a branch secretary of the Electrical Trades Union in Southend to the First Lord of the Admiralty demanding an investigation into the incidents depicted in the *Daily Worker* headhunting photographs, 2 May 1952, National Archives, ADM 1/25861, file ADM 149/52.
6. *Daily Worker* Reporter, "Shame and Disgrace: Malaya protests from factories," *Daily Worker*, May 9, 1952, 1.
7. *Daily Worker* Reporter, "Malaya Major Boosts Head-Hunters: Not for Identification'," *Daily Worker*, May 12, 1952, 1.

8. Mark Metcalf, "Betty Tebbs – A radical working class hero," Unite the Union, 2019, 24. Internet Archive Wayback Machine: https://web.archive.org/web/20201125154714/https://markwritecouk.files.wordpress.com/2020/02/6328-betty-tebbs-web.pdf
9. Maureen Shaw & Helen D. Millgate, *War's Forgotten Women: British Widows of the Second World War*, (Stroud: The History Press, 2011) 141.
10. *Daily Worker* Reporter, "'Disgrace on our troops in Malaya'," *Daily Worker*, May 9, 1952, 3.
11. *Daily Worker* Reporter, "Shame and Disgrace: Malaya protests from factories," *Daily Worker*, May 9, 1952, 1.
12. Caroline Elkins, *Legacy of Violence: A History of the British Empire*, (London: The Bodley Head, 2022) 529–530.
13. Peter Fryer, "The Ghastly Kenya Story," *Daily Worker*, December 12, 1953, 1.
14. A full account of Arthur Clegg's fight against Japanese imperialism can be found within his memoir *Aid China*.
15. George Matthews, "Obituary: Arthur Clegg," *Independent*, February 16, 1994. Internet Archive Wayback Machine: https://web.archive.org/web/20211214012015/https://www.independent.co.uk/news/people/obituary-arthur-clegg-1394476.html
16. Arthur Clegg, "Hunted, Murdered, Beheaded for daring to Strike: Tolpuddle Martyrs of Today," *Daily Worker*, May 12, 1952, 2.
17. *Daily Worker* Reporter, "Blood Stains Malaya Profits: Demonstrators Raid Shareholders," *Daily Worker*, June 10, 1952, 1.
18. Susan L. Carruthers, *Winning Hearts and Minds: British Governments, the Media and Colonial Counter-insurgency 1944–1960* (London: Leicester University Press, 1995) 110.
19. Wendy Webster, *Englishness and Empire 1939–1965*, (Oxford: Oxford University Press, 2005) 127.
20. Caroline Elkins, *Legacy of Violence: A History of the British Empire*, (London: The Bodley Head, 2022) 530.
21. Erik Linstrum, "Facts About Atrocity: Reporting Colonial Violence in Postwar Britain," *History Workshop Journal* 84 (Autumn 2017): 9. https://doi.org/10.1093/hwj/dbx032
22. Caroline Elkins, *Legacy of Violence: A History of the British Empire*, (London: The Bodley Head, 2022) 532.
23. H. D. Chaplin, *The Queen's Own Royal West Kent Regiment 1951–1961*, (Maidstone: Queen's Own Museum Committee, 1964) 41.
24. Ernie Trory, *Peace and the Cold War Part Two: The Crucial Years: 1952–60*, (Exeter: Crabtree Press, 1998) 19.
25. The script for this play can be found within the following book. Mona Brand, and Lesley Richardson, *Two Plays About Malaya* (London: Lawrence and Wishart LTD, 1954).
26. Erik Linstrum, "Facts About Atrocity: Reporting Colonial Violence in Postwar Britain," *History Workshop Journal* 84 (Autumn 2017): 4. https://doi.org/10.1093/hwj/dbx032
27. Alan Winnington, *I Saw the Truth in Korea* (London: People's Press Printing Society, 1950).
28. Winnington's eyewitness account of the discovery of the mass graves and his comments on the Labour Party's discussions of whether to have him hanged for treason, can be found in Winnington's posthumously published autobiography,

Breakfast with Mao. Alan Winnington, *Breakfast with Mao: Memoirs of a Foreign Correspondent* (London: Lawrence & Wishart, 1986) 113–117.
29. Caroline Elkins, *Legacy of Violence: A History of the British Empire*, (London: The Bodley Head, 2022) 531.
30. *Daily Worker* Special Correspondent, "Malaya Aroused by Massacre: Unarmed Workers were shot down in cold blood," *Daily Worker*, 4 January, 1949, 1.
31. See this book for a short description of how the *Daily Worker* reported on the Batang Kali massacre. Ian Ward and Norma Miraflor, *Slaughter and Deception at Batang Kali*, Singapore: Media Masters, 2008) 61–63.
32. Ian Ward and Norma Miraflor, *Slaughter and Deception at Batang Kali, Singapore*: Media Masters, 2008) 109.
33. Erik Linstrum, "Facts About Atrocity: Reporting Colonial Violence in Postwar Britain," *History Workshop Journal 84* (Autumn 2017): 4. https://doi.org/10.1093/hwj/dbx032
34. The CPGB both initiated and helped to maintain many anti-colonial and solidarity campaigns throughout Asia and Africa. A short list of key examples can be found here. Dave Cope, *Bibliography of the Communist Party of Great Britain*, (London: Lawrence & Wishart, 2016) 14–15.
35. James Hughes, *Chechnya: From Nationalism to Jihad*, (Philadelphia: University of Pennsylvania Press, 2007) 116.
36. The Morning Star article was released on the 3 January 1983 and was written by Chris Myant. *Ernie Trory, Peace and the Cold War Part Two: The Crucial Years: 1952–60*, (Exeter: Crabtree Press, 1998) 19–20.
37. Editor Mark Howe, *Is That Damned Paper Still Coming Out? The very best of the Daily Worker/Morning Star* 1930–2000 (London: People's Press Printing Society, 2001) 129–135.
38. Jon Swain, "The Telling Shots of War," *The Sunday Times*, January 23, 2005, 15.
39. A. T. Williams, *A Very British Killing: The Death of Baha Mousa*, (London: Jonathan Cape, 2012) 174–175.
40. According to Charles B. McLane, the decapitation photographs were published in Pravda on the 4th page of the 17th June 1952 issue. Charles B. McLane, *Soviet Strategies in Southeast Asia: An Exploration of Eastern Policy under Lenin and Stalin* (New Jersey: Princeton University Press, 1966) 397.
41. K. C. Chang, "Terror fails to bring a British victory: Malaya Fights Back," *China Monthly Review* (1950–1953), September 1, 1952, 268–273.
42. Unknown, "Against the "Dirty War" in Malaya," *New Times* (Trud), July 2, 1952, 15.
43. Message from Mr Lamb to the Foreign Office informing of Chinese media interests in Malaya that the Shanghai edition of the "Takungpao" on the 2nd June published British decapitation photographs from Malaya, 21 June 1952, National Archives, box FO 371/101228, file FZ 10110/65.
44. Message from British embassy in Peking informing the UK Foreign Office that Shanghai's "Ta Kung Pao" on the 2nd June had published two photographs "similar" to those published by the *Daily Worker*, 16 June 1952, National Archives, box FO 371/101228, file FZ 10110/70.
45. Glen Peterson, *Overseas Chinese in the People's Republic of China*, (Abingdon: Routledge, 2012) 113.
46. P.T.I. Reuter, "Malayan Red Terrorist: No Decapitation of Those Killed, The Times of India", May 9, 1952, 4.

47. Unknown, "Cutting Off Heads of Red Guerrillas Declared Taboo," *The Washington Post*, May 9, 1952, 4.
48. John Pittman, "Of Things to Come," The *Daily Worker* (USA), August 6, 1952, 4.
49. Unknown, "*Daily Worker* Prints Picture of Severed Head," *Singapore Standard*, April 29, 1952, 1. https://eresources.nlb.gov.sg/newspapers/Digitised/Article/singstandard19520429-1.2.4 (accessed 11 July 2022).
50. London Correspondent, "Lyttelton Clarifies *Daily Worker* Photos," *Singapore Standard*, May 8, 1952, 1. https://eresources.nlb.gov.sg/newspapers/Digitised/Article/singstandard19520508-1.2.18 (accessed 11 July 2022).
51. Unknown, "Mr. Lyttelton Explains That Severed Head," *Singapore Standard*, May 9, 1952, 7. https://eresources.nlb.gov.sg/newspapers/Digitised/Article/singstandard19520509-1.2.89 (accessed 11 July 2022).
52. Unknown, "The Head: Against Orders," *The Singapore Free Press*, May 8, 1952, 1. https://eresources.nlb.gov.sg/newspapers/Digitised/Article/freepress19520508-1.2.10 (accessed 11 July 2022).
53. Unknown, "Heads of bandits not to be cut off-Templer," *The Straits Times*, May 9, 1952, 7. https://eresources.nlb.gov.sg/newspapers/Digitised/Article/straitstimes19520509-1.2.109 (accessed 11 July 2022).
54. One example of the Straits Times publishing misinformation was through fake news reports claiming that Chin Peng had been replaced by a spy from the People's Republic of China. Chin Peng, *My Side of History* (Singapore: Media Masters, 2013) 314.

Chapter 5
1. Karl Hack, *The Malayan Emergency: Revolution and Counterinsurgency at the End of Empire*, (Cambridge: Cambridge University Press, 2022) 316.
2. There exist three separate accounts given by British soldiers of the killing and beheading of a man who is most likely Hen Yan, all of which were created by the British Army's Suffolk Regiment and describe the killing and beheading of a communist leader in April 1952. These include one recorded interview the Imperial War Museum, a personal diary, and a military intelligence diary.
3. Interview with British officer of the Suffolk Regiment James Patrick Macdonald, 1997, Imperial War Museum Sound Archive, Accession No. 17423, reel 1.
4. Diary of British officer James Patrick Macdonald of the British Army's Suffolk Regiment, entry on April 23 1952, documents 7805, Private Papers of Colonel J P Macdonald, Box 98/23/1, Imperial War Museum, London.
5. War diary belonging to a soldier of the Suffolk Regiment, 17 April 1952 – 5 January 1953, Suffolk Archives (Bury St Edmunds), GB554/B/2/10.
6. The author claims that Hen Yang, whom the author spells "Heng Yan", used the alias Foh Kwai and was a Branch Committee Member for the MNLA in Sungei Tingi before being killed near Sungei Beruang by the Suffolk Regiment's 4 platoon of B company commanded by a Major Dewar. Len Spicer, *The Suffolks in Malaya*, (Peterborough: Lawson Phelps Publishing, 1998) 93.
7. Many news articles often spell his name as either "Lim Tian Swui" or "Lim Tian Swee".
8. Karl Hack, *The Malayan Emergency: Revolution and Counterinsurgency at the End of Empire*, (Cambridge: Cambridge University Press, 2022) 125.

9. For a detailed examination of the Batang Kali Massacre and the investigations onto the massacre, see the following book. Ian Ward and Norma Miraflor, *Slaughter and Deception at Batang Kali, Singapore*: Media Masters, 2008)
10. The term "communist terrorist" or C.T was the official term used by the British government and military since 1952 to dehumanise Malayans that resisted British colonialism. Karl Hack, *The Malayan Emergency: Revolution and Counterinsurgency at the End of Empire*, (Cambridge: Cambridge University Press, 2022) 2.
11. Terri Judd, "High Court once again rejects investigation into Batang Kali 'massacre' during Malayan Emergency," *The Independent*, 4 September, 2012. Internet Archive Wayback Machine: https://web.archive.org/web/20211214011653/https://www.independent.co.uk/news/uk/crime/high-court-once-again-rejects-investigation-into-batang-kali-massacre-during-malayan-emergency-8104840.html
12. John Halford, "Batang Kali massacre: no public inquiry ordered, but instead a judgement exposing the slaughter of innocents and decades of Government-sanctioned deceit," Bindmans LLP, 4 September, 2012. Internet Archive Wayback Machine: https://web.archive.org/web/20211214011526/https://www.bindmans.com/news/batang-kali-massacre-no-public-inquiry-ordered-but-instead-a-judgement
13. Martin Vengadesan, and Lim Chia Ying, "Agony of massacre victims' descendants," *The Star*, 8 May, 2012, https://www.thestar.com.my/lifestyle/features/2012/05/08/agony-of-massacre-victims-descendants/ (accessed 27 November 2021).
14. Ibans served with the 2nd battalion of the Scots Guards. Robert Rizal Abdullah, *The Iban Trackers and the Sarawak Rangers 1948–1963*, (Kota Samarahan: UNIMAS, 2019) 39.
15. Transcript of an interview with Private Ron Harper of the Queen's Royal Regiment who fought in Malaya between 1954–1957, The Queen's Royal Surrey Regimental Association. https://web.archive.org/web/20220724025524/https://www.queensroyalsurreys.org.uk/video/07_1945to59/ron_harper_02_03-trans.html (accessed July 24, 2022).
16. Caroline Elkins, *Legacy of Violence: A History of the British Empire*, (London: The Bodley Head, 2022) 527.
17. Jenny's father's name was Derek Hargreaves MBE.
18. Anton Gill, *Empire's Children: Tracing Your Family History Across the World*, (London: Harper Press, 2007) 140–142.
19. Ewan Fletcher, "Jenny Éclair: My agony over my father's grisly wartime secret," *The Daily Mail*, June 16, 2007. Internet Archive Wayback Machine: https://web.archive.org/web/20220220121703/https://www.dailymail.co.uk/news/article-462494/Jenny-Eclair-My-agony-fathers-grisly-wartime-secret.html
20. Anton Gill, *Empire's Children: Tracing Your Family History Across the World*, (London: Harper Press, 2007) 140.
21. Calder Walton, *Empire of Secrets: British Intelligence, The Cold War and The Twilight of Empire*, (London: Harper Press, 2013) 195.
22. Album of photographs belonging to Sgt William Johnson of the Coldstream Guards regiment, 1946 onwards, National Army Museum, 2003-03-627, photographs 38–39.
23. Collection of Malayan atrocity photographs, Working Class Movement Library, Far East: Malaya, SLING/FAREAST/6
24. Simon Meddick, Liz Payne, and Phil Katz, *Red Lives: Communists and the Struggle for Socialism*, (London: Manifesto Press Cooperative Limited, 2020) 67–69.

25. Personal photograph album of Pte R Baldwin, 1st Battalion of the Suffolk Regiment, 1951 to 1952, Suffolk Archive, GB554/Y/1/532.
26. Folder of photographs and press cuttings, 1952 to 1993, Suffolk Archive, GB554/B/12/102.
27. The author of this book worked closely with Malayan Emergency veterans of the Suffolk Regiment. A copy of this photograph was published in the following book. Mike Forsdike, *The Malayan Emergency: The Crucial Years 1949–52*, (Barnsley, England: Pen & Sword, 2022) 62–63.
28. Annamaria Motrescu-Mayes and Susan Aasman, *Amateur Media and Participatory Cultures: Film, Video, and Digital Media*, (London: Routledge, 2019), chapter "Collective memories of an anonymous, global 'I'".
29. Eamonn McCann, McCann: *War & Peace in Northern Ireland*, (Dublin: Hot Press Books, 1998) 115.
30. The personal photography albums of soldiers belonging to the Suffolk Regiment stored in both GB554/Y/1/532 and GB554/Y3/17 contain copies of the same photographs of the corpses of suspected MNLA members.
31. Adrian Walker, *Six Campaigns: National Servicemen on Active Service 1948–1960*, (London: Leo Cooper, 1993) 44.
32. Ian Edwards who was in Malaya between 1956–1957 as a member of the South Wales Borderers regiment, owned a headhunting photograph despite never witnessing an MNLA corpse. Adrian Walker, *Six Campaigns: National Servicemen on Active Service 1948–1960*, (London: Leo Cooper, 1993) 50, 52.
33. Mike Forsdike, *The Malayan Emergency: The Crucial Years 1949–52*, (Barnsley, England: Pen & Sword, 2022) 139.
34. *Daily Worker* Reporter, "Headhunters are Reinforced: They like to take home scalps," The *Daily Worker*, June 18, 1952. Taken from cut out stored in the National Archives, box CO1022/45.
35. An excerpt from Globe and Laurel quoted in the *Daily Worker* newspaper. *Daily Worker* Reporter, "Malaya Major Boosts Head-Hunters: Not for Identification'," *Daily Worker*, May 12, 1952, 1
36. This is an excerpt from an article titled "The Ibans Go Home" which was published in the official journal of the Royal Marine's 3 Commando Brigade, Commando News, January 15, 1951. The article was then reprinted in the official journal of the Royal Marines, Globe and Laurel, March 1951. The *Daily Worker* then discovered the reprinted article in Globe and Laurel and quoted large parts for their article on headhunting titled "Malaya Major Boosts Head-Hunters: Not for Identification".
37. Unknown, "With 40 Commando on Monday, 6th November" *Globe and Laurel*, Vol. LIX, No. 1 (January 1951). Imperial War Museum archive, LBY E.5/125.
38. The ambush took place near the Caledonia Estate on the 22 October 1951. The Commonwealth personnel who were killed belonged to the Royal West Kent Regiment. 12 British soldiers and three Ibans died, along with 12 British soldiers wounded. The names of the three Ibans killed were Bulang, Kelambu, and Untang. Adrian Walker, Ron Harper, Paul Riches, *A County Regiment: 1st Battalion of the Queen's Own Royal West Regiment Malaya 1951–1954*, (Brockley Press, 2001) 37, 39, 43, 150.
39. Diary entry by Lieutenant John Norton Adrian Walker, Ron Harper, Paul Riches, *A County Regiment: 1st Battalion of the Queen's Own Royal West Regiment Malaya 1951–1954*, (Brockley Press, 2001) 41.

40. Jim Dove, "Jim Dove until 1954," Royal Signals Contact Site, https://web.archive.org/web/20220726002113/https://www.royal-signals.org.uk/of_interest/Signals%20Service.php (accessed 26 July 2022).
41. Sadly, despite the incredible quality of this research, the author did not mention which museum displayed the skull fragment. Simon Harrison, *Dark Trophies: Hunting and the Enemy Body in Modern War* (Oxford: Berghahn Books, 2012) 159.
42. Photographs of British troops wearing captured MNLA starred caps. Mike Forsdike, *The Malayan Emergency: The Crucial Years 1949–52*, (Barnsley, England: Pen & Sword, 2022) 106–107.
43. Herbert Andrew, *Who Won the Malayan Emergency?*, (Singapore: Graham Brash, 1995) 17.
44. Herbert Andrew, *Who Won the Malayan Emergency?*, (Singapore: Graham Brash, 1995) 101.
45. Interview with British Marine Francis Gerald Green, 1998, Imperial War Museum Sound Archive, Accession No. 18021, reel 2. https://www.iwm.org.uk/collections/item/object/80017724 (accessed 27 November 2021).
46. Interview with NCO Eddie Clarke of the 1st Battalion of the Cameronians, 2003, Imperial War Museum Sound Archive, Accession No. 26579, reel 12. https://www.iwm.org.uk/collections/item/object/80023609 https://www.iwm.org.uk/collections/item/object/80023609 (accessed 30 June 2022).
47. Joe Glenton, "Marine A-Style Killings Have Always Been a Feature of Britain's Dirty Wars – Ever Heard of Batang Kali?," *The Huffington Post*, February 9, 2014. Internet Archive Wayback Machine: https://web.archive.org/web/20211214010934/https://www.huffingtonpost.co.uk/joe-glenton/marine-a-style-killings-h_b_4422160.html
48. The official journal of the Royal Marines mentions that a Brigade Commander promised $20 for the first communist captured or killed by his men. Unknown, "3 Commando Brigade: 40 Commando R.M.," *Globe and Laurel*, Vol. LVIII, No.8, (August 1950): 204. Imperial War Museum archive, LBY E.5/125.
49. Royal Marines from 42 Commando are given cash rewards by a Brigade Commander for killing communists. Unknown "42 Commando RM," *Globe and Laurel*, Vol. LVIII, No. 8, (October 1950): 259. Imperial War Museum archive, LBY E.5/125.
50. Malaya (Guerrilla Activities), House of Commons debate, 9 December 1953. Hansard Parliamentary Debates Volume 521: House of Commons Official Report (London: Her Majesty's Stationary Office, 1953), 1970.
51. Ibans in Malaya were considered civilians by the British military until the creation of the Sarawak Regiment in 1953. Times Correspondent, "Sarawak Rangers to Become New Force," *The Times*, August 7, 1959, 8.
52. Dr Bonnar cites National Archive documents, CO 1022/57. David Bonner, *Executive Measures, Terrorism and National Security: Have the Rules of the Game Changed?*, (Aldershot: Ashgate Publishing Limited, 2007) 146.
53. Interview with trooper Alan Bradley Maybury of the 22nd Special Air Service, 2001, Imperial War Museum Sound Archive, Accession No. 22123, reel 3. https://www.iwm.org.uk/collections/item/object/80021040 (accessed 30 June 2022).
54. *Daily Worker* Reporter, "Severed heads: We ask three questions," *Daily Worker*, May 6, 1952, 1.
55. In November 1953 British war criminal Gerald Griffiths of the King's African Rifles regiment who had also been a perpetrator of the Chuka Massacre had admitted to providing these cash rewards.

56. John Chynoweth, *Hunting Terrorists in the Jungle*, (Stroud: Tempus Publishing Limited, 2005) 20.
57. John Chynoweth, *Hunting Terrorists in the Jungle*, (Stroud: Tempus Publishing Limited, 2005) 35.
58. John Chynoweth, *Hunting Terrorists in the Jungle*, (Stroud: Tempus Publishing Limited, 2005) 122.
59. John Chynoweth, *Hunting Terrorists in the Jungle*, (Stroud: Tempus Publishing Limited, 2005) 9.
60. John Chynoweth, *Hunting Terrorists in the Jungle*, (Stroud: Tempus Publishing Limited, 2005) 57.
61. John Chynoweth, *Hunting Terrorists in the Jungle*, (Stroud: Tempus Publishing Limited, 2005) 81.
62. John Chynoweth, *Hunting Terrorists in the Jungle*, (Stroud: Tempus Publishing Limited, 2005) 90.
63. John Chynoweth, *Hunting Terrorists in the Jungle*, (Stroud: Tempus Publishing Limited, 2005) 118.
64. John Chynoweth, *Hunting Terrorists in the Jungle*, (Stroud: Tempus Publishing Limited, 2005) 120.
65. John Chynoweth, *Hunting Terrorists in the Jungle*, (Stroud: Tempus Publishing Limited, 2005) 120.
66. J.P. Cross, *Jungle Warfare: Experiences and Encounters*, (London: Guild Publishing, 1989) 118–119.
67. Agnes Khoo, *Life as the River Flows: Women in the Malayan Anti-Colonial Struggle*, (Monmouth, Wales: Merlin Press, 2007) 67.
68. One example of such a photograph taken from the body of an MNLA guerrilla can be found here facing page 48. M. C. A. Henniker, *Red Shadow Over Malaya* (London: William Blackwood & Sons Ltd, 1955), pages 48
69. Four more examples of photographs found among the belongs of MNLA guerrillas depicting their fighters in the jungle can be found printed on pages 202–203. Len Spicer, *The Suffolks in Malaya* (Peterborough: Lawson Phelps Publishing, 1998) 202–203.
70. Another example can be found within this publication facing page 88. Major J. B. Oldfield, *The Green Howards in Malaya (1949–1952): The Story of a Post-war Tour of Duty by a Battalion of the Line* (Aldershot: Gale and Polden Ltd, 1953), 88.
71. Len Spicer, *The Suffolks in Malaya* (Peterborough: Lawson Phelps Publishing, Peterborough, 1998) 183.
72. Unknown, "Ipoh-Batu Gajah," *Commando News*, July 17, 1951.
73. Chynoweth cites the British military's Anti-Terrorist Operations in Malaya (ATOM) manual. John Chynoweth, *Hunting Terrorists in the Jungle*, (Stroud: Tempus Publishing Limited, 2005) 120.
74. J.P. Cross, *Jungle Warfare: Experiences and Encounters*, (London: Guild Publishing, 1989) 138.
75. J.P. Cross and Buddhiman Gurung, *Gurkhas At War: Eyewitness Accounts From World War II To Iraq*, (Barnsley: Frontline Books, 2016) 192, 198, 214.
76. J.P. Cross and Buddhiman Gurung, *Gurkhas At War: Eyewitness Accounts From World War II To Iraq*, (Barnsley: Frontline Books, 2016) 192.

77. Susan L. Carruthers, "Why Can't We See Insurgents? Enmity, Invisibility, and Counterinsurgency in Iraq and Afghanistan." *Photography and Culture* 8, no.2 (2015): 201. https://doi.org/10.1080/17514517.2015.1076246
78. Gerry Van Tonder, *Malayan Emergency: Triumph of the Running Dogs 1948–1960*, (Barnsley: Pen and Sword Military, 2017) 70.
79. Donald Mackay, *The Malayan Emergency 1948–60: The Domino That Stood*, (London: Brassey's, 1997) 137–138.
80. J.R. Dowling, *Helicopters in the Royal Air Force 1950–1960*, (Ministry of Defence, Air Historical Branch, 1978) 31, https://web.archive.org/web/20220514184001/https://www.raf.mod.uk/our-organisation/units/air-historical-branch/regional-studies-post-coldwar-narratives/helicopters-in-the-royal-air-force-1950-1960/
81. A. H. Peterson, G. C. Reinhardt, and E. E. Conger, Symposium on the Role of Airpower in Counterinsurgency and Unconventional Warfare: The Malayan Emergency, (Santa Monica: The RAND Corporation, July 1963) 15.
82. J.R. Dowling, *Helicopters in the Royal Air Force 1950–1960*, (Ministry of Defence, Air Historical Branch, 1978) 82, https://web.archive.org/web/20220514184001/https://www.raf.mod.uk/our-organisation/units/air-historical-branch/regional-studies-post-coldwar-narratives/helicopters-in-the-royal-air-force-1950-1960/
83. Interview with former SAS soldier Arpad Bacskai, 2004, Australians at War Film Archive, Archive Number 2029, timestamp 12:33–13:30. https://australiansatwarfilmarchive.unsw.edu.au/archive/2029 (accessed 5 July 2022).
84. A personal account of soldiers using this method in the deep jungles of Perak can be found within the following book. Herbert Andrew, *Who Won the Malayan Emergency?*, (Singapore: Graham Brash, 1995) 96–97.
85. This book contains three pages of photographs showing Commonwealth soldiers in the jungle receiving supplies via aircraft. Muhammad Azzam bin Muhammad Hanif Ghows, *The Malayan Emergency Revisited 1948–1960: A Pictorial History*, (Kuala Lampur: ARM HOLDING SDN BHD, 2007) 249–251.
86. Gerry Van Tonder, *Malayan Emergency: Triumph of the Running Dogs 1948–1960*, (Barnsley: Pen and Sword Military, 2017) 70.
87. Herbert Andrew, *Who Won the Malayan Emergency?* (Singapore: Graham Brash, 1995) 62.
88. Personal photograph album belonging to an officer of the Suffolk Regiment, 1951 to 1993, Suffolk Archive, GB554/Y/3/17.
89. The practice of taking trophy photographs of Commonwealth soldiers alongside the corpses of suspected MNLA members tied to wooden poles was not a practice unique to the British, but was also practiced by the Rhodesian African Rifles. Gerry Van Tonder, *Malayan Emergency: Triumph of the Running Dogs 1948–1960*, (Barnsley: Pen and Sword Military, 2017) 98.
90. Photographs of British troops having their photographs taken with the corpses of suspected MNLA members tied to poles. Mike Forsdike, *The Malayan Emergency: The Crucial Years 1949–52*, (Barnsley, England: Pen & Sword, 2022) 64.
91. Len Spicer, *The Suffolks in Malaya* (Peterborough: Lawson Phelps Publishing, 1998) 93.
92. Len Spicer, *The Suffolks in Malaya* (Peterborough: Lawson Phelps Publishing, 1998) 129–130.
93. Len Spicer, *The Suffolks in Malaya* (Peterborough: Lawson Phelps Publishing, 1998) 50.

94. In the opinion of former British military Intelligence Corps soldier Adrian Walker, the British military's decapitation of suspected MNLA members during the Malayan Emergency would be considered a war crime by the Geneva Convention. However it is important to note that at this time the Geneva Convention did not yet include civil conflicts. Adrian Walker, *Six Campaigns: National Servicemen on Active Service 1948–1960*, (London: Leo Cooper, 1993) 164.

Chapter 6

1. T. N. Harper, *The End of Empire and the Making of Malaya* (Cambridge: Cambridge University Press, 1999) 153.
2. Harper's sole piece of evidence to back his claim that Iban headhunters never decapitated anybody in Malaya is a single quote by a British military Major in a book on the Malayan Emergency published after the British Malayan Headhunting Scandal. Major J. B. Oldfield, *The Green Howards in Malaya (1949–1952): The Story of a Post-war Tour of Duty by a Battalion of the Line* (Aldershot: Gale and Polden Ltd, 1953) Xxii.
3. T. N. Harper, *The End of Empire and the Making of Malaya* (Cambridge: Cambridge University Press, 1999) 268–269.
4. Court documents incorrectly date the *Daily Worker* publication of decapitation photographs to 1951. John Halford, "Claimant's skeleton argument," (UK: Bindman and Partners, 2011) CO/1827/2011. https://www.bindmans.com/uploads/files/documents/Batang_Kali_Skeleton.pdf. (Accessed 27 November 2021).
5. Book incorrectly dates the *Daily Worker* publication of decapitation photographs to 1950. John Callaghan, *Cold War, Crisis and Conflict: The History of the Communist Party of Great Britain 1951–68* (London: Lawrence and Wishart, 2003), 133–134.
6. Barry Wynne, *A King's Shilling*, (Cambridge: Pegasus, 2012) 300.
7. Unknown, "Will the release of secret documents allow the real story of the Batang Kali Massacre to be told?," *The Independent*, July 11, 2009. Internet Archive Wayback Machine: https://web.archive.org/web/20211214012408/https://www.independent.co.uk/news/world/asia/will-the-release-of-secret-documents-allow-the-real-story-of-the-batang-kali-massacre-to-be-told-1739843.html
8. Ann Grey and Erin Bell, *History on Television*, (Abingdon: Routledge, 2013) 198.
9. Ann Grey and Erin Bell, *History on Television*, (Abingdon: Routledge, 2013) 198.
10. Ann Grey, "Televised Remembering," in *Research Methods for Memory Studies*, ed. Emily Keightley & Michael Pickering, (Edinburgh: Edinburgh University Press, 2013) 91.
11. Linstrum's ideas stem from Carolyn J. Dean's ideas on 'compassion fatigue'. Erik Linstrum, "Facts About Atrocity: Reporting Colonial Violence in Postwar Britain," *History Workshop Journal* 84 (Autumn 2017): 15. https://doi.org/10.1093/hwj/dbx032
12. Wen-Qing Ngoei, *Arc of Containment: Britain, the United States and Anticommunism in Southeast Asia* (New York: Cornell University Press, 2019) 89.
13. Simon Harrison, *Dark Trophies: Hunting and the Enemy Body in Modern War* (Oxford: Berghahn Books, 2012) 9.
14. Harrison's coverage and opinions of headhunting during the Malayan Emergency can be found within these pages. Simon Harrison, *Dark Trophies: Hunting and the Enemy Body in Modern War* (Oxford: Berghahn Books, 2012) 156–160.
15. Simon Harrison, *Dark Trophies: Hunting and the Enemy Body in Modern War* (Oxford: Berghahn Books, 2012) 157.

16. The most notable being officer Ronald Reid-Daly who both founded and commanded the Selous Scouts after fighting for the British in Malaya.
17. The author was most likely referencing the alleged beheading of two British SAS soldiers during a war known as the Aden Emergency. Rajani Palme Dutt, "A Jingo Election?" *The Labour Monthly* 46, no.6 (June 1964): 241.
18. The decapitated heads of two SAS soldiers were mounted on stakes in the town of Taiz. Tom Pocock, *East and West of Suez: The Retreat from Empire*, (London: The Bodley Head, 1986) 113.
19. John Newsinger, *The Blood Never Dried: A People's History of the British Empire*, 2nd edition (London: Bookmarks Publications, 2013) 215.
20. Among the archives Chin Peng visited is the Public Records Office in Kew (The UK National Archives), The London Imperial War Museum, and Rhodes House Library in Oxford. The documents held by Rhodes House are very often cited by historians of the Malayan Emergency, however they have since been moved to the Special Collections within the Bodleian Library's Weston Library.
21. Michael Vatikiotis, "Bitter Memories," *Far Eastern Economic Review*, Volume 166, issue 38, (September 25, 2003) 72–74.
22. Wai-Siam Hee, *Remapping the Sinophone: The Cultural Production of Chinese-Language Cinema in Singapore and Malaya before and during the Cold-War*, (Hong Kong University Press, 2019) 98.
23. Chin Peng, *Alias Chin Peng: My Side of History* (Singapore: Media Masters, 2003) 304.
24. Chin Peng, *Alias Chin Peng: My Side of History* (Singapore: Media Masters, 2003) 305.
25. This incident was the killing and mutilation of communist leader Ah Koek/Kuk. Chin Peng. *Alias Chin Peng: My Side of History* (Singapore: Media Masters, 2003) 313.
26. Chin Peng, *Alias Chin Peng: My Side of History* (Singapore: Media Masters, 2003) 307.
27. Victor Purcell, *Malaya: Communist or Free?* (London: 1954) 232.
28. Chin Peng, *Alias Chin Peng: My Side of History* (Singapore: Media Masters, 2003) 4.
29. Erik Linstrum, "Facts About Atrocity: Reporting Colonial Violence in Postwar Britain," *History Workshop Journal* 84 (Autumn 2017): 10. https://doi.org/10.1093/hwj/dbx032
30. Agnes Khoo, *Life as the River Flows: Women in the Malayan Anti-Colonial Struggle*, (Monmouth, Wales: Merlin Press, 2007) 12
31. This was the number 10 Platoon of the Suffolk Regiment. Mike Forsdike, *The Malayan Emergency: The Crucial Years 1949–52*, (Barnsley, England: Pen & Sword, 2022) 131.
32. Agnes Khoo, *Life as the River Flows: Women in the Malayan Anti-Colonial Struggle*, (Monmouth, Wales: Merlin Press, 2007) 9–10.
33. Agnes Khoo, *Life as the River Flows: Women in the Malayan Anti-Colonial Struggle*, (Monmouth, Wales: Merlin Press, 2007) 10.
34. These pages contain academic research on the MNLA's communication abilities. Rachel Leow, *Taming Babel: Language in the Making of Malaya*, (Cambridge: Cambridge University Press, 2016) 159–175.

Chapter 7

1. Christopher Bayly and Tim Harper, *Forgotten Wars: Freedom and Revolution in Southeast Asia* (Cambridge, Massachusetts: Belknap Press of Harvard University Press, 2007) 456.

2. Karl Hack, "Everyone lived in fear: Malaya and the British way of counterinsurgency, Small Wars & Insurgencies," *Small Wars and Insurgencies* 23, no. 4–5 (2012): 692. https://doi.org/10.1080/09592318.2012.709764
3. Examples of Malayan propaganda leaflets created by the Commonwealth containing photographs of dead MNLA members, unknown dates, Oxford Bodleian Libraries, Malaya Broadcasting & C. MSS. Ind.. Ocn. 216.
4. Chin Peng, *My Side of History* (Singapore: Media Masters, 2013), 307.
5. Recounting of the Malayan Emergency by a soldier of the Rifle Brigade who fought in Malaya between 1955–1957. Adrian Walker, *Six Campaigns: National Servicemen on Active Service 1948–1960*, (London: Leo Cooper, 1993) 128.
6. Interview with NCO Peter Arthur Woodhouse of the 13/18 Royal Hussars, 1991, Imperial War Museum Sound Archive, Accession No. 12216, reel 3. https://www.iwm.org.uk/collections/item/object/80011951 (accessed 30 June 2022).
7. While in Malaya Paul Richards was a craftsman for British military's Royal Electrical and Mechanical Engineers. Paul Richards, *Better a Friend than Foe: Life with the Gurkhas*, (London: Austin Macauley Publishers, 2014) 99.
8. Roy Follows and Hugh Popham, *The Jungle Beat: Fighting Terrorists in Malaya 1952–1961*, (London: Blandford, 1990) 17–18.
9. Peter Nolan, *Rebalancing China: Essays on the Global Financial Crisis, Industrial Policy and International Relations*, (Anthem Press, 2015) 218.
10. Souchou Yao, *The Malayan Emergency: Essays on a Small Distant War* (Copenhagen: NIAS Press, 2016) 46.
11. Catherine Lim, *Romancing the Language: a collection of essays*, (Singapore: Marshall Cavendish Corporation, 2018) 79–80.
12. Catherine Lim, *Romancing the Language: a collection of essays*, (Singapore: Marshall Cavendish Corporation, 2018) 80–81.
13. Eddie Wong, "the Unknown Person: Post-Colonial Fictioning, Personal Stories and Surveillance," *Leonardo* (Oxford) 53, no. 4 (2020): 442.
14. Melissa Foong, "#InTheNameOfArt: Eddie Wong Opens Up About The Idea Behind Portrait Of The Jungle People," *Yahoo News*, August 8, 2022, https://web.archive.org/web/20221006221407/https://malaysia.news.yahoo.com/inthenameofart-eddie-wong-opens-idea-065358886.html (accessed 6 October 2022).
15. Tan Teng Phee, *Behind Barbed Wire: Chinese New Villages During the Malayan Emergency, 1948–1960*, (Petaling Jaya, Selangor, Malaysia: Strategic Information and Research Development Centre, 2020) 119.
16. Tan Teng Phee, *Behind Barbed Wire: Chinese New Villages During the Malayan Emergency, 1948–1960*, (Petaling Jaya, Selangor, Malaysia: Strategic Information and Research Development Centre, 2020) 187–188.
17. Interview with a person who was present around a public corpse display in Bertam Valley New Village, Pahang. Tan Teng Phee, *Behind Barbed Wire: Chinese New Villages During the Malayan Emergency, 1948–1960*, (Petaling Jaya, Selangor, Malaysia: Strategic Information and Research Development Centre, 2020) 187.
18. Photograph of the body of a Malayan insurgent trussed onto a stake, brought in by a British patrol, 1952, The National Army Museum, 1963-09-163-1. https://web.archive.org/web/20221001131551/https://collection.nam.ac.uk/detail.php?acc=1963-09-163-1 (accessed October 1, 2022).
19. This is according to a history book about the Suffolk Regiment written by one of the co-leaders of the Friends of the Suffolk Regiment veterans organisation, with

the help and approval of Suffolk Regiment veterans who fought in Malaya. Mike Forsdike, *The Malayan Emergency: The Crucial Years 1949–52*, (Barnsley, England: Pen & Sword, 2022) 134.
20. Oliver Crawford was a Second Lieutenant of the Somerset Light Infantry (Prince Albert's) who fought in the Malayan Emergency between 1954–1955. Oliver Crawford, *The Door Marked Malaya*, (London: Rupert Hart-Davis, 1958) 215.
21. Karl Hack, *The Malayan Emergency: Revolution and Counterinsurgency at the End of Empire*, (Cambridge: Cambridge University Press, 2022) 320.
22. J.J. Raj (JR), *The Struggle for Malaysian Independence*, (Petaling Jaya, Malaysia: MPH Group Publishing, 2007) 137.
23. J.J. Raj (JR), *The Struggle for Malaysian Independence*, (Petaling Jaya, Malaysia: MPH Group Publishing, 2007) 137–138.
24. Interview with British officer of the Suffolk Regiment James Patrick Macdonald, 1997, Imperial War Museum Sound Archive, Accession No. 17423, reel 2.
25. Karl Hack, *The Malayan Emergency: Revolution and Counterinsurgency at the End of Empire*, (Cambridge: Cambridge University Press, 2022) 326.
26. Tan Teng Phee, *Behind Barbed Wire: Chinese New Villages During the Malayan Emergency, 1948–1960*, (Petaling Jaya, Selangor, Malaysia: Strategic Information and Research Development Centre, 2020) 118.
27. For an example of a photograph showing children being present during the public corpse displays, see episode 5 of Channel 4's Empire's Children (2007) featuring Jenny Éclair.
28. This book contains a photograph of the British Army's Suffolk Regiment performing this form of corpse identification via public display in front of children. Mike Forsdike, *The Malayan Emergency: The Crucial Years 1949–52*, (Barnsley, England: Pen & Sword, 2022) 65.
29. Wang Qiao Ying was also known as Hong Ying, and used the alias Wang Fen. Lin Yan, *Rainbow: An Epic Story of Heroic Fighters for Independence*, (Labis, Johor: Huai Lie Enterprise) 245–246.
30. Xiao Li was born in Singapore as He Tian Xin, and also used the alias He Xiao Li. Lin Yan, *Rainbow: An Epic Story of Heroic Fighters for Independence*, (Labis, Johor: Huai Lie Enterprise) 278–280.
31. Ye Guan Xi had many aliases, including Wen Guang, Ye Shui, and Ah Shui. Lin Yan, *Rainbow: An Epic Story of Heroic Fighters for Independence*, (Labis, Johor: Huai Lie Enterprise) 283–284.
32. Lin Yan, *Rainbow: An Epic Story of Heroic Fighters for Independence*, (Labis, Johor: Huai Lie Enterprise) 289.
33. Lin Yan, a veteran of the Malayan communist movement, insists that Liew Kon Kim's real name was Liu Guan Jin.
34. Lin Yan, *Rainbow: An Epic Story of Heroic Fighters for Independence*, (Labis, Johor: Huai Lie Enterprise) 335–356.
35. Christopher Hale, *Massacre in Malaya: Exposing Britain's My Lai* (Stroud: The History Press, 2013) 360–361.
36. Cited as coming from the Suffolk Regiment Old Comrades Association, Hemel Hempstead Branch Newsletter, March 2008. Mike Forsdike, *The Malayan Emergency: The Crucial Years 1949–52*, (Barnsley, England: Pen & Sword, 2022)

37. Liew Kon Kim was a famous and very effective MNLA leader, however many of his fellow guerrillas knew him as Liu Guan Jin. Lin Yan, *Rainbow: An Epic Story of Heroic Fighters for Independence*, (Labis, Johor: Huai Lie Enterprise) 267.
38. Liu Guan Geng used two aliases, Liu Ye Cheng, and Ah Geng. Lin Yan, *Rainbow: An Epic Story of Heroic Fighters for Independence*, (Labis, Johor: Huai Lie Enterprise) 285–287.
39. Mike Forsdike, *The Malayan Emergency: The Crucial Years 1949–52*, (Barnsley, England: Pen & Sword, 2022) 133–134.
40. Interview with British officer Richard Wilson of the 1st Battalion of the Suffolk Regiment, 2006, Imperial War Museum Sound Archive, Accession No. 27811, reel 7. https://www.iwm.org.uk/collections/item/object/80027039 (accessed 30 June 2022).
41. Unknown, "Queues to see Dead Bandits," *The Straits Times*, June 17, 1951, 5. https://eresources.nlb.gov.sg/newspapers/Digitised/Article/straitstimes19510617-1.2.55 (accessed 1 September 2022).
42. Lim Saw Hoon allegedly used an alias called Lim Suet Yin.
43. Unknown, "Crowds see dead bandits," *The Straits Times*, August 19, 1952, 5. https://eresources.nlb.gov.sg/newspapers/Digitised/Article/straitstimes19520819-1.2.85 (accessed 1 September 2022).
44. Reuter, "Corpses Exposed in Public: Malayan Terrorists," *The Manchester Guardian*, August 20, 1952, 8.
45. Correspondent, "Chinese Shot by Jungle Squad," *The Manchester Guardian*, May 19, 1951, 6.
46. Boon Kheng Cheah, *Red Star Over Malaya: Resistance and Social Conflict During and After the Japanese Occupation of Malaya, 1941–1946*, (Singapore University Press, 2006) 232.
47. J. W. Goodwin, "Bodies of Dead Rebels on Public View," *The Scotsman*, August 22, 1952. Taken from cut out stored in the National Archives, box CO1022/45.
48. Unknown, "Put dead bandits on show, govt told," *The Straits Budget*, August 21, 1952, 10. https://eresources.nlb.gov.sg/newspapers/Digitised/Article/straitsbudget19520821-1.2.49 (accessed 1 September 2022).
49. H. D. Chaplin, *The Queen's Own Royal West Kent Regiment 1951–1961*, (Maidstone: Queen's Own Museum Committee, 1964) 41–42.
50. Unknown, "Good Morale Value to Villagers: Put dead bandits on onshow, Govt told," *The Straits Times*, August 14, 1952, 5. https://eresources.nlb.gov.sg/newspapers/Digitised/Article/straitstimes19520814-1.2.95 (accessed 1 September 2022).
51. Unknown, "Unwisdom," *The Manchester Guardian*, August 29, 1952, 6.
52. Unknown, "Templer Shows off Patriot Corpses," *The Daily Worker*, August 20, 1952. Taken from cut out stored in the National Archives, box CO1022/45.
53. For more information on women in the Malayan communist movement, look for the following book. Agnes Khoo, *Life as the River Flows: Women in the anti-colonial struggle*, (Monmouth: Merlin Press, 2007).
54. Unknown, "We don't do this usually, says Govt.," *The Straits Times*, November 20, 1953, 6. https://eresources.nlb.gov.sg/newspapers/Digitised/Article/straitstimes19531120-1.2.110 (accessed 1 September 2022).
55. Unknown, "We don't do this usually, says Govt.," *The Straits Budget*, November 26, 1953, 9. https://eresources.nlb.gov.sg/newspapers/Digitised/Article/straitsbudget19531126-1.2.28 (accessed 1 September 2022) 136.

56. Although the online transcript of this quote says 25 December 1953, the actual date as confirmed by physical copies of Hansard Parliamentary records is 25 November 1953. Terrorists' Bodies (Photographing), House of Commons debate, 25 November 1953. Hansard Parliamentary Debates Volume 521: House of Commons Official Report (London: Her Majesty's Stationary Office, 1953) 42.
57. Telegraph from Gerald Templer sent to Oliver Lyttelton making excuses for the Kulim Tradegy,15 December, 1953, National Archives, box CO 1022/45, file SEA 10/162/02, page 59.
58. Leslie Plummer, "A Nation's Conscience," *The Times*, December 11, 1953.
59. Ghazali Shafie, "A Nation's Conscience," *The Times*, December 15, 1953.
60. Nigel Hunt, "Terrorists in Malaya: Identification of Dead Bodies," *The Times*, December 31, 1953.
61. Raja Uda, "Terrorists in Malaya," *The Times*, January 22, 1954.
62. Arthur Clegg, "Body of girl put on show in Malaya," *Daily Worker*, January 2, 1954, 1. Taken from cut out stored in the National Archives, box CO1022/45.

Additional Information
1. Maureen Kim Lian Sioh, "Fractured Reflections: Rainforests, Plantations and the Malaysian Nation-State," PhD Dissertation (The University of British Columbia, April 2000), 145. https://open.library.ubc.ca/soa/cIRcle/collections/ubctheses/831/items/1.0089657 (accessed 27 October 2021).
2. One of the most notable being the MA thesis of Howard John Clemente for San Jose State University, titled "Iban (Sea Dyaks) in the Malayan Emergency, 1948–1960", completed in 1983.
3. Noel Barber, *The Natives Were Friendly*, (London: Macmillan, 1977) 169–171.
4. See the Daily Mail's role in the Zinoviev letter hoax, their support for the British Union of Fascists, their attacks against Jewish refugees fleeing the Nazis, as well as their more recent attacks against Muslim refugees and the LGBT community.
5. Vincent Hancock, *Legends of the Dragonfly: Fighting the Communists During the Malayan Emergency 1947–1960*, (Bloomington, USA: Author House, 2020) 131, 134.
6. Tariq Ali, *Winston Churchill: His Times, His Crimes*, (London: Verso, 2022) 384–385.
7. Tariq Ali, *Street Fighting Years: An Autobiography of the Sixties*, (London: Verso Books, 2015) 94.
8. Nu'man Abd al-Wahid, *Debunking the Myth of America's Poodle: Great Britain Wants War*, (Winchester: Zero Books, 2020) 118.
9. E. B. Parkes, *No Drums to Beat no Flags to Fly*, (London: Minerva Press, 2000) 51–58.
10. J.P. Cross, *Jungle Warfare: Experiences and Encounters*, (London: Guild Publishing, 1989) 119.

Acknowledgements
1. Imperial War Museum, https://www.iwm.org.uk/collections/item/object/205359332 (accessed 14 September 2022).

Sources for Images/Figures

Figure 1: Mark Howe ed, *Is that Damned Paper Still Coming Out? The very best of the Daily Worker Morning Star*, (London: People's Press Printing Society Ltd, 2001) 135. (accessed through published book, copyright belongs to the People's Press Printing Society, the owners of the *Morning Star* newspaper)

Figure 2: *Stop This Horror in Malaya: Wipe out Britain's Shame!*, (London: Daily Worker Cooperative Society Ltd), 3. (accessed through Bodleian Library archive)

Figure 3: *Stop This Horror in Malaya: Wipe out Britain's Shame!*, (London: Daily Worker Cooperative Society Ltd), 4. (accessed through Bodleian Library archive)

Figure 4: Frank Gullett, "These are no Fakes: How head-hunting photographs came to Daily Worker." *Daily Worker*. April 30, 1952, 1. (accessed through Marx Memorial Library archive)

Figure 5: Editor, "This is the War in Malaya," *Daily Worker*, April 28, 1952, 1. (accessed through Marx Memorial Library archive)

Figure 6: Frank Gullett, "These are no Fakes: How head-hunting photographs came to Daily Worker," *Daily Worker*, April 30, 1952, 1. (accessed through Marx Memorial Library archive)

Figure 7: Gabriel, "Knights Templer of Malaya," *Daily Worker*, May 7, 1952, 2. (accessed through Marx Memorial Library archive)

Figure 8: Editor, "This Horror Must End: You must compel peace," *Daily Worker*, May 10, 1952, 1. (accessed through Marx Memorial Library archive)

Figure 9: National Archives, London, FO 371/101228, 1952. (accessed through National Archives)

Figure 10: National Archives, London, FO 371/101228, 1952. (accessed through National Archives)

Figure 11: National Archives, London, FO 371/101228, 1952. (accessed through National Archives)

Figure 12: *Stop This Horror in Malaya: Wipe out Britain's Shame!*, (London: Daily Worker Cooperative Society Ltd), 1. (accessed through Working Class Movement Library, Manchester)

Figure 13: *Stop This Horror in Malaya: Wipe out Britain's Shame!*, (London: Daily Worker Cooperative Society Ltd), 2. (accessed through Working Class Movement Library, Manchester)

Figure 14: *Stop This Horror in Malaya: Wipe out Britain's Shame!*, (London: Daily Worker Cooperative Society Ltd), 3. (accessed through Working Class Movement Library, Manchester)

Figure 15: *Stop This Horror in Malaya: Wipe out Britain's Shame!*, (London: Daily Worker Cooperative Society Ltd), 4. (accessed through Working Class Movement Library, Manchester)

Figure 16: Pollitt, Harry. "We Cannot Plead Ignorance: Act to Restore Britain's Honour." *Daily Worker.* June 14, 1952, 2. (accessed through Marx Memorial Library archive)

Figure 17: Clegg, Arthur. "Hunted, Murdered, Beheaded for daring to Strike: Tolpuddle Martyrs of Today." *Daily Worker.* May 12, 1952, 2. (accessed through Marx Memorial Library archive)

Figure 18: Daily Worker Reporter, "Blood Stains Malaya Profits: Demonstrators Raid Shareholders," *Daily Worker*, June 10, 1952, 1. (accessed through Marx Memorial Library archive)

Figure 19: War diary belonging to a soldier of the Suffolk Regiment, 17 April 1952 – 5 January 1953, Suffolk Archives (Bury St Edmunds), GB554/B/2/10. (accessed through Suffolk County archives)

Figure 20: Album of photographs belonging to Sgt William Johnson of the Coldstream Guards regiment, 1946 onwards, National Army Museum, 2003-03-627, photographs 38–39. (accessed through National Army Museum, London)

Figure 21: Collection of Malayan atrocity photographs, Working Class Movement Library, Far East: Malaya, SLING/FAREAST/6. (accessed through Working Class Movement Library, Manchester)

Figure 22: Folder of photographs and press cuttings, 1952 to 1993, Suffolk Archive, GB554/B/12/102. (accessed through Suffolk County archives)

Figure 23: Folder of photographs and press cuttings, 1952 to 1993, Suffolk Archive, GB554/B/12/102. (accessed through Suffolk County archives)

Figure 24: Personal photograph album of Pte R Baldwin, 1st Battalion of the Suffolk Regiment, 1951 to 1952, Suffolk Archive, GB554/Y/1/532. (accessed through Suffolk County archives)

Figure 25: Photograph album of a Suffolk Regiment officer, 1951–1993, Suffolk Archive, GB554/Y3/17. (accessed through Suffolk County archives)

Figure 26: Asoka Guikon, *A People's History of Malaya: The New Emergency,* (Oldham, England: Bersatu Press, 1980) 13. (author openly expresses inside this book that its contents are public domain)

Figure 27: Adrian Walker, Ron Harper, Paul Riches, *A County Regiment: 1st Battalion of the Queen's Own Royal West Regiment Malaya 1951–1954* (Brockley Press, 2001), 176.

Index

Absent Without Leave, 99
Admiralty, 3–4, 6, 12, 17, 61
Agent Orange, xvii, xviii
Al-Qaeda, 19
Alan Winnington, 32–3
Alias Chin Peng: My Side of History, 68
Ambrose Shardlow and Co, 28
Anthony Eden, 14, 18
Aphrodisiacs, 48, 55, 59
Archbishop of York, 17, 30
Arthur Clegg, 29–30, 92
Arthur Creech Jones, xxi, xxv, 61
Attorney General, 32
Australia, xvi, xix, xxii, xxvi
Awang anak Raweng, xxi

Bandits, xxv, 9, 15, 40, 43, 49, 74, 79, 84, 89, 95
Basra, 35
Batang Kali Massacre, xvii, 33, 41–42, 52, 62
Behind Barbed Wire, 77
Belsen, 29
Ben Tillett, 30
Bertrand Russell, 30
Betty Tebbs, 28
Blowpipe, xxi, xxv
Bodleian Library, 102, 110
Borneo, xi, xviii–xix, 5, 24–5, 43, 49–50
British Library, 101
Brooke family, xix
Bury St Edmunds, 101–2, 104

Calder Walton, 45
Camera, xi, 2, 4, 9, 11, 20, 26, 38, 52, 55–6, 58–60, 106
  Brownie camera, 4
Campbell Case, 6
Cannibalism, xxii, 104

Catherine Lim, 75–76
Channel 4, 44, 63
China, xiv, xvi, 27, 35, 37 84
China Monthly Review, 35
Chin Peng, xiv, 19, 68–9, 73, 99
Christopher Baird, xxii
Clement Attlee, 12, 32–3, 105
Clive Baillieu, 30
Coldstream Guards, xxi, 22, 52
Colonial Office, viii, 3, 11, 22, 53, 61, 69, 101, 103
Collective punishment, 16
Commando News, xxvi
Communist Party of Great Britain (CPGB), xxvii, 28–9, 33, 62, 95
Communist terrorists (CT), xxiv, 7, 42, 80
Corpse displays, 72–93, 95, 99, 103
Curfews, xvii, 16
Cyprus Emergency, 92, 103

Daily Mail, 104
Daily Telegraph, 68
Dakota aeroplane, 57
Dark Trophies: Hunting and the Enemy Body in Modern War, 65
David Maxwell Fyfe, 14
Douglas Porch, 26
Duchess of Kent, 22
Duke of Kent, 22
Dunlop Rubber Company, 27, 30–1

Eamonn McCann, 46–7
East Germany, 37
Eddie Clark, 51–2
Eddie Wong, 76–7
Edmund Frow, 46
Electrical Trades Union, 28–9
Ellen Wilkinson, 30
Empire's Children, 44, 63–5

Eric Gill, 30
Erik Linstrum, 65–6, 70
Experimental Iban platoons, xxii, 21

Far East Land Force (FARLAF), 4
Ferret Force, xxi
Fiji, xvi
Fingerprints, 25–6, 56
Flamethrowers, xvii
Foot guard regiments, 22
Francis Gerald Green, 51–2
Frederick Marquis, 14
Friendly fire, xxiv

Gateshead, United Kingdom, 28
Geneva Convention, xvi, 21, 51, 61
George Cross, xxi, 21
George Medal, xxi
Gerald Templer, viii, 13–4, 29, 52–3, 56, 69, 90, 102–3
Germ warfare, 33
Ghazali Shafie, 91
Globe and Laurel, xxvi, 48–9
Gordon Knapp, 10–1
Green Howards, xxii, 44, 86
Grenadier Guards, xxii, 22
Gurkhas, 8–9, 24, 55–6, 66

Hansard, 102
Harold Alexander, 14
Harold Laski, 30
Harry Pollitt, xxvii, 22
Harry Willcox, 48
Helicopters, 24, 57, 59
    Dragonfly helicopter, 57
Henry Brooke, 22
Henry Hopkinson, 21, 61
Hen Yan, 38–40
Herbert Andrew, 51
Herbert Morrison, 30
Holocaust, 29, 65, 98
House of Commons, 4, 12, 15–6, 20, 61, 90, 102
Hunger, 20
Hyde Park, xiv, 28

Imperial War Museum (IWM), 23–4, 51, 98, 102

Incorporated Society of Planters, 87
India, xvii, 35
Indonesia-Malaysia Confrontation, 24
Intelligence Gathering Theory, 38–61
Iraq, xviii, 35, 94
Irish Republican Army (IRA), 92
I Saw the Truth in Korea, 32
Islamic State (ISIS), 19
Is That Damned Paper Still Coming Out, 34

James Heartfield, 19
James Patrick Macdonald, 39–40
Jaweng ak Jugah, xxiv
Jenny Éclair, 44, 47, 63–5
John Chynoweth, 23, 52, 54
John Eber, 33
John Mackinnon, 24
John Norton, 49
John Strachey, 105
Johore, 80
J.P. Cross, 56
J.R. Campbell, viii, 6, 16–9

Kenya, xvi, 25–6, 29, 33, 54, 91, 94
Kenya Committee, 33
Korean War, 32, 65
Kuala Kangsar, 1
Kuching, xix, 24
Kulim, 7, 75–6, 86, 88–92
    Kulim Tragedy, 86, 88–92

Legends of the Dragonfly: Fighting the Communists During the Malayan Emergency, 1947–1960, 104
Leslie Plummer, 89–91
Liew Kon Kim, 79, 84–85
Lim Saw Hoon, 86, 88–9
Lim Tian Shui, 41–3
Lincolnshire Regiment, xxi, 23
Liu Guan Geng, 85
Longhouse, 24, 48
Lord Chancellor, 32

MacDonald family
    Malcolm MacDonald, Commissioner-General for Southeast Asia, 5–6
    Ramsay MacDonald, Prime Minister, 5–6

Malayan Communist Party (MCP), xiii, 68, 76
Malayan penal code, 21, 61
Malayan People's Anti-Japanese Army (MPAJA), xiii–xiv, xv, 84
Malay Regiment, 7, 23
Malnutrition, 29
Manchester Regiment, xxi
Margaret Mead, xxv
Marxist, 19, 34
  Marxist-Leninist, 2
Marx Memorial Library, 101, 110
Mau Mau Uprising, 25–6, 33, 103
Michael Stewart, 21
Min Yuen, 73
Mona Brand, 32, 37
Morning Star, 20, 34, 99
My Lai, 98–99

National Archives (UK), 101, 103
National Army Museum, 46, 78, 102
National Organisation of Cypriot Fighters (EOKA), 92
Nazi / Nazism, xxvii, 10, 26, 29, 36, 88, 93
Neil Ascherson, 9
Nepal, 7–8
New China News Agency, 35
New Times, 35
New Villages, xvii, 26, 29, 54–5, 66, 78
New Zealand, xvi, xxii
Nick Ut, 98
No Drums to Beat No Flags to Fly, 106
Noel Barber, 104

Officer Commanding Police District (OCPD), 51, 80
Official Secrets Act, 33
Oliver Lyttelton, viii, 12–8, 21, 28, 65, 90
Operation Legacy, 103
Orang Asli, 66
Order of the British Empire (OBE), xiv, 68, 91

Pagoh, 80
Palestine, 45
Parang, 22, 49
Peking, 35
Pengarohs, xx

Peter Nolan, 75
Peter Walls, 66
Phan Thi Kim Phuc, 98
Phillip Bolsover, 22
Port Dickson, xxi
Pravda, 35
Psychological warfare, 36, 73–8

Queen's Own Royal West Kent Regiment, xxii
Queen's Royal Regiment, 23, 42–3

Randall Swingler, xxvii
Rhodes House, 110
Rhodesia, xvi, 66
Robert Cecil, 30
Robert Clough, 19
Robert Gascoyne-Cecil, 14
Romancing the Language, 75
Ronald L. Haeberle, 98–99
Royal Air Force (RAF), xxii, 57
Royal Corps of Signals, 50
Royal Navy, viii, 2–4, 24, 28
Royal Inniskilling Fusiliers, 23
Ruth Frow, 46

Sarawak, xix, 24, 43
Sarawak Rangers, xxii, 21
Scots Guards, xxi, 22, 41
Scottish Rifles, Cameronians, xxi, 51–2, 109
Second World War (WWII), xiii–xiv, xix–xx, 10, 32, 65, 68, 84–5, 92
Segamat Massacre, xv
Senoi Praaq, 25
Sexual abuse, 35
Shanghai, 35
Shoreditch Trades Council, 28
Siam Railway, 30
Simon Harrison, 65–6
Singapore, 36–7, 75, 86, 96
Singapore Standard, 36
Somerset Light Infantry, 79
Souchou Yao, 75
Southend-on-Sea, 28
South Korea, 32
South Wales Borderers Regiment, 23, 47
Soviet Union (USSR), xvi, 2, 27, 35–7

Special Air Service (SAS), xxii, xxiv, 47, 53, 57, 63, 66
Special Branch, 23, 25, 80
Stamford Hill, 28
Stanley Stephen Awbery, 15
St George's Day, 39
Strangers in the Land, 32, 37
Strategic Hamlet, xviii
Suffolk Regiment, xvii, 14, 39–40, 46, 58, 70, 79, 81, 85
Sultan, 80
Surrendered Enemy Personnel (SEP), 58
Survivorship bias, 83
Susan Carruthers, 56

Taejon, 32
Ta Kung Pao, 35
Tan Teng Phee, 77–8
Tariq Ali, 105–6
Tattoos, xx, 49
Telok Anson Tragedy, 86–7
The Malayan Emergency: The Crucial Years, 99
The Manchester Guardian, 88
The Natives Were Friendly, 104
The People, xxvi–xxvii
The Planter, 88
The Scotsman, 87
The Singapore Free Press, 36
The Straits Times, xxvii, 36
The Suffolks in Malaya, 40
The Sunday Times, 35
The Times, 91–92
The Washington Post, 36
These are No Fakes, viii, 5
This is the War in Malaya, viii, 1
Tolpuddle Martyrs, 30

Tom Mann, 30
Torture, 19, 26, 33, 93, 103
Trade union, xii, xiv–xv, xvii, 27–31, 68, 87, 95
Treason, 32

UK National Army Museum, 46, 78, 102
Ulu Caledonia Estate Ambush, 49
Union of Shop Distributive and Allied Workers, 29
United States (USA), xviii, 27, 33, 36–7, 94
Unity Theatre, 32
University of British Columbia, 103

Veterans for Peace UK, 20, 52
Vietnam War, xvii–xviii, 98–99

Walter Heaton, 52–3
Wan Qiao Ying, 84
War of the Running Dogs, 104
War School, 99
Wen-Qing Ngoei, 65–6
Weston Library, 102, 110
Whistle-blower, 34
White Rajahs, xix
Who Won the Malayan Emergency, 51
Winston Churchill, viii, xii, xxviii, 4, 6, 12, 14–5, 17–9, 23, 25, 28, 47
Worcestershire Regiment, xxi
Working Class Movement Library (WCML), 46, 102

Xiao Li, 84

Ye Guan Xi, 84
Ye Shi Min, 84